Economic Warfare in the Communist Bloc

PRAEGER SPECIAL STUDIES IN
INTERNATIONAL ECONOMICS AND DEVELOPMENT

Economic Warfare in the Communist Bloc

A STUDY OF SOVIET ECONOMIC PRESSURE AGAINST YUGOSLAVIA, ALBANIA, AND COMMUNIST CHINA

Robert Owen Freedman

PRAEGER PUBLISHERS
New York · Washington · London

The purpose of Praeger Special Studies is to make specialized research in U.S. and international economics and politics available to the academic, business, and government communities. For further information, write to the Special Projects Division, Praeger Publishers, Inc., 111 Fourth Avenue, New York, N.Y. 10003.

66.895

PRAEGER PUBLISHERS
111 Fourth Avenue, New York, N.Y. 10003, U.S.A.
5, Cromwell Place, London S.W.7, England

Published in the United States of America in 1970
by Praeger Publishers, Inc.

Library of Congress Catalog Card Number: 79-123722

Printed in the United States of America

To Sharon, Deborah, and David, my precious jewels.

ACKNOWLEDGMENTS

The author is indebted to many individuals for assistance in preparing this book. First and foremost, I would like to thank Professor Zbigniew Brzezinski of Columbia University's Research Institute on Communist Affairs whose penetrating criticisms purged the study of a number of errors. I also owe a debt of gratitude to Professors Alexander Erlich, Istvan Deak, Joseph Rothschild, and Seweryn Bialer of Columbia University; John Montias of Yale University; and Amos Jordan of West Point, who commented on the manuscript at various stages of its preparation. While the comments and suggestions of these scholars have been of great assistance, the views expressed in this book are my own, and I take full responsibility for any errors that remain. Last, but certainly not least, a special word of thanks is due my wife Sharon, without whose support this book would never have been forthcoming.

CONTENTS

LIST OF TABLES

INTRODUCTION

Problems of discipline and control have long plagued the Russian leadership in its quest to maintain Soviet hegemony within the "Communist bloc."* Although the Soviet Union emerged from World War II as the second most powerful nation on the globe, centrifugal forces began to weaken Moscow's hold over the other members of the "bloc" even as the Russian leadership was endeavoring to spread Soviet influence into the rest of the world. As early as 1948, Tito's Yugoslavia came into open conflict with the USSR; Poland, Hungary, China, Albania, Rumania, North Korea, Cuba, and Czechoslovakia later followed its example.

Soviet leaders have reacted to these challenges in different ways. On two occasions, they resorted to military force to coerce an offending communist regime. At other times, the leadership limited itself to denunciations in the Soviet press. A broad spectrum of possible responses lies between these two extremes, and many of these intermediate responses can be grouped under the common heading of "economic pressure." Included in this category are minor forms of pressure like the postponement of trade negotiations, and major ones like the imposition of an economic embargo. In the period 1947-69, Russian leaders have in fact made frequent use of economic pressure as an instrument of policy toward other communist nations.

Stalin, the first Russian leader to employ economic pressure against a fellow communist state, imposed an economic embargo on Yugoslavia in 1949 and cancelled economic assistance agreements with that nation as well. Khrushchev utilized identical forms of economic pressure against Albania twelve years later. He also exerted economic pressure against Yugoslavia, which suffered the loss of two major capital loans in 1958; against China, which experienced both the loss of Soviet technical assistance in 1960 and a sharp reduction in Soviet exports in sub-

---

*In any study of Soviet relations with other communist nations, it is necessary to state at the beginning the terminology to be employed in discussing the various groupings of communist states. Here, the term "Soviet bloc" will be used to designate those countries whose foreign policies have been controlled by the USSR. Included in this group are: Bulgaria, East Germany, Czechoslovakia (except in the period February-August, 1968), Mongolia, Hungary (except for a brief period in 1956-57), Albania up to 1958, and Rumania up to 1960. These nations, up to 1953, will also be designated Russian "satellites." The term "Communist Camp" is a much broader one and will be used to designate both those nations in the "Soviet bloc" and the other communist nations (China, North Korea, North Vietnam, Cuba, Yugoslavia, Albania since 1958, and Rumania since 1960).

sequent years; and against North Korea, which was denied both military and economic assistance because of its alignment with China in the 1962-64 period. Less severe forms of economic pressure were exerted by Khrushchev's successors against Rumania in 1967 and Cuba in 1968.

Although Western analysts have examined many other facets of Soviet foreign policy, the USSR's frequent use of economic pressure against fellow communist nations has not been so carefully scrutinized.* This study will analyze the Soviet Union's use of economic pressure as an instrument of policy toward other communist countries in the period 1947-69. After an examination of the various weapons available in the Soviet economic arsenal, three case studies (Yugoslavia, 1947-58; Albania, 1960-69; and China, 1960-69) will be presented. These case studies will illustrate the degree to which there has been a common pattern in the employment of Soviet economic pressure throughout the period, and the degree to which changes in the strategy and tactics of its employment have reflected changes in the Soviet leadership.

Each of the case studies will be divided into four parts. The first section will contain a brief history of the developments that led to the conflict between the USSR and its fellow communist state (hereafter called a "target" state), highlighting the economic aspects of the two nations' relationship. The second section of the case study will analyze the major areas in which the target nation's economy was vulnerable to economic pressure from the USSR. Although the determination of the vulnerability of a given nation's economy to outside economic pressure is a very difficult task, this section will describe the probable Soviet *perception* of the target nation's economic vulnerability. Evidence in this area comes primarily from articles in the Soviet economic press (particularly *Vneshniaia Torgovlia*, the house organ of the Soviet Ministry of Foreign Trade), and also from the target nation's press, a source carefully scrutinized by Soviet officials. Next, each study will focus upon the Soviet strategy in exerting economic pressure against the target state and on the target nation's reaction to the pressure. The final section will discuss any changes in policy that occurred after the Soviet leader who initiated the policy of economic pressure against the target state was removed from the scene.

The study is based on three primary sources. The first consists of statements by the leaders of the nations against whom Soviet economic pressure has been employed. Whereas these leaders have not been reticent about describing their experiences, this source has provided a large amount of information both as to the forms of pressure the USSR exerted and as to the manner in which it was exerted. Although the author does not have a reading knowledge of Serbo-Croatian, Chinese, Albanian, or North Korean, he has been greatly assisted by the fact that most of the key documents have appeared in translation in documentary collections compiled either by Western scholars or by the target nation itself. Radio Free Europe press translations and situation reports have also been of great assistance in this regard.

---

*Robert Loring Allen's book *Soviet Economic Warefare* (Charlottesville: University of Virginia Press, 1960) deals with Soviet economic pressure against non-communist nations.

Trade statistics issued by the target nations, the Soviet Union, the United Nations, and the U.S. Government comprise the study's second primary source. These statistics have been cross-checked wherever possible to insure the greatest accuracy. Somewhat more ambiguous but still very useful sources are the Soviet press (particularly the economic press) and the Soviet radio. Although Soviet leaders have been relatively reticent in discussing their use of economic pressure, the Soviet press and radio, particularly during the early stages of a conflict, have often dropped "hints" as to what might happen should the target nation continue to oppose Soviet policies. In addition, as mentioned above, the Soviet economic press has been a major source of information on the Soviet perception of the economic vulnerability of the target nation's economy.

Economic relations between communist states is an increasingly complex field, and for this reason it is necessary to mention at the outset several areas that will not be covered in this analysis.[1] In the first place, the Mendershausen-Holzman debate on the Soviet Union's "exploitation" of other communist nations in their trade relations will not be rehashed here.[2] Secondly, the changing Soviet strategy toward the Council for Mutual Economic Assistance (COMECON)* will also not be dealt with in any detail.[3] Although this organization could eventually become a major lever of Soviet economic pressures, were all its members to accede to the Soviet scheme for a supra-national planning agency, this is not yet the case, and the organization remains relatively powerless.[4]

One final word is in order prior to beginning the study. The Soviet experience in the employment of economic pressure can be placed into a larger perspective by observing that the USSR was not the only super-power in the post-war period to exert economic pressure against nations within its sphere of influence. The story of the U.S. economic blockade of Castro's Cuba is well known, but lesser cases of U.S. economic pressure against its NATO allies should also be noted.[5] Lack of success in these endeavors, however, has prompted former American Secretary of State Dean Acheson to note in his memoirs: "Almost all recipients of our economic or military aid have shown us how useless threats to stop aid are in trying to pressure the recipients."[6]

It is hoped that the following study will indicate whether a high official in the Soviet Union's Ministry of Foreign Affairs would, in examining the USSR's use of economic pressure against fellow communist states over the past twenty years, come to the same conclusion as to the efficacy of economic pressure as a foreign policy instrument as did Dean Acheson.

---

*This organization is also referred to as CMEA.

NOTES

1. For an ambitious attempt to cover the entire field in a single volume, see Peter J. Wiles, *Communist International Economics* (New York: Frederick A. Praeger, 1969).

2. A useful summary of the Mendershausen-Holzman debate is found in Marshall I. Goldman, *Soviet Foreign Aid* (New York: Frederick A. Praeger, 1967), pp. 8-9. The Chinese have recently "out-mendershausened" even Mendershausen in describing Soviet exploitation in its trade relations with other communist states. See *Peking Review,* Vol. 12, No. 7 (February 14, 1969), pp. 16-17.

3. This subject has been well covered in Michael Kaser, *Comecon* (London: Oxford University Press, 1967).

4. For a recent Soviet view of the problems and prospects of the Council for Mutual Economic Assistance, see Y. Akimov, "Problems of CMEA Countries' Economic Integration," *International Affairs* (Moscow), Vol. 15, No. 12 (December, 1969).

5. U.S. policies and practices in employing economic pressure are described in detail in Gunnar Adler-Karlsson, *Western Economic Warfare 1947-67* (Stockholm: Almqvist and Wiksell, 1968). In the early 1950's, the U.S. Government exerted a considerable degree of economic pressure against its NATO allies in an effort to compel them to follow a common economic policy toward the Soviet bloc. Given the present interest in comparative analysis among political scientists in the field of communist studies, a comparison of Soviet and American techniques and experiences in the employment of economic pressure could provide a useful contribution to the field of international relations by illustrating how nations governed by very different political systems attempt to solve problems in their international environments through the use of identical instruments of policy. On this point, see Frederic J. Fleron (ed.), *Communist Studies and the Social Sciences: Essays on Methodology and Empirical Theory* (Chicago: Rand McNally, 1969).

6. Dean Acheson, *Present at the Creation* (New York: W. W. Norton, 1969), p. 61.

Economic Warfare in the Communist Bloc

CHAPTER 1

SOVIET CAPABILITIES FOR EXERTING ECONOMIC PRESSURE

There has always been a close relationship between Soviet foreign policy and Soviet foreign economic relations. The Russians themselves have stated that "between foreign policy and foreign economic policy there exists an intimate and indissoluble connection and a mutual dependence."[1] Although the USSR often cultivates a "non-political" image in its foreign trade with the industrialized nations of the West in order to obtain sophisticated industrial machinery,[2] it is under no constraints to act similarly in its economic relations with other members of the Communist Camp.

The direct relation between Soviet foreign economic relations and Soviet foreign policy can be seen in Table 1, which presents the statistics on Soviet-Yugoslav trade from 1946 to 1968. Following the establishment of Yugoslavia as a full-fledged communist state after World War II, Yugoslav trade with the USSR rose rapidly. The onset of the conflict between Tito and Stalin, however, caused Soviet exports to fall in 1948, and by 1949 all trade between the two countries had come to a halt. A complete trade embargo was imposed on Yugoslavia in the 1949-53 period as Stalin cast Yugoslavia out of the Soviet bloc. Then, under Khrushchev, a rapprochement was consummated and trade between the two nations again rose sharply. (A detailed discussion of this period is found in Chapter 2.) Khrushchev's displeasure with the Yugoslav position on the Hungarian Revolution as well as on other issues, however, led to another decline in Soviet-Yugoslav trade after 1957. Then, in 1962, as a result of the increasingly bitter Sino-Soviet conflict, Khrushchev again sought a rapprochement with Yugoslavia. This was to lead to yet another sharp increase in trade. Indeed, the statistics on Soviet-Yugoslav trade have been a very effective barometer of the state of Soviet-Yugoslav relations in the 1946-68 period.

The Russians have given an explanation for this type of manipulative economic relationship in an article summarizing the Soviet Union's economic role in the Communist Camp since 1945:

The creative role in the foreign policy of the USSR and other Socialist states in the sphere of their mutual economic cooperation is manifested in the carrying out of close inter-party cooperation in the

3

elaboration of a coordinated course of party and state policy, in concluding bilateral and multi-lateral political agreements, in the working out of a common line in international economic policy and so on. . . . The belief in Marxism-Leninism and Proletarian Internationalism is the basic criterion of a correct foreign policy course and its positive influence on international economic relations. *A deviation from Marxism-Leninism, from Proletarian Internationalism leads to a transformation of foreign policy into a negative historical force which draws to itself grave consequences for the course of Socialism, for the real national interests of the state and the development of its economic relations* [emphasis added] .[3]

TABLE 1

Soviet-Yugoslav Trade, 1946-68
(value in new rubles; one ruble = 1.11 U.S. dollars)

Year	Soviet Exports	Yugoslav Exports	Total Trade
1946	16.6	22.3	38.9
1947	33.9	26.6	60.5
1948	31.0	41.7	72.7
1949	2.6	9.6	12.2
1950	0	0	0
1951	0	0	0
1952	0	0	0
1953	0	0	0
1954	1.8	1.0	2.8
1955	14.8	15.7	30.5
1956	62.2	44.7	106.9
1957	65.8	51.1	116.9
1958	46.0	45.8	91.8
1959	41.6	47.8	89.4
1960	49.6	47.8	97.4
1961	32.3	49.1	81.4
1962	65.1	41.5	106.6
1963	86.7	78.3	165.0
1964	121.4	108.8	230.2
1965	130.6	169.8	300.4
1966	192.5	173.5	366.0
1967	252.5	209.3	461.8
1968	260.2	195.4	455.6

Sources:
  1946-66: *Vneshniaia Torgovlia SSSR 1918-1966* (Moscow: Mezhdunarodnye
        Otnosheniia, 1967), pp. 66-67.
  1967-68: *Vneshniaia Torgovlia*, Vol. 49, No. 7 (July, 1969), p. 57.

This chapter will analyze the different forms of economic pressure the USSR can employ against communist countries which, in the view of the Soviet leaders, have "deviated from Marxism-Leninism and Proletarian Internationalism."

There is a broad spectrum of economic pressures the Soviet Union can exert against a communist state with which it has come into conflict. These range from a delay in trade negotiations to a complete embargo of all trade, and from the withdrawal of technical assistance to the cessation of all economic aid. We will first analyze Soviet capabilities for exerting economic pressure in its foreign trade relations, and then examine the USSR's ability to exert economic pressure through its economic assistance policies. Although in some instances the two areas overlap, for the sake of greater clarity each will be treated separately. The concluding section of the chapter will discuss the possibilities of resistance to economic pressure from the Soviet Union.

SOVIET TRADE WITH TARGET NATIONS

As the main supplier of both raw materials and machinery in the Communist Camp, the Soviet Union occupies the major position in intra-Camp trade relations. Many Western economists have pointed out, quite validly, that the communist trade partners of the USSR have sacrificed considerable economic gain because of the bilateral nature of their trade with the Soviet Union.[4] One should not overlook, however, certain advantages that accrue to communist nations—particularly the less-developed ones—from trade with the Soviet Union. In the first place, because of the bilateral or barter nature of trade between communist states, imports can be paid for directly by exports instead of through hard currency, a commodity which is often in short supply in non-communist as well as communist developing nations. Indeed, in paying for imports from the USSR in this manner, a communist nation can sometimes find a market for its so-called soft goods—those goods which could not be easily sold on the world market, either because of poor quality or absence of demand. Thus in 1955, at the time of the first Soviet-Yugoslav rapprochement, Dr. Milan Aleksic, secretary of Yugoslavia's Federal Foreign Trade Chamber, stated:

The Yugoslav economy is specially interested in the development of economic cooperation with the economies of the USSR, Poland, and Czechoslovakia. In these countries one can purchase, on the one hand, some of the important raw materials such as cotton, naphtha, coal, coke, etc. as well as various machines, industrial equipment and precision machine products which are not produced in Yugoslavia. On the other hand, these markets are no less attractive in view of their almost limitless possibilities for absorbing many *Yugoslav products which cannot always be placed on the markets of Western Europe.* These products are primarily livestock and meats, wines, fresh and dried fruits and vegetables, tobacco and hemp [emphasis added].[5]

The less-developed communist nations whose exports are primarily agricultural commodities or raw materials find still another advantage in trade with the USSR. A long-term trade agreement with the Soviet Union in effect insulates them from the price fluctuation of their commodities on the world market. Thus the Soviet agreement to purchase Cuban sugar at a stable price for a set period of years could only have been an aid to Cuban planners in a period when world sugar prices gyrated wildly.[6]

In listing these advantages, one cannot, of course, overlook the fact that the more a communist nation trades with the USSR (the higher the percentage of its total trade taken by the Soviet Union), the more vulnerable it is to Soviet economic pressure. Indeed, some Western observers have gone one step further and asserted that this economic vulnerability has given the USSR control over the economies and hence the governments of the East European communist states.* Recently, Communist China has begun to echo this argument. On November 15, 1967, Radio Peking in an English language broadcast to Western Europe stated:

> In the name of the "international division of labor," the Soviet revisionist ruling clique has secured control over the industries of other "COMECON" member countries, reduced their factories into Soviet subsidiaries, and deepened their economic dependence. Many Eastern European countries have to import raw materials from the Soviet Union, turn out products to Soviet requirements and specifications and then sell them to the Soviet Union. Take Poland for instance. It depends on the Soviet Union for a considerble part of the raw materials required for its industries, in some cases the percentage being as high as 80 per cent, while most of its principal exports such as ships and railway cars go to the Soviet Union. *By such means the Soviet revisionist clique controls the economic arteries of the other "COMECON" members and utilizes this for political blackmail against them* [emphasis added] .[7]

Whether the economic leverage possessed by the USSR can be transformed into political leverage, however, is not so clear. In order to ascertain the validity of this assertion, it is necessary to examine in detail Soviet capabilities for exploiting its trade position in the Communist Camp to secure political obedience. This analysis will begin with an examination of the intra-communist foreign trade process itself.

The very nature of intra-communist foreign trade affords the Soviet Union a variety of techniques for exerting economic pressure—many more than the United States possesses in its trade with non-communist states.[8] Intra-communist trade is basically bilateral, and all trade relations take place between government agencies rather than between private merchants, as in the West. For this reason, the Soviet Union can exert pressure at many different junctures of

---

*Harry Trend of Radio Free Europe is a leading exponent of this view.

the foreign trade process. Thus the USSR can begin to exert economic pressure in the early stages of intra-governmental trade negotiations, or it can wait until it is scheduled to make deliveries of equipment and raw materials and then refuse to do so. An examination of the mechanics of intra-communist foreign trade will illustrate the numerous gradations of potential Soviet pressure.

Intra-communist foreign trade is a complex process. In drawing up a set of national material balances, central planners consider imports as an input category for certain of their industries—that is, as materials necessary for the successful completion of the national economic plan. Exports, on the other hand, are treated as an output category. Once the central planners have agreed on import requirements and export capabilities, the next step is trade negotiations with a potential foreign trade partner. These negotiations, which take place annually, are complex in nature. There is a long, drawn-out five-step process in which both sides seek to gain the maximum in imports for the minimum in exports.[9] Any unnecessary delay in the negotiations can disrupt a nation's planning for the next year.

When such a delay occurs in negotiations with a nation's primary supplier, a serious economic disruption can result—especially if there is no readily available alternate supplier. The Soviet Union, which at one time or another during the period 1947-69 was the main supplier and market for *every* communist country, has often used a delay in trade negotiations in an attempt to pressure a recalcitrant communist nation into adopting the Soviet line. This is the first gradation of Soviet economic pressure in the trade process. In late 1960, for example, when the Soviet-Albanian conflict had increased in intensity and the Albanians were completing preparations for their third five-year plan, the Russians deliberately delayed trade negotiations between the two countries. Until this point, Albania had depended on the Soviet Union for the vast majority of its imports (a large percentage of which were delivered on credit) and as its main export market. When the Soviet deputy foreign trade minister finally contacted his Albanian counterpart, the latter was told that "it would be advisable to postpone the matter of signing a long term commercial agreement for 1961-65 and the agreement for credits to Albania in view of the need to discuss this question on a higher level."[10]

Once trade negotiations have begun, there are a number of areas in which the USSR can apply pressure. First, the Russians can refuse to purchase some of the target nation's "soft goods" despite the fact that they had previously purchased these goods. Thus in a period of deteriorating relations between the USSR and Yugoslavia in 1958, the Russians refused to accept some agricultural goods that normally had been included in their commodity purchases from Yugoslavia.[11]

Another pressure the USSR can exert is its refusal to sell to a target nation as much of a certain commodity as it desires. Although this type of refusal may be interpreted as a limitation on the capacity of the Soviet economy, its practice in the past gives evidence of political rather than economic motivation. Thus Cuba, which requested a 10 per cent increase in oil shipments for 1968, was promised only a 2 per cent increase—with the result that the Cuban government had to institute fuel rationing.[12]

The Russians can go one step further and simply refuse to sell certain goods to a target nation. Following the open confrontation with China at the Bucharest Conference in 1960, the USSR began to selectively eliminate certain goods from Sino-Soviet trade. The Chinese Communists have described this technique in an open letter to the CPSU (Communist Party of the Soviet Union):

> In pursuance of your policy of further imposing restrictions on and discriminating against China in the economic and commercial fields, since 1960 you have deliberately placed obstacles in the way of economic and trade relations between our two countries and *held up or refused supplies of important goods which China needs.* You have insisted on providing large amounts of goods which we do not really need or which we do not need at all, while holding back or supplying very few of the goods which we need very badly. *For several years you have used the trade between our countries as an instrument for bringing political pressure to bear on China* [emphasis added].[13]

In addition to refusing to sell economic goods such as oil and machinery, the Soviet Union can also refuse to sell high-quality military equipment to a target nation during the trade negotiations. When the North Koreans opted for the Chinese position in late 1962, they found themselves unable to purchase either high-performance military aircraft or jet fuel from the Soviet Union. This type of sanction can be very serious for a communist nation such as North Korea which considers war with the United States or a U.S. ally a likely possibility. Although raw materials and machinery can be purchased in the West (assuming sufficient hard currency or loans are available), certain key types of military equipment rarely can. The U.S. bombing of North Vietnam could only have increased the sense of insecurity felt by the North Koreans, and this was one of the factors which weakened Pyongyang's alignment with Peking in 1965 and 1966 (see Chapter 4).

The next stage in the trade process where the USSR can exert economic pressure is its refusal to sign the trade agreement, even though the trade negotiations have been concluded. There is considerable evidence that the Russians, unhappy at Rumania's independent economic plans, delayed signing the five-year trade agreement with that country for the 1961-65 period.[14] Indeed, the treaty was not signed until November 10, 1960—the day of the opening of the Conference of Eighty-one Communist Parties in Moscow, where Khrushchev needed Rumania's support against the Chinese.

Once the trade agreement has been signed, the next gradation of Soviet economic pressure is its ability to delay deliveries of goods which a target nation is in great need of. Such goods include basic raw materials, the absence of which will cause an immediate slow-down in the target nation's industrial production. The Russians appear to have exerted this form of pressure against

Rumania in the fall of 1967 when they delayed shipments of coke and iron ore to that country. (In 1966, Rumania had obtained 84 per cent of its iron-ore imports from the Soviet Union.[15]) Nicolae Ceausescu, the leader of the Rumanian Communist Party, described this form of Soviet pressure in a veiled way in a speech on December 6, 1967, to the national conference of the Rumanian party:

> In practice sometimes the provisions of long-term agreements are not fully respected, which diminishes the importance of these agreements and causes damage to both partners . . . particularly the renouncing by one or the other parties of undertakings contained in these agreements have a negative influence on economic collaboration and cooperation and infringe on long-term planning. . . . It is necessary to make sure that, in the practice of relations among states, the existence of differences of opinion on one or another problem should not affect economic collaboration and cooperation, and these should base themselves in an effective manner on economic principles and criteria.[16]

The final form of economic pressure the USSR can exert in the foreign trade process is the ultimate one: refusal to sell any goods to the target nation or purchase any goods from it. So far, the Soviet Union has taken these extreme measures against only two communist states: Yugoslavia in the 1949-53 period and Albania from 1962 to the present (1970). The effects of such a trade embargo will be discussed below.

SOVIET ECONOMIC ASSISTANCE POLICIES

The second major classification of Soviet economic pressure lies in the area of economic assistance. Here again, it is the less-developed nations that, as the main recipients of Soviet economic aid, are the most vulnerable to Soviet manipulation of the aid as an instrument of economic pressure. To the less-developed communist nations, the USSR (or nations controlled by it) is usually the only source of capital and technical assistance. Whereas the ruling elites of these nations have devoted themselves to the goal of "building socialism" (a term in communist parlance that is usually synonymous with industrialization), Soviet assistance is vital for the realization of this goal.

The two basic forms of Soviet economic aid are capital aid and technical assistance. Capital aid consists of the supply of capital goods such as machinery, equipment, or even complete factory installations either as gifts or on long-term loans at low interest. Soviet technical assistance may take several forms. Perhaps the most important is the provision of Soviet experts to aid the recipient nation in setting up factories, in geological exploration for raw materials, in planning, or in a number of other areas vital to the nation's economy.

For a country beginning industrialization, this form of technical assistance can be as important as the provision of capital. This is clearly illustrated by the case of China, where Russian loans during the first Chinese five-year plan played a relatively minor role in China's economic development, but Soviet willingness to sell complete plants together with the men who had the know-how to put them into operation was the key factor. Soviet specialists also directed the restoration and reconstruction of existing Chinese factories.

The training of foreign students in Russian educational institutions and foreign workers in Russian factories are other forms of Soviet technical assistance. The creation of a technical intelligentsia is a vital necessity for a developing country, and both students and workers can acquire valuable technical skills in the Soviet Union—skills that are in short supply in their own country. The USSR can also offer blueprints and technical processes as still another form of technical assistance.

There are a number of ways the USSR can exploit its position as an aid donor to exert political pressure. First, its economic advisors and technicians can be abruptly withdrawn from a target nation. Indeed, this form of pressure was employed against Yugoslavia in 1948, China in 1960, and Albania in 1961. The Chinese have aptly described this form of pressure in an open letter to the CPSU:

> You were well aware that the Soviet experts were posted in over 250 enterprises and establishments in the economic field and the fields of national defense, culture, education and scientific research, and that they were undertaking important tasks involving technical design, the construction of projects, the installation of equipment, trial production and scientific research. As a result of your peremptory orders to the Soviet experts to discontinue their work and return to the Soviet Union, many of our country's important scientific research projects had to stop halfway, some of the construction projects in process had to be suspended, and some of the factories and mines which were conducting trial production could not go into production according to schedule. Your perfidious action disrupted China's original national economic plan and inflicted enormous losses upon China's socialist construction.
>
> Your action fully demonstrates that you violate the principle of mutual assistance between socialist countries and *use the sending of experts as an instrument for exerting political pressure on fraternal countries, butting into their internal affairs and sabotaging their socialist construction* [emphasis added].[17]

Another form of Soviet economic pressure is the expulsion of a target nation's students and workers from the USSR—sometimes, in the case of the students, in mid-semester. The Albanian newspaper *Zeri i Popullit* has described how the USSR employed this form of pressure (together with a number of others) against Albania:

N. Khrushchev, unilaterally and with the sole aim of obstructing the building of Socialism in Albania, cancelled the credits granted by normal agreement to the Albanian People's Republic by the Soviet Union for the third five year plan 1961-65, arbitrarily violated and annulled the 1961 trade agreement, unilaterally withdrew Soviet technicians, liquidated in fact the agreements on cultural cooperation, *expelled on false grounds a number of Albanian students and cadets from the Soviet Union, cancelled the agreement on the granting of scholarships to Albanian cadets and students studying in the Soviet Union,* violated the military agreements and organized a strict economic, political and military blockade of the Albanian People's Republic [emphasis added].[18]

This form of economic pressure can be particularly damaging in the long run if the target nation, for political reasons, has nowhere else to send its students. The only place to which Albania could send its expelled students (many of whom had not even been permitted to bring their textbooks with them from the USSR) was to underdeveloped Communist China.

A related pressure the USSR can employ is depriving a target nation of the benefits of belonging to the Council for Mutual Economic Assistance (CMEA*), the intra-communist economic organization. Although CMEA has not fulfilled Soviet hopes of becoming the integrative mechanism for communist unity, it has nonetheless served as a central processing center where many of the less-developed communist nations have been able to acquire patents and technical processes donated primarily by the USSR free of charge.[19] Consequently, exclusion from CMEA means loss of access to these technical documents. The USSR has twice excluded Yugoslavia from membership in CMEA, once by denying it admission in 1949 and the second time by depriving it of the "observer" status it had acquired in 1956. Albania, a full member of CMEA since 1949, was for all intents and purposes exluded from the organization in 1962—allegedly for not paying its dues. The USSR can also simply stop providing technical documents to a target nation.

The most serious form of economic pressure in the area of economic assistance is the cancellation of promised loans or grants. The usual Soviet explanation for a cancellation of credit agreements lies in the statement, "The USSR can only offer aid to friends." In cancelling aid projects to Yugoslavia in 1948 at the time of their first clash, the Russians stated:

They (the Yugoslav leaders) should also bear in mind that retaining this (anti-Soviet) attitude means depriving themselves of the right to demand material and any other assistance from the USSR, because the Soviet Union can only offer aid to friends.[20]

A Soviet note to Albania thirteen years later was similar in tone and content:

---

*This organization is sometimes referred to in the West as COMECON.

The Soviet People and the peoples of the other socialist countries
would not understand us if we, while depriving our country of
material resources, should continue to satisfy the demands of the
Albanian leaders who, to the detriment of the interests of the
Albanian people have trampled on elementary norms in relations
with the USSR and its government. . . . It is understandable that the
Albanian leadership cannot expect in the future that the USSR will
help it as it has in the past, with aid from which only true friends and
brothers have a right to benefit. . . . As concerns future relations
between our countries, and USSR aid to Albania, these will depend
entirely on the attitude adopted by the Albanian party.[21]

Although for the purpose of this analysis Soviet economic pressure in the
areas of trade and economic assistance have been presented separately, it
should be pointed out that in actual practice the two forms of economic
pressure have been closely orchestrated. Indeed, the Soviet Union has
combined many forms of economic (and political) pressure in its attempts to
force recalcitrant communist nations into line. Although in this chapter only
the main forms of economic pressure have been discussed, the case studies to
follow will reveal many variations of the primary techniques.

Having thus considered the main forms of Soviet economic pressure, an
analysis will now be made of the impact of Soviet pressure on the target
nation's economy and the various capabilities a target nation may possess to
counteract this pressure.

A TARGET NATION'S ABILITY TO RESIST
SOVIET ECONOMIC PRESSURE

A delay in Soviet shipments of vitally needed goods or the complete
cessation of all deliveries will have a number of negative effects on the target
nation's economy. A shortage in raw materials will have an immediate effect,
for without the raw materials many of its industries would cease to operate.
(The slow-down can be avoided or at least postponed if the target nation
possesses a large stockpile of the raw material; the taut nature of central
plans, however, usually precludes such a possibility.[22]) Although raw
materials can usually be purchased on the world market, this will require
both time and an outlay of scarce hard currency. In addition, because of the
need to obtain the raw materials rapidly, the target nation will usually have
to pay more than world market prices to acquire them.

A more lasting form of damage to the target nation's economy may be
its inability to obtain spare parts for Soviet-built machinery. The damage is
again most severe to the less-developed communist nations which possess
neither the domestic capacity to fabricate the necessary spare parts nor
(usually) sufficient hard currency to purchase substitute machinery in the
West.

The cessation of Soviet economic and technical aid will also have a major effect on the target nation's economy. Industrialization plans will usually have to be sharply curtailed, and factories only partially completed when Soviet advisors were withdrawn will have to be completed with the target nation's own resources or else abandoned. In addition, if Soviet raw materials and machinery exports were financed by credits, additional sources of these products must be found.

As impressive as this list of Soviet economic pressures and their potential effects might appear, the target nation is not totally defenseless. The optimum solution to the dilemma posed by Soviet economic pressure is for the target nation to find another nation or nations willing to supply—on credit—the goods that were previously imported from the USSR. Yugoslavia's relations with the United States in the 1949-53 period somewhat approximate this situation; Yugoslavia obtained no less than $376.8 million in loans and grants from the United States during this period.[23] Nonetheless, Yugoslavia encountered serious problems because of the Soviet embargo and had difficulty marketing its exports in non-communist countries. Albania, which acquired Communist China as a substitute benefactor in 1961, ran into far greater difficulty than did Yugoslavia. Because China was far poorer than the USSR, it was unable to supply Albania either with as much machinery or with machinery of as high quality as the USSR had supplied. As a result, Albania had to accept a major retardation in its industrialization. Both Yugoslavia and Albania were able to secure "benefactor nations"; China, however, managed to avoid the necessity of relying on another nation in this manner. Nonetheless, beginning in 1963, China began to acquire a number of long-term credits from Western European nations and Japan for the purchase of complete factories and equipment.[24]

In the absence of an alternate supplier willing to extend credits—or with only a limited amount of credit available from such a supplier—the target nation must still acquire hard currency for imports from the West to make up for the unavailability of goods it had originally planned to import from the USSR or nations controlled by it. It may be difficult to sell the goods originally destined for the USSR on Western markets. This was the Yugoslav experience in the 1949-53 period. Such a situation may occur because the goods in question were either built to Soviet specifications—and hence perhaps unusable in the West—or else because of a lack of Western demand. In this event, the ruling elite of the target communist nation, faced by the necessity of acquiring the required amount of hard currency, might choose to tighten the national belt and export goods (usually agricultural goods or consumer goods) originally planned for domestic consumption.

This belt-tightening process may be made more palatable to its population, initially, if the ruling elite treats the Soviet embargo as a national insult. Indeed, the Chinese, Albanian, and Yugoslav leaders have all attempted to appeal to the population of their countries with the cry, "The USSR is trying to prevent the building of socialism in our country."

But even if agricultural products and consumer goods are made available for export, they may not yield the desired amount of foreign exchange needed to purchase goods in the West. First, the agricultural goods to be sold may not be in demand on Western markets at the time and consequently may be marketable only at a large discount. Second, producers of consumer goods, which have low national priorities, will not be accustomed to the quality demands of the world market. Low quality means that these goods, if they can be sold at all, will usually bring low prices on Western markets.[25] The Albanian economic journal *Ekonomia Popullore* discussed this situation in describing the difficulties encountered by Albanian exports in Western markets:

> The production enterprises are faced with no problems regarding the question of quantity. However the same cannot be said about the quality, packaging, wrapping and labelling of export products. In this respect there are many shortcomings which in the final analysis harm the profits of Albanian exports, i.e. they lower their value and their volume.[26]

Another possibility for overcoming the problems caused by the absence of Soviet goods is to raise norms for existing production and thus produce the same output with less input. Alternatively, an attempt can be made to use import substitutes that are produced domestically or inputs diverted from goods originally planned for shipment to the USSR. In either case, the quality of production is likely to decline. It should be noted, however, that the more highly developed a target nation's economy, the greater its ability to produce import substitutes.

The Soviet embargo may also stimulate the target country to find domestic supplies of the raw materials it had previously imported from the USSR. The Chinese Communists exultantly declared in 1964 that they had discovered sufficient oil to end China's dependence for this commodity on the "revisionist Russians." Alternatively, the target nation may develop new technological processes that allow it to produce the same products with lesser amounts of these raw materials. Thus the Rumanians have begun to develop new processes for making steel requiring less coke and iron ore (raw materials the deliveries of which the USSR began to delay in 1967). The Chairman of Rumania's State Planning Committee, Maxim Berghianu, in an article on Rumanian economic development, wrote in July, 1968:

> As for metal production, because of our relatively limited resources of metallurgical raw materials, output is to be increased through the use of technological methods requiring minimum consumption of raw materials; the proportion of alloyed steel in the production process is to be increased. This is to be met, for instance, by the new 1,700 cubic meter blast furnace recently put into operation at the Galati iron and steel plant, where the consumption of coke is to be 20 per cent below the average for the national economy.[27]

The effect of Soviet economic pressure on a target state may also be related to the timing of the form of economic pressure employed. In order for a trade embargo to achieve its maximum effect, for example, it must be applied as rapidly as possible so as to afford the target nation the minimum amount of time to acquire vital imports elsewhere. Similarly, a delay between a Soviet threat to cut off economic aid and its actual termination may give the leaders of the target nation sufficient time to find an alternate supplier of economic aid. Thus in analyzing the effect of the various forms of Soviet economic pressure, it is necessary to examine the timing as well as the nature of each type of economic pressure employed.

In sum, the Soviet Union has the capability to exert a large number of forms of economic pressure against a target state, both in foreign trade and in economic assistance. For its part, the target nation has a number of defensive measures it can take to alleviate the effects of the Soviet pressure. In the case studies to follow, an examination will be made of the nature and timing of the various forms of economic pressure the Soviet Union has exerted against Yugoslavia, Albania, and China in an effort to ascertain the different Soviet leaders' strategy in employing economic pressure as an instrument of their foreign policy toward other communist states.

NOTES

1. B. P. Miroshnichenko, "Vneshniaia Politika i Ekonomicheskoe Sotrudnichestvo SSSR s Inostrannymi Gosudarstvami," in *Vneshnee-konomicheskie Sviazi SSSR za 50 Let* (Moscow: Nauchno-Issledovatel'skii Kon''iunkturnyi Institut MVT, 1967), p. 35.

2. For a discussion of Soviet trade strategy toward Western industrialized states, see *East-West Trade,* ed. Philip E. Uren (Toronto: Canadian Institute of International Affairs, 1966). For a Soviet critique of this book and other Western studies of Soviet foreign economic policy, see Abram Frumkin, *Modern Theories of International Economics* (Moscow: Progress Publishers, 1969), pp. 470-90.

3. Miroshnichenko, *op. cit.,* pp. 38-40.

4. For a recent discussion of this issue, see *International Trade and Central Planning,* ed. Alan Brown and Egon Neuberger (Berkeley: University of California Press, 1968), pp. 3-28.

5. Milan Aleksic, "Yugoslav Exports and Relations with Eastern Europe," *Review of International Affairs* (Belgrade), Vol. 6, No. 138 (January 1, 1956), pp. 16-18.

6. Marshall I. Goldman, *Soviet Foreign Aid* (New York: Frederick A. Praeger, 1967), Chapter 9. For a Soviet view of the sugar agreement, see I.

Shvartsshtein, "Rynok Sakhara—Problema Pereproizvodstva," *Vneshniaia Torgovlia*, Vol. 49, No. 2 (February, 1969), pp. 56-59.

7. Radio Peking (NCNA), November 15, 1967. For a recent Chinese evaluation of the political implications of Soviet attempts at economic integration, see Hai Chen, "The Aggressive Nature of Soviet Revisionism's 'New Stage of Economic Integration,' " *Peking Review*, Vol. 12, No. 36 (September 3, 1969), pp. 16-19.

8. For a comparative study of American economic warfare policies, see Gunnar Adler-Karlsson, *Western Economic Warfare 1947-67* (Stockholm: Almqvist and Wiksell, 1968).

9. Frederick Pryor, *The Communist Foreign Trade System* (Cambridge: MIT Press, 1963), Chapter 2.

10. *Zeri i Popullit*, March 25, 1963 (translated in William Griffith, *Albania and the Sino-Soviet Rift* [Cambridge: MIT Press, 1962], p. 341).

11. M. Pericic, "Trade with Countries of Eastern Europe," *Review of International Affairs* (Belgrade), Vol. 10, No. 216 (April 1, 1959), pp. 4-5.

12. Radio Havana, January 4, 1968.

13. *Peking Review*, Vol. 7, No. 19 (May 8, 1964), pp. 14-15.

14. David Floyd, *Rumania* (New York: Frederick A. Praeger, 1965), p. 60.

15. Radio Free Europe Situation Report: Rumania, November 15, 1967.

16. *Radio Bucharest*, December 7, 1967.

17. *Peking Review*, Vol. 7, No. 19 (May 8, 1964), p. 14.

18. *Zeri i Popullit*, December 10, 1961 (translated in Griffith, *op. cit.*, p. 284).

19. Michael Kaser, *Comecon* (London: Oxford University Press, 1967), pp. 153-55.

20. Letter of the Central Committee of the Communist Party of the Soviet Union to the Central Committee of the Communist Party of Yugoslavia, May 4, 1948, published in *The Soviet-Yugoslav Controversy, 1948-58: A Documentary Record*, ed. Robert Bass and Elizabeth Marbury (New York: Prospect Books, 1959), p. 29.

21. *Zeri i Popullit,* March 25, 1962 (translated in Griffith, *op. cit.,* p. 342).

22. For a brief summary of the principles and problems of central planning, see the appendix of Brown and Neuberger, *op. cit.*

23. John C. Campbell, *Tito's Separate Road* (New York: Harper and Row, 1967), p. 171.

24. A list of these agreements is found in Robert L. Price, "International Trade of Communist China 1950-65," *An Economic Profile of Mainland China,* Joint Economic Committee, Congress of the United States (Washington, D.C.: U.S. Government Printing Office, 1967), pp. 595-99.

25. For a discussion of these problems, see Brown and Neuberger, *op. cit.,* p. 76.

26. Translated in Radio Free Europe Situation Report: Albania, June 11, 1964.

27. Maxim Berghianu, "Rumania's Economic Development at the Present Stage," *International Affairs* (Moscow), Vol. 14, No. 9 (September, 1968), p. 15.

CHAPTER 2

YUGOSLAVIA: THE FIRST VICTIM OF SOVIET ECONOMIC WARFARE

Yugoslavia, the first communist nation to oppose Soviet domination openly, was also the first victim of Soviet economic warfare. In this case study, an examination will be made of Stalin's use of various instruments of economic pressure to force the Yugoslavs back into line. Although Stalin combined economic pressure with various forms of political pressure and even military pressure, this study will concentrate on his use of economic pressure in an effort to abstract it for comparison with later cases where Soviet leaders employed economic pressure to discipline recalcitrant communist nations.

THE POLITICAL BACKGROUND OF THE CONFLICT

There was conflict in the relationship between the communist leaders of Russia and Yugoslavia almost from the beginning of Tito's uprising against the Germans in 1941. As Milovan Djilas has related in *Conversations with Stalin*, Stalin simply could not understand that the Yugoslav resistance movement had a spirit of its own—apart from Russian leadership.[1] This conflict was to permeate post-war relations between the two nations and culminate in the expulsion of Yugoslavia from the Cominform in 1948.

The basic issue in the conflict between Stalin and Tito was the latter's refusal to accept dictation from the USSR. Unlike the leaders of most of the other communist states of Eastern Europe who had come to power on the tips of Soviet bayonets,* Tito had taken power primarily through his own efforts and he displayed no sign of becoming a servile follower of the Russian dictator.

---

*The threat of a move by the Red Army was a major factor enabling the Czech Communists to seize power. The Albanian Communist leaders had come to power with the help of the Yugoslavs. See Chapter 3.

In the years following the war, Tito and Stalin came into conflict on a number of issues. First, Tito was outspokenly unhappy because of the Soviet Union's failure to give sufficient backing to his territorial claims against Italy and Austria. Second, there was a serious difference of opinion over the proper organization and training of Yugoslavia's army, which Stalin tried to make an adjunct of the Russian Army. Another irritant to Tito was the widespread activity of the Soviet secret police in Yugoslavia which, the Yugoslav leader later claimed, tried to recruit individuals who were "negatively inclined toward the new [Tito-controlled] Yugoslavia."[2]

Neither were the economic relations between Yugoslavia and the Soviet Union devoid of conflict. The Yugoslavs were very unhappy at the operation of the two joint stock companies they had agreed to set up with the USSR. Soviet attempts to exploit Yugoslavia economically through the joint stock companies, as it was doing to the other nations of Eastern Europe, caused increasing resentment on the part of the Yugoslavs. In his biography of Tito, which appeared in 1953, Vladimir Dedijer described the Soviet manipulation of the joint stock companies in these words:

> These agreements on the joint stock companies more than anything up to then in our experience with the Soviet Union opened the eyes of our people to Russia's real intentions toward Yugoslavia, her unwillingness to see Yugoslavia develop its economic potential freely and her endeavors to enslave us economically.[3]

Other conflicts of an economic nature included Yugoslavia's dissatisfaction at the amount of economic assistance the Russians were willing to provide for its five-year plan and clashes as to the proper level of pricing in their trade relations. The overriding conflict, however, was the one cited by Djilas—the Yugoslav refusal to become an obedient satellite of the Soviet Union.

As the USSR began to tighten its hold over Eastern Europe following the U.S. offer of Marshall Plan aid to several of the nations of the region, Stalin saw the need to curb Tito's independent activities throughout the area. These included satellization of Albania, assistance to the Greek communist guerrillas, and sponsorship of the idea of a Balkan Federation. Although Stalin permitted these independent activities during the 1945-47 period of relative flux in Eastern Europe, Tito's apparent desire to set himself up as the "Stalin of the Balkans" could no longer be tolerated when Stalin decided to solidify Russian control. Tito's brand of independent "nationalist" communism became anathema to Stalin (who was soon to brand it "anti-Soviet"), and in December, 1947, he took action to curb it. Although none of the documents yet published reveal Stalin's precise motivation for turning to the economic weapon in the Soviet arsenal for use against Tito, this must have appeared to Stalin as an effective way of curbing the Yugoslav leader's independent proclivities since, as the next section will indicate, Yugoslavia was quite vulnerable to Soviet economic pressure.

YUGOSLAVIA'S ECONOMIC VULNERABILITY

There is no question but that Yugoslavia's economic vulnerability, much of it self-created, was substantial. Yugoslavia had suffered great destruction during the war, and Stalin, who had sent numerous advisors to Yugoslavia, was well aware of the fact. Yugoslavia's transportation system was badly disrupted with no less than 43 per cent of its railway track (6,100 kilometers), 76 per cent of the locomotives, and 84 per cent of the railway carriages destroyed or severely damaged. In addition, 88 per cent of its inland river fleet was destroyed. Yugoslavia's small industrial base was also hit hard. One Yugoslav economist has estimated that no less than 40 per cent of his country's industrial capacity was destroyed, with 3,438 industrial enterprises, 50 per cent of its mines, and 251 electric stations knocked out of operation. Yugoslavia's civilian population suffered greatly, with 59,810 houses in urban areas and 372,660 peasant homes destroyed. Yugoslavia lost 1,700,000 people including 90,000 of its 295,105 industrial workers.[4]

Despite these losses, the Yugoslav leaders in numerous speeches and statements proclaimed that Yugoslavia's future lay in its rapid industrialization and transformation from an agrarian to an industrial country. For this reason, the Yugoslav leaders embarked in 1947—well before Yugoslavia had recovered from the effects of the war—on a very ambitious, if not grandiose, five-year plan which had as its aim a 323 per cent increase in industrial production over Yugoslavia's pre-war production level. In the words of Tito:

Industrialization and electrification on a modern technical base and especially the creation of heavy industry as the main element in developing the other branches of the economy—this is the developmental plan of our national economy.[5]

The successful completion of the plan, however, was heavily dependent on imports of such raw materials as coke, oil, and cotton as well as capital goods such as machinery and equipment. Other prerequisites included capital loans and technical assistance, because not only capital but skilled labor and trained managers were in short supply in post-war Yugoslavia. With Yugoslavia's trade primarily geared to the Soviet-controlled nations during this period, and the USSR its only source of capital loans and technical assistance, Yugoslavia was vulnerable to Soviet economic pressure in a number of areas. (Yugoslavia had received UNRRA aid up to the middle of 1947; Milutin Bogosavljevic has estimated that total UNRRA aid amounted to only 2.3 per cent of total war damage.[6])

Yugoslavia was the first of the East European communist nations to embark on a five-year plan. The plan sought to triple the amount of steel produced (235,000 tons to 750,000 tons) and increase the annual extraction of iron ore from 613,000 tons to 1,500,000 and of coal from 6,068,000 tons to 16,500,000. In addition, many products such as trucks, tractors, heavy locomotives, and heavy construction machinery were to be produced for the first time in Yugoslavia.[7] Yet Yugoslavia's domestic capabilities to achieve this goal were limited due to a lack of capital and raw materials. Indeed, there was a major debate between Tito and two of his lieutenants, Andrija Hebrang and Sreten Zujovic, who from their positions in Yugoslavia's economic bureaucracy questioned the viability of such an ambitious plan. (See below for a later Yugoslav view of their opposition.) Nonetheless, Tito pushed on with his industrialization plans, and both Hebrang and Zujovic lost power within the economic bureaucracy as a result of their opposition. They were to emerge several years later, however, as opponents of Tito and spokesmen for the USSR during the Stalin-Tito conflict.

Tito pursued two policies to overcome Yugoslavia's shortage of capital goods and raw materials. The first was the acquisition of capital aid and technical assistance from the Soviet Union, and the second was extensive trade relations with that nation and the others of Eastern Europe whereby Yugoslavia would exchange its raw materials and agricultural goods in return for capital goods and other raw materials. In July, 1947, the first of Tito's policies bore fruit when he obtained a capital goods credit of $135 million from the Soviet Union. Although not completely satisfactory to the Yugoslavs, the loan was to provide Yugoslavia the following industrial installations: "steel plants complete with a coking plant; installations for extracting and refining oil; a zinc electrolysis plant; a sulphuric acid factory; copper and aluminum rolling mills and molybdenum installations."[8] The USSR, which in 1946 had given Yugoslavia a $9 million loan, also gave Yugoslavia a $78 million grant for the purchase of armaments and "military-technical" supplies.[9]

Soviet technical aid was of equal importance to Yugoslavia. In Chapter 1, mention was made of a developing country's need for technical assistance; Yugoslavia was no exception to the pattern. Indeed, in a speech to a group of Bulgarian correspondents in June, 1947, Tito himself was very explicit in his recognition of Yugoslavia's weakness in this area. In discussing the problems Yugoslavia was encountering in its five-year plan, the Yugoslav leader stated that "the greatest problem of the five-year plan is the training of skilled workers and technicians."[10] One year later, Boris Kidric, Yugoslavia's Minister of Heavy Industry, gave the following description of the quality of Yugoslavia's managerial cadres and the effect the short supply of skilled managers was having on the Yugoslav economy:

Our new [managerial] cadres were drawn into employment haphazardly.... They as yet do not have solid technical knowledge ... [but] to mark time owing to the shortage of cadres or to pursue detrimental competition with other institutions or enterprises for personnel is an extremely harmful activity.[11]

Kidric also disclosed the problems faced by the Yugoslav central planners:

One of the gravest shortcomings in the organization of our trade is the inability of our poorly developed operative planning to embrace both concrete regions which are to be supplied and the sources of supply.[12]

The Russian economic advisors thus performed a very valuable function in training Yugoslav workers, technicians, managers, and planners and played an important role in the early stages of Yugoslavia's five-year plan.

The second policy followed by the Yugoslavs in acquiring the necessary imports for their five-year plan was trade with the East European countries and the USSR. The basic pattern lay in the supply of Yugoslav raw materials such as iron ore, lead, zinc, copper, and timber in return for oil, coke, and machinery; and Yugoslavia signed long-term economic agreements with Poland, Czechoslovakia, Hungary, and the USSR to coincide with its five-year plan. In all, Yugoslavia planned to obtain 95 per cent of its capital imports during the period of the five-year plan from the USSR or Soviet-controlled countries.[13]

The USSR was clearly aware of Yugoslavia's dependence on foreign trade. In an otherwise glowing article in the June, 1947, issue of *Vneshniaia Torgovlia* describing the goals of Yugoslavia's five-year plan and the determination of the Yugoslav people to achieve it, the Soviet economist V. Shvetz stated:

> For the realization of the basic goals of the five year plan for the industrialization of the state, Yugoslavia must purchase abroad a great quantity of equipment, particularly for ferrous and non-ferrous metallurgy, for the power generation industry, and for transportation. In order to acquire the necessary equipment from abroad Yugoslavia must develop its own exports, especially those goods such as copper, antimony, mercury, pyrites, lumber, tobacco, hemp, calcium soda, caustic soda, cement, iron ore, brown coal, tanin extract, cigarette paper, prunes, wine, vodka, alcohol, livestock, meat, poultry, and other agricultural products.[14]

Trade statistics for the period 1945-48 indicate the dependence of Yugoslavia on nations in the Russian sphere of influence for both its reconstruction and economic development. In 1947, for example, the year before the Cominform break, no less than 56.1 per cent of Yugoslavia's total imports came from these countries and 52.7 per cent of her exports were directed to them.[15] A commodity study of Yugoslavia's trade with the nations of East Europe and the USSR for the entire 1945-48 period further indicates the extent of Yugoslavia's dependence on this area as a source of its imports and as a market for its exports. Yugoslavia imported the following percentages of its import needs from these countries: 100 per cent of its coal and coke, 85 per cent of its fertilizer, 60 per cent of its oil, all of its rolling stock, and almost all of its steel tubing. In return, Yugoslavia sent the following share of its exports to the Soviet-controlled nations: 100 per cent of its iron ore, 97 per cent of its zinc, 72 per cent of its copper, 62 per cent of its antimony, and 40 per cent of its lead.[16] But in June, 1947, Tito apparently saw these trade relations as of benefit to his country, not as a handicap. Indeed, in his talk to the Bulgarian correspondents, he stated that because of trade with the nations of Eastern Europe and the USSR "we have assured fulfillment of the five year plan and we are not dependent on the Western powers."[17] He was to change his views radically sixteen months later.

Thus by the end of 1947, because of its dependence on Soviet economic aid and on trade with countries controlled by Stalin, Yugoslavia was markedly vulnerable to Soviet economic pressure. But before the pattern of Stalin's economic pressure is examined, it would be well to discuss the nature of Yugoslavia's relations with the industrial nations of the West, its only alternative sources of capital aid and technical assistance should Soviet aid be cut off.

With the exception of neutral Sweden, Yugoslavia's relations with the industrialized nations of the West were far from good, and the Yugoslav leadership in retrospect has asserted that Stalin exploited the situation to bring pressure on their country:

> He (Stalin) made abundant use of the fact that during the early postwar years Yugoslavia was threatened by other great powers; he himself endeavored to complicate these relations so as to make us easier prey. And indeed we were compelled to be silent for a long time because a greater danger at one time threatened us from the West. Finally, considering that conditions were ripe, Stalin resolved on an open blow.[18]

Yugoslavia and the West were in serious conflict even before the end of World War II over Trieste and the Austrian border. The proclamation of a Soviet-type republic, nationalization of Western-owned property, and the rapid repression of all non-communist groups served to further lower Yugoslavia's reputation in the West.[19]

From the Yugoslav point of view, the West was also the enemy. Their communist ideological suspicion of the capitalist West was heightened by a series of conflicts of a purely nationalistic nature. In addition to the Austrian and Trieste disputes, the Yugoslavs were angered that the gold the Royal Yugoslavian Government had deposited in the United States for safekeeping at the beginning of World War II remained frozen and was not returned to Yugoslavia's new government. In addition, Tito and his followers resented the fact that men whom they considered "war criminals" had been allowed to pass freely through the West. A further note of discord stemmed from the fact that Yugoslavia's river shipping which the German occupation forces had seized and brought to Germany remained in Western hands and was not returned to Yugoslavia.[20] This was particularly serious in that, as stated above, Yugoslavia's internal transportation system had been shattered by the war.

In 1946, relations between Yugoslavia and the West deteriorated still further with the shooting down of an American transport plane that had strayed over Yugoslavia. Although the Yugoslav government grudgingly apologized for the incident and paid compensation, the Western nations saw this as but further evidence of Yugoslavia's hostility. To the West throughout 1946 and 1947, Yugoslavia gave the appearance of being the most aggressive and most Sovietized of any of the new communist regimes in Eastern Europe. Its aid to the communist rebels in Greece only enhanced this image. For these reasons, it must have seemed unlikely to Stalin that Yugoslavia would receive aid from the West in the case of conflict.

THE PATTERN OF SOVIET ECONOMIC PRESSURE

In December, 1947, Stalin began to exploit Yugoslavia's economic vulnerability in an attempt to curb Tito's independent activities. It was at this point that the Soviet dictator began to delay the scheduled trade negotiations between the two nations. Whereas the existing trade agreement was to expire in April, 1948, and the successful fulfillment of the Yugoslav five-year plan was to a large extent dependent on Soviet supplies, the postponement of the trade talks became a matter of considerable concern to Tito.[21]

The Yugoslav leader, however, wasted little time in beginning the search for alternate suppliers. On January 3, 1948, he requested an audience with American Ambassador Cavendish Cannon. At this meeting in which Tito was reported to be "considerably friendlier" than in earlier talks, the Yugoslav leader made a new proposal for the disposition of the Yugoslav gold held in the United States. Instead of continuing to demand the return of all the gold (some $50 million), he now suggested that $20 million be held by the United States until American claims against Yugoslavia (primarily for nationalized American enterprises) were adjudicated. Tito further proposed that the remaining $30 million be utilized for the purchase of machinery and industrial equipment in the United States.[22] Although the Yugoslav proposal was rejected by Secretary of State Marshall on January 14, 1948,[23] Tito's meeting with the U.S. ambassador indicated that he was willing to do business with the United States if this would be in Yugoslavia's national interest.

Indeed, Tito made a further attempt to improve relations with the United States on January 22 when an official military ceremony was held honoring the American fliers who had died while bombing the German and Italian troops occupying Yugoslavia during World War II.[24] These efforts, however, were to have no immediate effect on improving relations with the United States.

Stalin's next move against Yugoslavia came in February, 1948. In early February, Tito and Georgi Dimitrov (the Bulgarian party leader) were summoned to Moscow. Tito, sensing a trap, did not go himself but sent Milovan Djilas in his place. At this meeting, the two Balkan leaders were severely criticized by Stalin, who upbraided them for signing a treaty of alliance he had told them to postpone. Djilas was then singled out for the Kremlin leader's wrath because Yugoslavia had sent troops and airplanes into Albania without first informing him and had sent aid to the Greek communist guerrillas even though their cause, in Stalin's opinion, was hopeless.[25] Following this meeting, Edvard Kardelj, another Yugoslav Politburo member who attended the meeting, was forced to sign an agreement with the USSR for "mutual consultation" on foreign policy.[26]

In the latter part of February, Stalin underscored this political pressure with increased economic pressure on the Tito regime. The Soviet Deputy Minister for Foreign Trade, Aleksei D. Krutikov, told his Yugoslavian counterpart, Bogdan Crnobrnija, that the Yugoslav trade delegation that had been waiting in Belgrade for two months need not come to Moscow "since the Soviet Government would not be able to sign a protocol on the further exchange of goods for 1948, and talks on this question could be resumed only towards the end of 1948."[27] Tito's response to these pressures was to call a special meeting of his Central Committee on March 1, 1948, at which he discussed the worsening relations with the USSR. Although Boris Kidric, Minister of Heavy Industry, pointed out the pernicious effects of the delay in trade negotiations for Yugoslavia's five-year plan, he, together with almost all the other Central Committee members, agreed with Tito that Yugoslavia had to "endure the pressure" for the sake of its independence.[28]

Stalin, who was informed of the meeting by one of the participants (Sreten Zujovic), then began to increase the pressure. On March 19, he ordered the withdrawal of all the Russian technical experts who were acting as advisors in Yugoslavia (he had withdrawn all military advisors one day earlier). The stated reasons for the withdrawal of advisors was that, unlike the "friendly reception" the advisors had been accorded in the other Peoples Democracies, in Yugoslavia they had been shown "a lack of hospitality and a lack of confidence." In particular, the Yugoslav regime was admonished for denying the Soviet advisors freedom to gather economic information and for placing them under the surveillance of the Yugoslav secret police.[29]

It is difficult to overestimate the consequences of this withdrawal to an economy as lacking in skilled managers, planners, and workers as the Yugoslav. Mention has already been made of the critical shortage facing Yugoslavia in these areas. Stalin's employment of this form of economic pressure, coupled with the earlier delay in trade negotiations, seems clearly intended to pressure the Tito regime into submission or, barring this, to split it. It is possible that Stalin assumed that members of the Yugoslav economic apparatus who would be particularly sensitive to Soviet economic pressure would persuade the other Yugoslav leaders to give in to Soviet demands. Indeed, he may have been encouraged in this belief by the fact that two of the key members of Yugoslavia's economic apparatus—Andrija Hebrang, President of the Economic Council, and Sreten Zujovic, Minister of Transport (both of whom the Yugoslavs later branded as Soviet agents)— had, as seen above, clashed with Tito earlier on the pace of development of the Yugoslav economy.

Eight days after the advisors were withdrawn, Stalin gave further evidence of his desire to split the Yugoslav party. In a letter to the Yugoslav Central Committee in which he castigated Tito for his "anti-Soviet policies," the Soviet leader openly threatened to appeal to the Yugoslav "Party masses" over the head of Tito and his close associates—Djilas, Kardelj, Alexander Rankovic, and Kidric:

We do not doubt that the Yugoslav Party masses would disown this anti-Soviet criticism as alien and hostile *if they knew* about it. We

> think this is the reason why the Yugoslav officials make these [anti-Soviet] criticisms in secret, behind the backs of the masses [emphasis added].[30]

Following receipt of this letter, Tito decided to convene another meeting of the Yugoslav Central Committee. In his biography of Tito, Vladimir Dedijer reveals that Tito considered the "most difficult period" of his conflict with Stalin was between March 27, when Stalin's letter arrived, and April 12, when the meeting of the Yugoslav Central Committee was held—a meeting in which, in Dedijer's words, "Stalin hoped Zujovic would draw the majority of the Central Committee to his side."[31]

Tito himself, however, was not idle during this period. Although the Yugoslavs were later to claim that at this time their relations with the West were at their worst level since World War II because of the conflict over Trieste,[32] Tito had evidently not given up hope of acquiring the United States as an alternate supplier, and he continued his behind-the-scenes work to arrange for the release of the U.S.-held gold. Significantly, on April 2, it was officially announced that Yugoslavia had engaged the prestigious Washington law firm of Pehle and Lesser (already the agent of France in the United States) to act as its agent in the United States for this purpose.[33]

When the Central Committee meeting was held, Tito received its almost unanimous support (with the exception of Zujovic). Backed by a united Central Committee, Tito replied to Stalin's letter on April 13 not only by rejecting charges of carrying on anti-Soviet policies but even by brashly requesting *further* Soviet aid:

> Even though we know that the USSR has tremendous difficulties with the reconstruction of devastated lands, we rightfully expect the assistance of the USSR in the development of our country and the realization of the five year plan without material deprivation to the people of the USSR, because we feel it is to the interest of the USSR for the new Yugoslavia to be stronger, since it is face to face with the capitalist world which is endangering not only its peaceful development but the development of other countries of people's democracy and even the development of the USSR.[34]

On April 23, Tito made another move to strengthen his country in the growing confrontation with the Soviet Union by announcing a 27 per cent increase in defense expenditures in order to build up Yugoslavia's armament industry.[35] Although Kardelj in a speech to the Second Postwar Congress of the Liberation Front later justified the increased expenditure on "the warmongering actions of the Western Powers,"[36] there is no question that the Yugoslav rifles could point both ways—and hitherto Yugoslavia had purchased most of its war material from the USSR.

Stalin's next move did not take place until May 4, 1948. In a letter to the Yugoslav Central Committee on that date, Stalin further castigated the "narrow circles of Yugoslav Party cadres" for their anti-Soviet policies and again threatened to go over the heads of the Central Committee to the party masses. In addition, Stalin proposed bringing the Yugoslav-Soviet conflict to the Cominform—a body in which the USSR had overwhelming influence. As for Tito's brash request for further Soviet economic aid, Stalin's answer was brief and to the point:

> They [the Yugoslav leaders] should also bear in mind that retaining this [anti-Soviet] attitude means depriving themselves of the right to demand material and any other assistance from the USSR, because the Soviet Union can only offer aid to friends.[37]

In the period between the Soviet letter and the Cominform meeting, Tito took several steps to further strengthen his position. In the latter part of May, Zujovic and Hebrang were officially purged and in early June the Yugoslav government ordered pre-military training for all high school boys and girls under military service age. The official justification for this order was as follows: "Every Yugoslav must educate himself in love of and fidelity to the fatherland, and must become capable of defending its freedom and independence."[38]

The Soviet-dominated Cominform meeting, which the Yugoslavs refused to attend, denounced the "anti-Soviet" attitude of the Tito regime as "incompatible with Marxism-Leninism and only appropriate to *nationalists*"[39] (emphasis added). Its final resolution contained an open appeal to the Yugoslav party to overthrow Tito:

> The Information Bureau does not doubt that inside the Communist Party of Yugoslavia there are enough healthy elements, loyal to Marxism-Leninism, and to the international traditions of the Yugoslav Communist Party and to the united Socialist front.
>
> Their task is to compel the present leaders to recognize their mistakes openly and honestly and to rectify them; to break with nationalism, return to internationalism; and in every way to consolidate the united front against imperialism.
>
> Should the present leaders of the Yugoslav Party be incapable of doing this, their job is to replace them and to advance a new internationalist leadership of the Party.[40]

But perhaps to Stalin's surprise, the Yugoslav party did not split and Tito remained in power. Indeed, Tito and his followers decided to publish the Cominform resolution throughout Yugoslavia to rally support for their regime. To bolster the regime economically, a 3,500,000,000 dinar ($70 million) internal loan was floated which the Yugoslav government claimed on July 6 was 80 per cent subscribed because "the patriotic feelings of the Yugoslav people had been aroused by the Cominform resolution."[41] Yugoslavia's economy was further strengthened by the announcement on July 4 that the United States had agreed to unfreeze most of the Yugoslav gold it had been holding since the war, although the American officials responsible for the agreement stated that the timing of their announcement "had no bearing whatsoever on Yugoslavia's quarrel with the Cominform."[42]

Tito's next major step was to hold a Party Congress on July 21 in which he informed the members of the Yugoslav party of his regime's position in its conflict with the Cominform. The speeches delivered at the Congress by Tito, Kardelj, Djilas, Rankovic, and Kidric dealt with two main issues. The first was a profession of Yugoslavia's continued loyalty to the Soviet Union and the socialist system. Having made this point, Yugoslav leaders went on to state their determination to "build Socialism" in Yugoslavia the Yugoslav way.* Indeed, Hebrang and Zujovic were repeatedly singled out for criticism because they had attempted to "artificially" adopt the methods of the USSR.

> Attempts were made to transplant the direct ways and forms from the first years after the October Revolution mechanically, without comprehensive analysis of their contents, without realistic analyses of our internal conditions, without a dialectical analysis of our general conditions.
> We know that such automatism, that such opposition to Marxist dialectics had its original source in Hebrang and Zujovic.[43]

Although Kardelj remarked in his speech that "there were some honorable comrades in our party who wavered as a result of the Cominform resolution,"[44] most of the party stood firm behind Tito,** and this fact could not have been lost to the Kremlin. Consequently, whereas Stalin's earlier attempts at limited economic pressure had failed and his attempt to split the Yugoslav party had met a similar fate, in the middle of August he began to exert increased economic and political pressure. It is interesting to note, however, that Stalin escalated the economic pressure against Yugoslavia only gradually, and there was a full year between the Cominform resolution and the imposition of the total economic blockade in July, 1949. If it is remembered that the more rapidly an embargo is effected, the more likely it is to disrupt a target nation's economy, it is necessary to examine Stalin's motivations in waiting so long. A tentative hypothesis explaining Stalin's "gradualism" will be offered below after a detailed description has been presented of the kinds of pressures he employed and the defensive measures taken by Tito.

Less than a month after the Yugoslav Congress, Stalin began to increase the economic pressure. In August, Yugoslavia lost an important "invisible export" when tourists from Cominform countries ceased coming to Yugoslavia.[45] At the same time, Rumania began to delay shipments of oil derivatives.[46] On September 8, *Pravda* printed a one-half page editorial that signaled the exclusion of Yugoslavia from the Communist Camp, at least insofar as the Russians were concerned. The editorial stated that "Tito had not drawn the necessary conclusions from the Cominform's resolution and had not understood that his nationalist policy leads to the loss of Yugoslavia's truest

---

*The Yugoslav government translated and reprinted these speeches in pamphlet form.

**Tito purged many of the remaining opposition in August and September.

allies—the communist parties of the world." The editorial went on to say that the Yugoslav Communist Party was isolated both inside and outside the nation and indeed was "presently in one general camp with the imperialists."[4][7]

Following the *Pravda* editorial, economic pressure against Yugoslavia increased. Its communist trade partners began to delay shipments of cotton, oil, and coke. In addition, in October Poland cancelled meetings of the Joint Polish-Yugoslav Commission for Economic Cooperation, and Rumania refused to answer a Yugoslav request for trade negotiations.[4][8] The Yugoslavs, however, were already taking steps to meet the threat. On October 3, it was revealed that the Yugoslav government had been trying to convince skilled Yugoslav workers living abroad to come back to Yugoslavia to "build up the homeland."[4][9] On October 10, in a speech to the workers of the Bor copper mine, Tito stated that Yugoslavia was short of oil and other commodities because of her political difficulties with the Cominform nations and as a result had to seek alternative suppliers in the West.[5][0] On November 18, the Yugoslav party paper *Borba* announced new targets for the five-year plan. These targets raised the goals for timber and raw material production—items that Yugoslavia could export to the West in return for badly needed imports.[5][1]

It was not until November 25, however, that the Yugoslavs tacitly admitted that the growing Cominform economic pressure was having some effect. In a speech to the Second Congress of the Croatian Communist Party on that date, Tito revealed that in the Yugoslav five-year plan "secondary projects" would have to be eliminated. In fact, Tito bluntly told the Yugoslav people that consumer goods would have to be sacrificed for industrialization:

> We must never lose sight of the principal targets—the blast furnaces,
> foundries, coke, coal, oil and housing projects for our workers. . . .
> After we have created the basic conditions of our industrialization,
> then we will throw ourselves entirely into the production of those
> articles which are needed by our people and which will give our
> people more material proof of what socialism means.[5][2]

On November 27, it was announced that Yugoslavia had sought metallurgical coke from the coal committee of the Economic Commission for Europe and had been allocated 50,000 tons for the first quarter of 1949.[5][3] Previously, Yugoslavia had obtained all its metallurgical coke from Czechoslovakia and Poland. Yugoslavia further strengthened its economic position on December 23 when, after prolonged negotiations, a $120 million trade agreement was signed with England.[5][4] Although this agreement did not provide Yugoslavia with the capital goods necessary for its five-year plan, it nonetheless supplied many of the raw materials, such as gasoline and cotton, which the Cominform nations had begun to embargo.

Although the Cominform nations had delayed or discontinued deliveries to Yugoslavia, Stalin had not yet decided to institute a complete embargo. On December 27, the USSR signed a trade protocol with Yugoslavia, but for a very sharply reduced amount of goods. The TASS communique clearly stated the political reasons for the drop in trade:

> Owing to the hostile policy of the Yugoslav government towards the Soviet Union, in consequence of which it is impossible to maintain large scale economic exchange between the USSR and Yugoslavia, the Protocol provides for reduced exchange of goods between the USSR and Yugoslavia for 1949. This exchange of goods will be reduced by eight times as compared with 1948.[55]

At the same time that Stalin was officially curtailing trade with Yugoslavia, Tito was informing his nation of the reasons for Yugoslavia's turn to the West in its economic relations. In a speech to Parliament on December 27, Tito stated:

> If our allies do not want to help us industrialize, if they violate various obligations they made with us, then of course we must sell our raw materials elsewhere even if it be to capitalist countries in order to buy the machines we need for the mechanization of our mines and heavy industry. . . . We had to ask our working people, our workers, our youth, our People's Front to intensify their efforts in extraction of different ores, in the felling of trees and so forth, so that we might be able to export and sell and purchase that material which was denied us through this incomprehensible economic pressure.[56]

The Yugoslav leader also proclaimed that Yugoslavia would now exploit its own capacities to the maximum extent to ensure the successful completion of the five-year plan.[57] On December 28, Boris Kidric revealed in a speech to Parliament that Yugoslavia had had to spend $20 million in the West in 1948 to obtain such products as cotton, oil, construction steel, asbestos, and rubber which the Cominform nations had failed to deliver. Kidric also stated that the Soviet bloc nations had delivered only 35 per cent of the machinery Yugoslavia had ordered and that the mining machinery they had sent had arrived without motors. Kidric attributed the failure of the mining industry to meet its quota (only 58.3 per cent fulfilled) to this factor.[58] Whereas Yugoslavia now depended to a large extent on the export of mined raw materials to pay for its purchases in the West, this was a particularly serious form of pressure. Following these speeches, the Yugoslav Parliament voted to increase capital investment and military spending by 8 billion dinars ($160 million).[59]

In February, 1949, Stalin increased the economic pressure one more notch when the USSR reneged on the long-term capital aid agreement it had signed with Yugoslavia in 1947.[60] At the same time, Stalin emphasized the exclusion of Yugoslavia from the Communist Camp by rejecting its request to join the Council for Mutual Economic Assistance (COMECON), the intra-bloc economic organization that had just been founded as a response to the Marshall Plan. In his note of February 11, Stalin made it clear to the Yugoslavs that they would gain no benefits from economic cooperation unless their policies were radically altered:

The Council for Mutual Economic Assistance has not been set up for purposes of ordinary economic cooperation of the type that exists between the USSR and Belgium and Holland in the field of commerce, for instance. This Council was set up for purposes of extensive economic cooperation among countries which are *mutually pursuing an honest and friendly policy. . . .*

The Soviet Government considers the participation of Yugo-slavia in the Council for Mutual Economic Assistance as desirable. Participation in the Council for Mutual Economic Assistance, however, will be possible only if the Yugoslav Government renounces its hostile policy towards the USSR and the countries of peoples democracy and if it returns to the former policy of friendship. The Soviet Government has no doubt that only a resolute break with the policy of hostility, and a return to the policy of friendship, can correspond to the essential interests of the Yugoslav peoples, *the interests of their economic prosperity* and the independence of the Yugoslav State [emphasis added].[61]

The Yugoslavs, meanwhile, continued their efforts to withstand the Soviet pressure. On February 5, 1949, the Yugoslav government announced that 171,500 youths had been mobilized for work on public works projects such as railroads and highways.[62] By resorting to youth brigades, the Yugoslav government was attempting to substitute large amounts of manpower for the capital goods they were no longer receiving from Cominform countries.* In March, the Yugoslav government began negotiations with British and American firms to purchase steel mills, and on April 24, these efforts bore fruit when it was announced that Yugoslavia had made a raw-material-for-capital-equipment deal with an American firm.** On this date, Paul F. Langer, a consulting engineer for Youngstown Sheet and Tube Company, announced that his company, through a subsidiary, would supply Yugoslavia with several million dollars worth of oil drilling equipment in return for "considerable quantities" of lead, copper, antimony, and chromium.[63]

Even by exporting raw materials, however, Yugoslavia was having difficulty acquiring all the needed imports for its five-year plan.*** Conse-quently, the next Yugoslav move was to request economic aid from Western nations. On May 4, 1949, American Secretary of State Dean Acheson revealed that the Yugoslav government had approached the International Bank for Reconstruction and Development for a loan and had requested that the U.S.

---

*The same pattern on a much larger scale was to be repeated ten years later by the Communist Chinese in their "Great Leap Forward" (see Chapter 4).

**Early in 1949, the U.S. government had removed Yugoslavia from the list of communist nations subject to the American embargo.

***Yugoslav exports fell 37 per cent in 1949 compared with 1948, as the country had difficulty in restructuring its export trade to Western markets.

representative on the bank take a "friendly attitude" toward the loan request.[64]

The complete Soviet bloc trade embargo was implemented shortly thereafter. In June, 1949, one Cominform nation after another denounced its trade agreement with Yugoslavia. The documents on the rupture of trade between Hungary and Yugoslavia offer a good example of the ideological justifications employed by the Soviet bloc in sundering trade. Hungary by an agreement of July 24, 1947, was to send Hungarian equipment for the establishment of a Yugoslav aluminum industry for which it was to be repaid by Yugoslav exports of aluminum over a period of years. In addition, Hungary was committed to sending heavy electrical installations in return for Yugoslav exports of iron ore, copper, and non-ferrous metals.[65] In all, Hungary was to obtain 50 per cent of its timber imports, 50 per cent of its iron ore imports, and 20 per cent of its non-ferrous metal imports from Yugoslavia.[66] Thus it can be seen that any trade rupture would damage Hungary's five-year plan as well as Yugoslavia's. Nonetheless, on June 18, 1949, the Hungarian government unilaterally broke the trade agreement:

> On July 24, 1947 the Hungarian and Yugoslav governments signed a five-year economic agreement on cooperation which the Hungarian government signed with a view to strengthening the ties between the two countries on the basis of planned economy both as regards production and foreign trade. . . . The attitude of the government of the FPRY (Federal Peoples Republic of Yugoslavia) towards this question proves that the Yugoslav government, on the one hand, *is not capable of pursuing a policy of planned economy or does not desire to continue pursuing it,* and, on the other hand, has a hostile stand towards the states which are proceeding along the road of socialism, and does not wish to strengthen its economic ties with us, but with the imperialist powers.
>
> *Owing to these circumstances all the prerequisites have ceased to exist on the basis of which the Hungarian government signed the five year Hungarian-Yugoslav economic agreement on cooperation.*
>
> *The agreement could be carried out only if both countries were to continue along the road of socialism but Yugoslavia has digressed from that road* [emphasis added].[67]

Thus, approximately one and one-half years from the time that the first form of economic pressure was applied by the USSR, the ultimate form of economic pressure, an economic blockade, was imposed. The question arises, however, why Stalin did not impose the economic blockade on Yugoslavia more quickly, because in the year and a half interval since the USSR began to delay trade negotiations, the Yugoslav leaders clearly had had ample time to arrange for alternate (though not yet equivalent) supplies of raw materials and machinery and even had time to initiate negotiations for economic aid from the West.

There are several possible explanations for this comparatively long period. The first is a purely economic one; namely, that both the USSR and its satellites were in such need of Yugoslav raw materials that they could not afford to break off relations too rapidly. There is some merit to this explanation, although it does not appear to be the most important one. The Soviet Union, which strictly dictated to its satellites after June, 1948, was not particularly vulnerable to Yugoslav economic counterpressure. Although Soviet exports to Yugoslavia in 1947 accounted for 16.8 per cent of the latter's total imports, Yugoslavia's exports to the USSR in 1947 comprised only .4 per cent of all Russian imports. Figures for 1948 were similar. Russia accounted for 10 per cent of Yugoslavia's imports in 1948 whereas Yugoslavia still comprised only .4 per cent of Soviet imports.[68] According to the commodity statistics published by the USSR, the Soviet Union in 1949 was able to increase its total imports of all commodities it had previously imported from Yugoslavia with the exception of lead, berries, fresh fruit, and dried fruit.[69] The last three commodities were not vital for the Soviet economy, and by 1950 the Soviets were able to partially make up their shortage of lead by imports from North Korea. The other Cominform nations had greater problems. The Hungarians, for example, who had built a large steel mill in the expectation of obtaining iron ore from Yugoslavia, now had to import it at great cost from the USSR.[70] The other Cominform nations also turned to the USSR for most of the raw material imports they had previously acquired from Yugoslavia.

Although economic considerations may have played some role in the delay of the total embargo, the very pattern in which economic pressure was exerted indicates that political considerations played a more important one. Stalin seems to have followed a measured policy of escalation in exerting economic pressure on Yugoslavia; that is, he expected at each juncture that an increased amount of economic pressure coupled with continued political attacks would suffice to either break the Tito regime or force it to capitulate to Soviet demands. A review of the steps taken by Stalin will illustrate the pattern. First came the delay in trade negotiations, a relatively minor form of pressure that was easily reversible. The next step, the withdrawal of Soviet advisors, was more serious but also reversible with a minimum of harm to the Yugoslav economy. Stalin stepped up the pressure, however, following the failure of the Cominform resolution to topple Tito. First he brought about a delay in the shipment of goods (particularly raw materials), then an abrogation of capital delivery contracts, and finally a total embargo. It was as if at each stage Stalin expected Tito's regime to crack under the pressure.

By the end of August, 1949, however, it must have appeared even to Stalin that economic pressure alone would not be enough to overthrow the Tito regime. Following the completion of a $94 million trade agreement on August 4 between Yugoslavia and Italy, through which Yugoslavia was to obtain both raw materials *and* industrial machinery,[71] and the announcement several days earlier that the International Bank for Reconstruction and Development would send a mission to Yugoslavia to investigate conditions for a loan,[72] Stalin moved three Soviet divisions to staging areas near Hungary's border with Yugoslavia.[73] Their presence, coupled with the increasing number of incidents on Yugoslavia's borders with Cominform nations, presented another form of threat against Tito. On September 5, *Pravda* called for an entirely new Yugoslav Communist Party and a new Central Committee because "the present situation requires the formation of a new party organization consisting of healthy forces from the Communist Party of Yugoslavia, honest workers, working peasants and intelligentsia . . . remaining true to friendship with the USSR."[74]

Following the publication of this article, Stalin increased military maneuvers on Yugoslavia's borders, and he was to continue this dual policy of military pressure—though not attack—and economic blockade until he died in 1953. Soviet propaganda during this period concentrated on the three themes that under Tito's "fascist rule," Yugoslavia had become a colony of the "imperialists"; that the Yugoslavs were no longer building socialism; and that the Yugoslav economy and the standard of living of the Yugoslav people had suffered terribly. The goals of Tito's five-year plan, which as late as November, 1947, had been characterized in the Soviet economic press as "viable" and "realistic," were now characterized as "grandiose" and unrealistic. In an article in the November, 1949, issue of *Vneshniaia Torgovlia* with the title "The Fall of the Economy of Yugoslavia and the Enslavement of the State to Anglo-American Capital," A. Kuibyshev, after citing an Italian correspondent who predicted the imminent collapse of the Yugoslav economy because of the raw material shortage caused by the Cominform blockade, then justified the blockade in these terms:

> The anti-Soviet policy of the Yugoslav government has made impossible the continuation of economic cooperation between the USSR and Yugoslavia. In view of the inimical and subversive activities of the Yugoslav government against the USSR and Peoples Democracies, the governments of the USSR, Hungary, Czechoslovakia, Poland, Rumania and Bulgaria have informed the Yugoslav government that they consider themselves free from the obligations flowing from agreements concluded with Yugoslavia.
>
> It is characteristic that at a time when the foreign trade of Yugoslavia in 1949 contracted compared to 1948 more than one fifth, the trade of the Peoples Democracies continues to grow.[75]

In an article in the same journal in September, 1950, the Soviet economist V. Shvetz, who before the Cominform break had praised Yugoslavia's march toward socialism, joined in the Soviet chorus attacking Tito. After describing the "horrendous" condition of the Yugoslav economy and the suffering of the Yugoslav working class, Shvetz went on to predict the destruction of the Tito regime. Significantly, however, the Soviet economist stated that domestic, not foreign, forces would be responsible for Tito's fall:

> The opposition of the workers of Yugoslavia, who feel the *moral* support of all the progressive forces of humanity, is getting stronger. The Yugoslav people will find *in itself* sufficient strength to

overthrow the hated fascist dictatorship of Tito and Rankovic and return Yugoslavia to the camp of democracy and socialism [emphasis added] .[76]

Although much Soviet writing describing the failures of the Yugoslav economy during the blockade period was propaganda aimed at discrediting the Tito regime, there is no question but that the Yugoslav economy was in dire straits for almost the entire period. A *New York Times* correspondent who visited Yugoslavia in March, 1950, reported:

Worn trucks are now being run with tires on only two of their rear wheels. Half constructed factories planned for new industrial projects are idle because the Soviet Union, Czechoslovakia and Hungary refused delivery on promised machinery.[77]

Toward the end of September, 1950, after the outbreak of the Korean War, another *New York Times* reporter had an even more discouraging report:

Observers in Belgrade who are acquainted with the true character of the Yugoslav economic crisis and of the financial position of the Yugoslav government have come to the conclusion that only a substantial grant-in-aid by the United States Government, given in time, can prevent this country from becoming a tempting prey to the Soviet leaders next spring.[78]

The survival of the Yugoslav regime of Marshal Tito can in large part be credited to a very astute policy on the part of the United States.[79] As early as September, 1949, the Export-Import Bank agreed to a $20 million loan to Yugoslavia. This was to be the first in a long series of U.S. loans and grants. Loans from France, England, and West Germany were also soon forthcoming.

Plagued by a severe drought in 1950 which added to the problems caused by the blockade, Yugoslavia requested further American aid. It was not long in coming. Seeing the political and military advantages of an independent (albeit communist) Yugoslavia, the U.S. Congress passed the Yugoslav Emergency Relief Act which authorized the expenditure of $50 million to help Yugoslavia. This was in addition to the shipment of $26.5 million in agricultural goods to alleviate the effects of the drought.[80]

U.S. military aid soon began to accompany this economic assistance. Facing a buildup of Russia's satellite forces on her borders and fearing the possibility of a "new Korea," Yugoslavia was definitely interested in U.S. military aid. Edvard Kardelj, the Yugoslav Foreign Minister, said in a speech before the Foreign Political Committee of the Yugoslav National Assembly:

We shall not allow anyone to stage a new Korea in Yugoslavia; that is to say to throw this or that satellite or several of them against Yugoslavia while he himself is supposedly protecting peace.[81]

Thus only three years after Yugoslavia had bitterly attacked the United States as "the bulwark of world imperialism," an American Military Assistance Advisory Group was established in Belgrade.[82]

Thanks to this aid from the West, the Yugoslav economy was kept afloat and Yugoslavia did not crumble before Russian economic, military, and political pressure. But despite all the foreign aid Yugoslavia obtained, her economy remained in deep trouble during this period. Mention has already been made of the fact that the Yugoslav five-year plan was unrealistic, considering her small resource base and low standard of technology. Added to the difficulties caused by the blockade were severe droughts in 1950 and 1952 which, together with Tito's collectivization policies, severely limited agricultural production.[83] The dangerous situation on her borders led to a tripling of the defense share of the national budget between 1949 and 1951,[84] and by 1952 military expenditures totaled 22.3 per cent of Yugoslavia's national income.[85] Still another economic problem the Yugoslavs faced stemmed from the fact that Tito had appointed to the industrial ministries high party officials who, although loyal (an important consideration during Stalin's attempts to split the party), had had no economic experience. The lack of trained personnel and the inefficiency of the centralized economic administration, together with Yugoslavia's other economic difficulties, doomed the five-year plan.

A major area of difficulty for the Yugoslav economy was its inability to restructure its trade rapidly. In attempting to shift its sources of imports and acquire new markets for its exports, Yugoslavia had run into difficulty. Although the Western nations were both willing and able to provide Yugoslavia with imports (although partially on credit), the Yugoslavs had a very hard time finding new markets for many of their exports. Yugoslavia's copper and lead found eager customers among the NATO countries, particularly during the Korean War, but other commodities such as livestock, fruit, tobacco, hemp, and alcohol, for which Yugoslavia had had ready markets in the Soviet bloc countries, were far more difficult to sell in the West.[86] Although imports dropped only 7 per cent in 1949, exports dropped 37 per cent. Total Yugoslav trade dropped 22 per cent in 1949 and another 19 per cent in 1950.[87] For this reason, the Yugoslavs faced a serious balance-of-payments problem throughout the early and middle 1950's. Grants from the United States, UNRRA aid, and German reparations covered part of the deficit, but short- and medium-term loans accounted for much of the rest, and these loans came due in the middle 1950's. By 1955, 61 per cent of Yugoslavia's foreign debt consisted of short- and medium-term loans.[88] The Yugoslav economist Stane Pavlic described the situation in these words:

> Of our total financial obligations which amount to $400 million, 42 per cent are the so-called medium term debts. These were mostly incurred in the period from 1950 to 1952 through purchases of investment goods in the countries of Western Europe. These purchases were made at a time when our country was in a very difficult situation—the economic blockade, droughts—and when the

international situation reached an alarming stage—the Korean War—so that Yugoslavia had to accept the terms dictated by her creditors, terms which were unfavorable to our country both in prices and on our balance of payments, so that in 1953 and 1954 we already approached a partial revision of our medium term obligations to some of the creditor countries.[89]

All in all, the Yugoslav leaders had considerable difficulty in adjusting their economy to meet its many problems. At first, even after Yugoslavia was expelled from the Cominform, Tito tried to continue the rapid drive toward heavy industrialization. Indeed, the government economic reports to Parliament at the close of 1948 and 1949 both proclaimed successful fulfillment of the annual goals of the five-year plan. But before long, the effects of the blockade, the drought, and Yugoslavia's other economic problems forced sharp modifications in the plan. In December, 1950, the goals of the five-year plan were sharply contracted in scope. *Borba* on December 14 stated:

The development of our planned economy has reached the point where it requires complete concentration on the basic branches of industry. . . . It is therefore necessary to abandon a wider front.[90]

The article went on to say that henceforth all manpower and resources would be concentrated on the completion of a number of "key projects": a new coking plant, blast furnaces, a rolling mill, electric power plants, coal, copper, and lead mines, and plants for the assembly of capital equipment.[91]

Other moves taken by Tito to increase production in the face of economic difficulty included attempts to decentralize the Yugoslav government's control over major industries; inauguration of a profit-sharing scheme for the workers; establishment of so-called workers councils; and finally, in 1952, a government deflation policy and devaluation of the dinar (from 50 to 300 per U.S. dollar). Despite these efforts, Yugoslavia's industrial production decreased in 1952,[92] and on December 28, 1952, Svetozar Vukmanovic-Tempo, the President of Yugoslavia's Council for Industry and Production, made the startling statement that Yugoslavia had on hand only a fifteen-day supply of raw materials.[93]

This continual shortage of raw materials, coupled with Yugoslavia's other economic problems, such as its chronic balance-of-payments difficulties, helped make Tito amenable to the rapprochement overtures of the post-Stalin leadership of the USSR. Even a partial return to the pre-1948 trade pattern would alleviate some of Yugoslavia's balance-of-payments problems by enabling it to obtain a number of vital imports without spending scarce foreign exchange to acquire them. Offers of loans, given Yugoslavia's economic difficulties, would be even more welcome. An examination of the rapprochement will be found in the next section.

ECONOMIC ASPECTS OF
KHRUSHCHEV'S RAPPROCHEMENT

It is not the purpose of the present section to deal with all the factors involved in the rapprochement; this material is well covered elsewhere.[94] Instead, the economic aspects of the rapprochement will be highlighted and a detailed description given of Khrushchev's use of expanded trade and offers of economic aid to rebuild a community of interest with Yugoslavia.

Relations with Yugoslavia began to improve soon after the death of Stalin. On June 6, 1953, the USSR requested an exchange of ambassadors with Yugoslavia, but relations remained cool for the rest of the year. In April, 1954, at a meeting of the European Economic Commission, Soviet bloc trade representatives contacted their Yugoslav counterparts and arranged for a resumption of trade.[95] In the trade agreement signed on October 1, 1954, the Russians agreed to supply Yugoslavia with $2.5 million worth of oil, gasoline, cotton, anthracite, and magnesium ore—items the embargo of which had caused the Yugoslav economy such difficulties in the 1949-53 period.

In return, Yugoslavia supplied the Soviet Union with $2.5 million worth of meat, tobacco, hemp, ethyl alcohol, prunes, and caustic soda.[96] *Vneshniaia Torgovlia* characterized the trade agreement in these terms:

> The negotiations for the conclusion of the bilateral trade agreement proceeded in a businesslike atmosphere and showed the presence of possibilities for the realization of mutually profitable trade relations.[97]

Less than three months later, the Soviet government had apparently become considerably more interested in this "mutually profitable trade," for it invited Yugoslavia to send a trade delegation to Moscow at the end of December, with the result that on January 5, 1955, another trade agreement was signed, this one for no less than $20 million.[98]

Following Khrushchev's trip to Belgrade in June, 1955, both political and economic relations grew warmer. In his famous airport speech, Khrushchev blamed Beria for the 1948 break and officially proclaimed that Yugoslavia was "building socialism." Following his talks with Tito, Khrushchev publicly endorsed a number of principles for which the Yugoslavs had long been fighting—such as "respect for the sovereignty, independence, integrity and equality of states" and "noninterference in the internal affairs of another state for any reason whatsoever."[99]

Relations between the two countries improved still further in July when it was announced that the USSR had cancelled a $90 million debt Yugoslavia owed for military and economic supplies delivered before 1948, and the Yugoslavs dropped their claim to damages resulting from the Cominform blockade. In August, Tito disclosed that he was ready to revive relations between the Soviet and Yugoslav parties—something he had pointedly refused to do when Khrushchev had visited Belgrade earlier in the year.

Toward the end of August, major trade talks were held in Moscow and an agreement was signed on the first of September which provided for a total trade of $70 million in 1956 and a raw material credit from the USSR. In the words of the Yugoslavs: "These talks were held in an atmosphere of complete understanding and in the spirit of the new higher forms of international economic cooperation."[100] The Yugoslavs had reason to be pleased. A major benefit to Yugoslavia from the sharp increase in trade lay in her acquisition of markets for many Yugoslav products that could not be sold easily or profitably in the West. In addition, by paying for her raw material and capital equipment imports from Soviet bloc countries with her own exports, Yugoslavia was able to conserve her very limited reserves of foreign exchange. In discussing the advantages of trade with the Soviet Union and its satellites at this time, Dr. Milan Aleksic, Secretary of the Federal Foreign Trade Chamber of Yugoslavia, stated:

> The Yugoslav economy is specially interested in the development of economic cooperation with the economies of the USSR, Poland and Czechoslovakia. In these countries one can purchase, on the one hand, some of the important raw materials such as cotton, naphtha, coke, coal, etc. as well as various machines, industrial equipment, and precision mechanics products which are not produced in Yugoslavia. On the other hand, these markets are no less attractive in view of their almost limitless possibilities for absorbing many Yugoslav products which cannot always be placed on the markets of Western Europe. These products are primarily livestock and meats, wines, fresh and dried fruits and vegetables, tobacco and hemp.[101]

The September agreement also helped alleviate some of Yugoslavia's credit problems. As discussed above, the country was in a difficult economic position because of her burden of foreign debt, much of which was becoming due. Attempts to renegotiate loan terms with its creditors had thus far proven unsuccessful. On August 22, 1955, for example, the Yugoslav government had asked the Western powers to help her settle some pressing foreign debts amounting to $100 million.[102] In addition, American aid had sharply dropped (see Table 2), and Yugoslavia continued to have difficulty acquiring the necessary foreign exchange to finance needed imports, particularly raw materials. Many of these problems were alleviated when the Soviet Union promised to deliver to Yugoslavia over a three-year period, on credit, important raw materials such as cotton, petroleum, and coking coal, for which the Yugoslavs had been spending large amounts of their scarce foreign exchange. This raw material credit was worth $54 million and was to be repaid over a ten-year period at 2 per cent interest.[103] The head of the Yugoslav economic delegation to Moscow, Svetozar Vukmanovic-Tempo, stated the advantages of the raw material credit to his country:

TABLE 2

U.S. Foreign Assistance to Yugoslavia
(in millions of dollars)

			Public Law 480		
Fiscal Year	Loans	Grants	Title I Sales for Dinars	Titles II and III Emergency Relief and Grants to Voluntary Relief Agencies	Title IV Dollar Credit Sales
1950	40.0	---			
1951	15.0	92.9a			
1952	---	81.5		24.8b	
1953	---	122.4		0.2b	---
1954	---	66.5		1.1b	---
1955	---	42.7	49.5	61.9	---
Total	55.0	406.0	49.5	88.0	---
1956	15.0	14.8	70.8	8.7	---
1957	13.5	1.3	99.3	32.8	---
1958	8.0	3.4	71.9	28.8	---
1959	59.2	3.9	94.8	27.9	---
1960	40.8	3.8	19.2	14.2	---
Total	136.5	27.2	356.0	112.4	---
1961	102.7	3.3	30.4	14.1	---
1962	---	0.5	93.1	15.1	17.3
1963	−0.8	−0.2	92.1	14.3	16.2
1964	---	−0.4	18.2	13.4	46.1
1965	−0.3	−0.1	---	3.6	94.1
Total	101.6	3.1	233.8	60.5	173.7
Grand Total	293.1	436.3	639.3	260.9	173.7

aIncludes $50 million under Yugoslav Emergency Relief Act of 1950 (using funds appropriated for Economic Cooperation Administration).

bExtended under Agricultural Act of 1949 (prior to PL 480). The 1952 total covers fiscal years 1950-52.

Source: John C. Campbell, *Tito's Separate Road* (New York: Harper and Row, 1967), p. 171.

At this point I would like to stress that we have actually received credits under the following conditions: payments over a ten year period will bear an interest rate of only 2% and the first payment does not have to be made for three years. *These conditions certainly have surpassed any we have previously had or are being offered on other markets. . . .*

We are assured credit for the procurement of specific raw materials (primarily coking coal and cotton) from the Soviet Union during the course of the next three years in the amount of approximately 18 million dollars, or 54 million dollars for three years. In addition to which we can obtain an amount of 30 million dollars in gold or convertible currencies. . . . Through the establishment of credit for the procurement of raw materials, we facilitate our situation in meeting our balance of payments and the needs for convertible currency, particularly dollars, since most of the indispensable raw materials must be purchased on the so-called dollar market. Through this credit our economy will not be compelled to purchase raw materials on short-term credit deals which frequently become exorbitant and subjected to price increases at times over 20% [emphasis added].[104]

Khrushchev seemed equally pleased with the trade and aid agreements that had been signed. The lead article in the October, 1955, issue of *Vneshniaia Torgovlia* was effusive in its praise for the rapprochement between the two countries and the aid agreements:

The normalization and strengthening of relations between the USSR and Yugoslavia is one of the most important events in international relations in recent times. . . . The two peoples are tied in bonds of eternal friendship from their struggle in the war against a common enemy—the German Fascist conquerors.

The Soviet Union, as a great industrial power, . . . can offer significant aid to the Yugoslav people in the development of their economy by supplying necessary materials, different types of machines and equipment including complete factories, specialists and trained cadres.

The Yugoslav people, solving great and complicated problems in the reconstruction of the economy of their country know that *with the fraternal aid of the Soviet people they could more quickly and more successfully solve these problems* [emphasis added].[105]

Thus Tito, who had been called a fascist by the same journal only three years before, received a warm economic embrace similar to the political one he had received from Khrushchev in June. This article also made it clear that Tito would be well rewarded if he continued on the path of rapprochement with the Soviet Union. The reward was not long in forthcoming.

In January, 1956, the USSR signed an agreement with Yugoslavia stipulating that the Soviets would give Yugoslavia a $110 million credit to pay for blueprints and equipment for a nitrogenous fertilizer factory with an annual capacity of 360,000 tons of calcium ammonium nitrate, a super-phosphate factory with a 250,000-ton capacity, a thermal power plant with a 100,000-KW capacity, and equipment for two zinc lead plants and one foundry plant. The Soviet credit was repayable in ten years at 2 per cent interest and the Yugoslavs could conserve their foreign exchange by repaying the Soviet credit with their own exports.[106]

At the same time, Yugoslavia also obtained a joint Russian-East German 20-year credit worth $175 million for the construction of an aluminum combine complex together with its hydroelectric plants, which was to have an annual aluminum production of 50,000 tons.[107] Czechoslovakia then offered the Yugoslavs a $50 million capital investment credit (repayable in ten years) and a $25 million consumer goods credit (repayable in seven years), and Poland gave Yugoslavia a $20 million investment credit repayable in ten years.[108] Both Czechoslovakia and Poland followed the Soviet pattern of charging 2 per cent interest on their credits.

In May, 1956, Tito received further satisfaction when Hungary and Yugoslavia reached an accommodation on the reparations question. Hungary, which had ceased paying reparations after the Cominform break in 1948, signed an agreement in May, 1956, to pay Yugoslavia a sum of $85 million in goods over a period of five years.[109]

Thus Yugoslavia, which for so long had felt the stick of Soviet economic power, was again being enticed by the carrot. By June, 1956, Russia and her satellites were offering loans and credits that totaled $360 million. This compared quite favorably with U.S. non-military loans and grants which totaled only $30 million in 1956. The U.S. aid program to Yugoslavia was under heavy attack in Congress because of the rapprochement, and despite visits by John Foster Dulles and Robert Murphy, relations between the United States and Yugoslavia had declined markedly from the 1950-53 period.[110] On the other hand, closer relations with the Soviet Union brought not only large credits and profitable trade but still another benefit to the Yugoslav economy—a sharp drop in defense expenditures. And, as a political bonus, the Soviet government announced on June 1, 1956, the day before Tito's arrival in the USSR, that Molotov, the man most responsible after Stalin for the break with Yugoslavia and a bitter foe of Khrushchev's rapprochement policy, had been relieved as foreign minister.

All in all, the post-Stalin policy of rapprochement with Yugoslavia seemed by June, 1956, to have borne major dividends for the Soviet Union. Whereas Stalin had attempted to crush the Tito regime by preying on its economic weaknesses, Krushchev exploited Yugoslavia's economic weaknesses in order to bring Tito into closer alignment with the Soviet Union. Khrushchev was prepared to grant Tito considerably more freedom of action within the Communist Camp than was Stalin, and he was willing to expend large amounts of economic aid to bring him back. But for the Yugoslavs, this favorable political and economic situation was not to last much longer.

Political though not yet economic difficulties began to darken Soviet-Yugoslav relations in the early fall of 1956. Khrushchev, fearing that Yugoslavia had become too much of a divisive force in Eastern Europe, circulated a letter among the Eastern European communist parties which warned against a "mechanical" imitation of Yugoslavia's system of socialism.[111] Tito reacted angrily to the letter and, although Khrushchev later mollified him, suspicion still lingered.[112] When several months later the Hungarian Revolution broke out, Tito came into open political conflict with the USSR.

In his first public reaction to the Soviet suppression of the Hungarian Revolution, Tito stated that the revolt had occurred because the reforms that had come were too little and too late. It was tragic that "reactionaries should have found there a very fertile ground and that they should have been able gradually to take the situation into their hands, exploiting for their aims the justified revolt which took place."[113] Tito also blamed Stalinism not only on the personality of Stalin but on the Soviet system itself.

Pravda responded to Tito's speech on November 23 by stating that it was not right to denigrate the socialist system of other countries and praise one's own as universal. After all, "Yugoslavia has received capitalist aid and all the countries of the camp cannot rely on such aid."[114]

Following a speech by Kardelj on December 6 that attacked the USSR for taking a critical view of the Hungarian Revolutionary Workers Councils, Khrushchev began to apply economic pressure. In early 1957, on the pretext that the lack of diplomatic relations between Yugoslavia and East Germany impeded economic relations between the two countries, the joint Soviet-East German offer for the construction of the promised aluminum combine was "postponed."[115] By doing this, the USSR accomplished two goals: it penalized Yugoslavia for her position on the Hungarian Revolution and conserved credits which could be better used to aid more "friendly" Eastern European nations. If one recalls the tremendous outpouring of Soviet aid following the Hungarian Revolution, the economic as well as political motivations behind the postponement of aid become apparent.[116]

The situation took a temporary turn for the better, however, after the so-called anti-party (and anti-Yugoslav) group was removed from the Soviet leadership by Khrushchev in June, 1957. On July 29, 1957, the aluminum agreements were renegotiated to the satisfaction of the Yugoslavs[117] and in August the meeting between Khrushchev and Tito in Rumania was comparatively friendly. In October, Tito, perhaps hoping for a further reconciliation, finally recognized East Germany, despite the fact that he must have known that the West Germans would immediately break diplomatic relations with Yugoslavia. This move, which further alienated Yugoslavia from the Western powers, did not lead to closer ties with the Soviet bloc; the November Moscow Party Conference proved to be a major diplomatic defeat for Tito. At this meeting, the Yugoslavs refused to sign the conference "Declaration" which acknowledged the leading position of the USSR in the "socialist camp."[118] Several months later, relations between Yugoslavia and the Soviet bloc deteriorated still further when the Yugoslavs brought forth a new party program to bolster their ideological position. Of particular offense to the Soviet Union was the Yugoslav proposition that the USSR had, in the past, utilized its position of hegemony to exploit other socialist states.

The USSR replied on April 19, 1958, that "Socialist mutual aid essentially excludes the possibility of an advantageous position of some countries at the expense of others."[119] When the Yugoslavs did not sufficiently alter their program to suit the wishes of the USSR, Moscow on May 9 made some not-so-veiled threats of cutting off "Socialist mutual aid":

> The authors of the Draft Program of the Yugoslav League of Communists flagrantly distorted the nature of the ties linking the Socialist countries, accused them in an unfriendly and even slanderous way of a desire for hegemony. They claimed that in the initial phases of the development of Socialism in individual nations or states there exists the possibility of utilizing economic exploitation of other countries in one form or another.

> *Do certain persons in Yugoslavia feel that the tendency toward exploitation also exists in economic relations between the Soviet Union and Yugoslavia? If so, it would be possible to free Yugoslavia from such exploitation* [emphasis added].[120]

It was not long before the USSR carried out its threat. On May 30, 1958, the Yugoslavs made public a Soviet statement that the implementation of the credit agreements would have to be postponed for five years in view of "new plans to expand the USSR's own chemical industry." To add insult to injury, Khrushchev stated on June 3 that the Cominform resolution of 1948 that had expelled the Yugoslavs was "fundamentally correct."[121]

In addition to suffering the loss of economic aid, Tito saw Yugoslavia's trade relations with the Soviet Union also begin to reflect the strained political relations. Shipments of vitally needed wheat and coking coal were delayed,[122] and it was only after "many difficulties" that a trade agreement between the two countries was signed for 1959, but it was 15 per cent below the 1958 figure.[123] The economic aid agreement between Czechoslovakia and Yugoslavia was another victim of the renewed political conflict, as only a small percentage of the $50 million credit was ever committed.[124] And, as an added slap at Yugoslavia, the Soviet Union withdrew from the 1959 Zagreb International Fair, despite the fact that it had constructed a permanent pavilion there in 1956.[125]

In sharp contrast to the situation following the 1948 split, however, there was no cessation of trade between Yugoslavia and the Soviet bloc, nor was there any economic blockade. Khrushchev evidently did not want to have Yugoslavia completely alienated a second time. Having placed his prestige in the original rapprochement with Yugoslavia in 1955, Khrushchev seems to have hoped that by maintaining continued, though cool, relations with Belgrade there was always the possibility of a renewed rapprochement in the future. Indeed, in a speech to a visiting Polish delegation on November 10, 1958, Khrushchev clearly indicated that, unlike Stalin, he was prepared to differentiate between relations on the party and on the state levels:

> Unfortunately, the leaders of Yugoslavia, those who stand at the head of the Party, are slipping down from the position of the working class to the position of its enemies. Therefore, today we can hardly count on mutual understanding with the Yugoslav League of Communists along Party lines, although we would not like to give up hope in this regard. . . .

> Along state lines we will strive to develop friendly relations with Yugoslavia, and to encourage trade and cultural ties. And we are ready in the future to trade with Yugoslavia on *mutually advantageous* terms [emphasis added].[126]

Nonetheless, for several years trade relations between the Soviet Union and Yugoslavia were not particularly good (see Table 1), and Yugoslavia, which had been invited to participate in COMECON sessions in 1956 and 1957 as an observer, was refused an invitation in 1959.[127]

So matters stood until 1960. In June, 1960, the conflict between the USSR and Communist China burst out into the open at the Rumanian Party Congress. As Russia's conflict with China deepened, Khrushchev began to draw closer to Yugoslavia. Here economic relations once again paved the way for closer political relations. One month after the November, 1960, Moscow Conference of Eighty-one Communist Parties in which for the first time the USSR had to openly lobby for support among the communist parties, Yugoslavia secured long-term trade agreements for the 1961-65 planning period with Rumania, East Germany, and Poland. Three months later in March, 1961, the USSR itself signed a long-term trade agreement with Yugoslavia which called for an increase in trade to twice the 1960 level. (Actually, due to the rapid improvement in Yugoslav-Soviet relations, trade more than tripled by 1965.)[128]

Meanwhile, relations between the United States and Yugoslavia, which had improved in the 1958-59 period, began to deteriorate both economically and politically in 1960. In 1961, at a time of high cold-war tensions, a furor developed in the United States when a Dallas newspaper published an article on the training of Yugoslav airmen in the United States. A bitter debate in Congress arose over the issue of "selling aircraft to the enemy."[129] The Yugoslavs, sensing as a result of the congressional debate that the United States might not be a very secure future source of armaments, then began to purchase arms from the Soviet Union. In addition, the failure of Tito to condemn the Soviet Union for breaking the nuclear test ban during the Belgrade conference of uncommitted nations further angered both the American public and certain influential congressmen. A direct result of this anger was the U.S. government's postponement of Yugoslavia's annual request for surplus food aid.[130]

It was at this juncture of heightened Sino-Soviet tensions and deteriorated U.S.-Yugoslav relations that a new political rapprochement took place between Yugoslavia and the Soviet Union. In December, 1962, Tito was invited to Moscow where he delivered a speech to the Supreme Soviet. It was a major political triumph for the man who only four years before had been vilified as the "Trojan Horse of the Imperialist Camp."[131] Although Khrushchev's interest in the renewed rapprochement was primarily political—Yugoslavia provided useful access to the non-committed nations of the world which the Soviet leader wished to keep out of the Chinese sphere of influence—Tito's reasons were more economic in nature. Britain's decision in 1961 to join the Common Market threatened one of Yugoslavia's main export markets. In addition, Yugoslavia's domestic economic situation had begun to deteriorate, and Tito sought increased trade with the CMEA (COMECON) nations to help alleviate his nation's shortage of hard currency.

In August, 1963, on a visit to Yugoslavia, Khrushchev discussed the subject of COMECON participation with Tito, and one year later Yugoslavia became what might be termed an "associate member" of the organization. The Yugoslavs were admitted to seven COMECON commissions (Foreign Trade, Currency and Finance, Coordination of Scientific and Technical Research, Ferrous Metals, Non-Ferrous Metals, Engineering, and Chemicals).[132] Despite her participation, however, Yugoslavia was not obligated to abide by any COMECON decisions and thus was able to continue her position as an independent nation unbound by any economic or military alliance.

During the 1963-65 period, Yugoslavia's trade with nations of COMECON increased steadily, and by 1967 Russia had become Yugoslavia's leading trade partner.[133] This "second rapprochement" with the USSR was further sweetened in September, 1965, when the new Russian leaders offered Tito a $160 million loan for the purchase of industrial equipment, possibly to gain Yugoslavia's backing for an international communist meeting that would expel the Chinese communists.[134]

With the improvement in economic relations came a corresponding improvement in political relations, and Yugoslav-Soviet ties became particularly close following the defeat of their common ally, Nasser of Egypt, in his June, 1967, war with Israel. Nonetheless, the Soviet invasion of Czechoslovakia in August, 1968, which was criticized by Tito even more vehemently than the invasion of Hungary twelve years earlier, cast a deep shadow on Yugoslav-Soviet relations. Although the trade statistics for 1968 show only a slight diminution in trade (in contrast, however, to the sharp rises of the three previous years), the future of economic and political relations between the two communist states remains very clouded at the time of this writing (January, 1970). Indeed, the latest (1970) revision of the *History of the CPSU*, unlike the 1967 edition which appeared at a high point in Soviet-Yugoslav relations, once again blames Yugoslavia for the 1948 split.[135]

LESSONS OF THE YUGOSLAV EXPERIENCE

The issue that provoked Stalin's use of economic sanctions against Yugoslavia was that of Yugoslav nationalism vs. Stalinist "internationalism"—or subordination to the USSR. It seems evident that Stalin decided to employ economic pressure as a means of dealing with Tito because Yugoslavia was extremely vulnerable to such pressure through its dependence on Soviet economic assistance for its five-year plan and through its need for trade with nations Stalin controlled. Stalin had first-hand knowledge of the economic vulnerability of the Yugoslav economy through Soviet economic advisors.

The relatively mild nature of the early economic sanctions against Yugoslavia (the delay in trade negotiations and the withdrawal of economic advisors) indicates that Stalin's original motivation was simply to force Tito to toe the Soviet line. When Tito failed to comply, Stalin's subsequent actions were aimed at splitting the Yugoslav party and ousting Tito from power. After the failure of Stalin's efforts to split the Yugoslav party through Zujovic and the publication of the Cominform resolution, the Soviet leader resorted to more severe economic pressure to force Tito to capitulate. First raw materials and then capital goods shipments from Cominform countries were curtailed. Next the capital goods agreements themselves—so vital for the completion of Yugoslavia's five-year plan—were abrogated. Finally a total economic blockade was instituted. The pattern was one of gradual "escalation" in which Stalin appeared to feel at each juncture that one additional economic pressure would be sufficient to break the Tito regime or force it to capitulate.

Considering that Stalin's original expectations about the efficacy of economic pressure to break the Tito regime proved unfounded, the question arises as to why he maintained the policy of economic blockade until he died. Several explanations are possible. First, the Yugoslav economy was in dire straits throughout this period, and Stalin may have entertained the hope that it would yet collapse. At the very least, Stalin could utilize Yugoslavia as an example of what might happen to a nation that defied the USSR and went over to the "Imperialist camp."

Second, Stalin's action can be seen as the result of the fact that by the time he realized economic pressure alone would not suffice to eliminate Tito, the option of using military force to oust the Yugoslav leader was precluded by U.S. involvement in the country. The Soviet dictator, clearly aware of (and perhaps overestimating) American strength, had no wish to risk a confrontation with the United States by military intervention. Consequently, economic pressure alone was the only meaningful weapon available to Stalin with which he could demonstrate his opprobrium for Tito's regime.*

A third possible reason for Stalin's behavior is more ideological in nature. If Tito and his clique remained in power, argued the Soviet journals, it was only

---

*U.S. trade policy toward Cuba and Communist China seems to be governed by similar considerations.

because he had become a lackey of the "Imperialists" and existed on their alms; Yugoslavia in this condition, the argument went, not only was not "building socialism," but had reverted to its pre-war position of raw material supplier to the West.

Finally, Stalin had staked a great deal of his prestige in the conflict with Tito. He had engineered a whole series of purges in Eastern Europe in the name of anti-Titoism (i.e., anti-nationalism), and to make any kind of accommodation with Yugoslavia would hurt not only his own prestige but would also weaken the not yet stable communist regimes of Eastern Europe. In addition, in his later years, Stalin was not a man to admit that he had made a mistake.

It appears then, for all of these reasons, that maintenance of the economic blockade—even if it meant the complete exclusion of Yugoslavia from the Communist Camp and its virtual addition to the anti-communist camp—was deemed a necessity by Stalin.

Stalin's successors, and particularly Khrushchev, had not invested as much prestige in the conflict with Yugoslavia. Khrushchev, coming to power in 1955, had a far more flexible image of the "bloc" than had Stalin, and he was willing to go to some lengths in order to bring Yugoslavia back into the fold. One of his chief weapons was also economic, but this time in the form of the carrot rather than the stick. He too exploited the weaknesses of the Yugoslav economy, but in a positive rather than a negative way. Khrushchev attempted, principally through the use of expanded trade and economic aid, to rebuild the community of interests between the Soviet Union and Yugoslavia. In this, he was relatively successful, until he too deemed the independent activities of the Yugoslav leader to be a threat to Soviet hegemony in Eastern Europe, and then he reacted in a neo-Stalinist way.

What then are the lessons the Soviet leaders should have learned from this—their first experience in the use of economic pressure as an instrument of foreign policy toward a fellow communist regime? First, they should have learned that if a communist leader is in firm control of his party, no amount of economic pressure will cause his regime to collapse if alternate suppliers of raw materials, capital goods, and economic aid are available.[136] A second lesson the Soviets should have learned is that extreme economic pressure such as a blockade only serves to drive the nation against which it is imposed over to the side of the West. A third lesson to be derived is that although Soviet economic pressure alone may not be sufficiently strong to compel a communist regime to change its political stand, Soviet economic pressure can severely damage another nation's economy as well as put a major stumbling block on that nation's road to industrialization. Conversely, as Khrushchev's early experience with Yugoslavia demonstrated, economic aid and trade can serve as major instruments in building (or rebuilding) a community of interests between the USSR and another nation. In addition, the fact that Khrushchev's subsequent economic pressures, which were quite limited in scope, did not prevent a renewed rapprochement with the Yugoslavs, should also have been a useful lesson for the Soviet leadership.

In the case studies to follow, an analysis will be made of what lessons—if any—the Soviet leadership has learned from their experience with Yugoslavia in both their expectations as to the efficacy of resorting to economic pressure and in their techniques in applying it once the decision to use it is made.

NOTES

1. Milovan Djilas, *Conversations with Stalin* (New York: Harcourt Brace and World, Inc., 1962), p. 9. The official Yugoslav view of the conflict is found in Vladimir Dedijer's biography *Tito* (New York: Simon and Schuster, 1953).

2. Letter from the Central Committee of the Communist Party of Yugoslavia to the Central Committee of the Communist Party of the Soviet Union, April 13, 1948. The Yugoslavs have made public most of their correspondence with the Russians in the critical period from February to June, 1948. These documents have been published in the United States under the title *The Soviet-Yugoslav Controversy, 1948-58: A Documentary Record*, ed. Robert Bass and Elizabeth Marbury (New York: Prospect Books, 1959). The documents will hereafter be referred to as *The Soviet-Yugoslav Controversy.*

3. Dedijer, *op. cit.,* p. 285. For a description of Soviet policy in exploiting the joint stock companies in other East European countries, see Nicholas Spulber, *The Economics of Communist Eastern Europe* (London: Chapman and Hall, 1957), Chapter VII.

4. V. Shvetz, "Piatiletni Plan Razvitiia Narodnogo Khoziaistva Iugoslavii," *Vneshniaia Torgovlia,* Vol. 27, No. 6 (June, 1947), p. 11; Shvetz's information is similar to that given by the Yugoslav economist Milutin Bogosavljevic in *The Economy of Yugoslavia* (Belgrade: Prosveta, 1961), pp. 7-11.

5. Cited by Shvetz, *op. cit.,* pp. 11-12.

6. Bogosavljevic, *op. cit.,* p. 9.

7. Cited by Shvetz, *op. cit.,* pp. 14-15.

8. Dedijer, *op. cit.,* p. 288.

9. Tito cited these additional grants in a speech to a People's Front meeting in Dvar, Yugoslavia. The speech was reprinted in *Yugoslav Newsletter,* No. 54 (New York: Yugoslav Information Agency, March 17, 1950), p. 1. In his generally negative portrayal of the Soviet aid, Tito stated that the military aid "left much to be desired" because of its poor quality.

10. *The New York Times,* June 3, 1947.

11. Speech by Kidric to the Fifth Congress of the Communist Party of Yugoslavia, translated and reprinted in pamphlet form by the Foreign Language Press of Yugoslavia (Belgrade, 1948), p. 76.

12. *Ibid.,* p. 73.

13. Dedijer, *op. cit.,* p. 390.

14. Shvetz, *op. cit.,* p. 18.

15. *Economic Survey of Europe 1953* (New York: United Nations, 1954), p. 112.

16. Nicholas Spulber, "On Yugoslavia's Economic Ties with the Soviet Bloc," *Economia Internazionale,* Vol. 9, No. 2 (May, 1956), pp. 308-10.

17. *The New York Times,* June 3, 1947.

18. Dedijer, *op. cit.,* p. 259.

19. Adam B. Ulam, *Titoism and the Cominform* (Cambridge: Harvard University Press, 1952), p. 79.

20. Dedijer, *op. cit.,* pp. 250-53.

21. *Ibid.,* p. 326.

22. *The New York Times,* January 22, 1948.

23. *Ibid.*

24. *The New York Times,* January 23, 1948.

25. Djilas has given a first-hand account of this meeting in *Conversations with Stalin,* pp. 174-83.

26. Dedijer, *op. cit.,* p. 324.

27. Document No. 179, *White Book on Aggressive Activities by the Governments of the USSR, Poland, Czechoslovakia, Hungary, Rumania, Bulgaria and Albania toward Yugoslavia* (Belgrade: Government Printing Office, 1951), p. 292. This documentary collection, hereafter referred to as *White Book,* contains numerous statements from both Yugoslav and Cominform-nation sources.

28. Dedijer, *op. cit.*, pp. 327-28.

29. Letter from the Central Committee of the Communist Party of the Soviet Union to Tito, *et al.*, March 27, 1948, *The Soviet-Yugoslav Controversy*, pp. 8-9.

30. *Ibid.*, p. 10.

31. Dedijer, *op. cit.*, p. 379.

32. *Ibid.*, p. 336. Although it is possible that the Yugoslavs may have perceived the possibility of war over Trieste at this time, in my opinion, Dedijer has played it up for dramatic effect in his book.

33. *The New York Times*, April 3, 1948.

34. *The Soviet-Yugoslav Controversy*, p. 22.

35. *The New York Times*, April 24, 1948.

36. *The New York Times*, May 4, 1948.

37. *The Soviet-Yugoslav Controversy*, pp. 28-30.

38. *The New York Times*, June 4, 1948.

39. Resolution of the Information Bureau Concerning the Situation in the Communist Party of Yugoslavia, June 28, 1948, *The Soviet-Yugoslav Controversy*, p. 42.

40. *Ibid.*, p. 46.

41. *The New York Times*, July 7, 1948.

42. *The New York Times*, July 5, 1948.

43. Kidric, *op. cit.*, pp. 8-9.

44. Report of Edvard Kardelj to the Fifth Congress of the Communist Party of Yugoslavia, translated and reprinted in pamphlet form by the Foreign Language Press of Yugoslavia (Belgrade, 1948), p. 24.

45. *The New York Times* (C. L. Sulzberger), August 27, 1948.

46. Document No. 178, "Note of the Yugoslav Embassy in Bucharest, No. 1661 of December 4, 1948 to the Rumanian Government in Connection with Trade Agreement Violations by the Latter," *White Book*, p. 288.

47. *Pravda,* September 8, 1948.

48. Document No. 183, "Letter from the President of the Polish Delegation in the Permanent Polish-Yugoslav Commission Postponing Indefinitely the Meeting of the Permanent Commission," *White Book,* p. 298; Document No. 178, *White Book,* p. 289.

49. *The New York Times,* October 3, 1948.

50. *The New York Times,* October 12, 1948.

51. Cited by *The New York Times,* November 19, 1948. The timber goal was, in 1948, to exceed the 1951 planned goal by 40 per cent.

52. *The New York Times,* November 27, 1948.

53. *Ibid.*

54. *The New York Times,* January 4, 1949.

55. Document No. 181, *White Book,* p. 293.

56. Josef Broz Tito, "Real Reasons Behind the Slanders Against Yugoslavia," address delivered during the debate on the budget in the Federal Assembly of the Federal People's Republic of Yugoslavia on December 27, 1948 (translated and reprinted in pamphlet form, Belgrade, 1949), p. 23.

57. *Ibid.,* p. 32.

58. *The New York Times,* December 30, 1948.

59. *The New York Times,* December 31, 1948.

60. Document No. 182, *White Book,* pp. 294-98.

61. Document No. 175, *White Book,* pp. 284-85.

62. *The New York Times,* February 6, 1949.

63. *The New York Times,* April 24, 1949.

64. *The New York Times,* May 5, 1949.

65. Spulber, "On Yugoslavia's Economic Ties with the Soviet Bloc," pp. 311-12.

66. Document No. 194, *White Book,* p. 316.

67. Document No. 193, *White Book*, p. 315.

68. Yugoslav trade statistics taken from *Economic Survey of Europe 1953,* p. 112; Soviet trade statistics taken from *Vneshniaia Torgovlia SSSR 1918-1966* (Moscow: Mezhdunarodnye Otnosheniia, 1967), pp. 64, 66. Hereafter *VT SSSR 1918-1966.*

69. *VT SSSR 1918-1966,* pp. 110, 158, 202. Soviet imports of berries and dried fruit which totaled 8.3 thousand tons in 1948 (14.3 thousand in 1947) dropped to 4.1 thousand in 1949, but rose again in 1950 to 5.9 thousand and in 1952 reached 15.9 thousand tons. Total lead imports dropped from 23.3 thousand tons in 1948 (of which Yugoslavia supplied 14.6 thousand tons) to 17.6 thousand tons in 1949 and only 11.1 thousand tons in 1950.

70. In 1947, Yugoslavia exported 397,000 tons of iron ore to Hungary. This figure dropped to 344,000 tons in 1948 and 95,000 in 1949. At the same time, the USSR increased its exports of iron ore to Hungary from 170,000 in 1947 to 231,000 in 1948, 404,000 tons in 1949, and 539,000 tons in 1950. Yugoslav trade statistics taken from *Statistics of the Foreign Trade of Yugoslavia 1946-49* (Belgrade: Federal Statistical Office, 1953), pp. 58-59. Soviet trade statistics taken from *VT SSSR 1918-1966,* p. 128.

71. *The New York Times,* August 5, 1949.

72. *The New York Times,* July 29, 1949.

73. *The New York Times,* August 29, 1949.

74. *Pravda,* September 5, 1949.

75. A. Kuibyshev, "Upadok Ekonomiki Iugoslavii i Zakabalenie Strany Anglo-Amerikanskim Kapitalom," *Vneshniaia Torgovlia,* Vol. 29, No. 11 (November, 1949), p. 30.

76. A. Shvetz, "Zakabalenie Iugoslavii Anglo-Amerikanskim Kapitalom," *Vneshniaia Torgovlia,* Vol. 30, No. 9 (September, 1950), p. 31.

77. *The New York Times* (C. L. Sulzberger), March 2, 1950.

78. *The New York Times* (M. S. Handler), September 24, 1950.

79. An excellent description of U.S. policy toward Yugoslavia in this period is found in John C. Campbell, *Tito's Separate Road* (New York: Harper and Row, 1967).

80. *Ibid.*, pp. 23-24.

81. The speech was reprinted in *Yugoslav Newsletter*, No. 89 (July 6, 1951), p. 3.

82. Campbell, *op. cit.*, p. 26.

83. For a discussion of Yugoslavia's agricultural problems during this period, see Ranko M. Brashich, "Yugoslavia's Agriculture," in *Yugoslavia*, ed. Robert F. Byrnes (New York: Frederick A. Praeger, 1957), Chapter 12.

84. *Economic Survey of Europe 1953*, p. 112.

85. R. Barry Farrell, *Yugoslavia and the Soviet Union 1948-1956* (Hamden, Conn.: Shoe String Press, 1956), p. 30. As Farrell points out, p. 29, Yugoslavia's military expenditures between 1949 and 1954 constituted a higher percentage of its gross national product than did the defense expenditures of any non-communist state in Europe.

86. Milan Aleksic, "Yugoslav Exports and Relations with Eastern Europe," *Review of International Affairs*, Vol. 6, No. 138 (January 1, 1956), p. 18.

87. *Direction of Trade*, January-December, 1950 (New York: United Nations, April 10, 1951), p. 87; *Economic Survey of Europe 1953*, p. 112.

88. Svetozar Vukmanovic-Tempo, "Some Basic Characteristics of Economic Development in Yugoslavia," *Yugoslav Review*, Vol. 4, Nos. 2-3 (February-March, 1955), p. 21.

89. Stane Pavlic, "Yugoslavia's Economic Relations with Foreign Countries," *Yugoslav Review*, Vol. 5., Nos. 3-4 (March-April, 1956), pp. 16-17.

90. *The New York Times*, December 15, 1950.

91. *Ibid.*

92. Bogosavljevic, *op. cit.*, p. 12.

93. *The New York Times*, December 29, 1952.

94. See Campbell, *op. cit.*, Chapter 3. Other descriptions are found in Zbigniew K. Brzezinski, *The Soviet Bloc* (2d ed. rev.; Cambridge: Harvard

University Press, 1967), Chapters 8 and 9; and Richard Lowenthal, *World Communism* (New York: Oxford University Press, 1964), Chapter 1.

95. Milan Aleksic, "Trade Relations with Eastern Countries," *Review of International Affairs*, Vol. 5, No. 1 (December, 1954), p. 15.

96. A. Korolenko, "Kompensatsionnoe Soglashenie Mezhdu Sovetskimi i Iugoslavskimi Vneshnetorgovlimi Organizatsiiami," *Vneshniaia Torgovlia*, Vol. 34, No. 11 (November, 1954), p. 21.

97. *Ibid.*, p. 22.

98. Vladimir Sajcic, "Yugoslav-Soviet Economic Relations," *Review of International Affairs* (Belgrade), Vol. 6, No. 131-2 (October 1, 1955), p. 10; *Vneshniaia Torgovlia*, Vol. 35, No. 9 (September, 1955), p. 23.

99. The text of the declaration is found in *The Soviet-Yugoslav Controversy*, pp. 56-60.

100. Sajcic, *op. cit.*, p. 11.

101. Aleksic, "Yugoslav Exports and Relations with Eastern Europe," p. 18.

102. *The New York Times*, August 23, 1955.

103. Vladimir Bakaric, "New Stage in the Development of Yugoslav-Soviet Relations," *Review of International Affairs* (Belgrade), Vol. 6, No. 149 (June 15, 1956), p. 10.

104. *Yugoslav Review*, Vol. 5, Nos. 8-9 (October-November, 1955), pp. 7-8.

105. V. Michkov, "Razvitie Sovetsko-Iugoslavskikh Ekonomicheskikh Otnoshenii," *Vneshniaia Torgovlia*, Vol. 35, No. 10 (October, 1955), p. 1.

106. Bakaric, *loc. cit.*

107. Stane Pavlic, "Yugoslav Economic Relations with Foreign Countries in 1956," *Review of International Affairs*, Vol. 8, No. 162 (January 1, 1957), p. 22.

108. *Ibid.*

109. *Ibid.*

110. For a study of the interrelationship among U.S., Soviet, and Yugoslav policies during the 1954-57 period, see Campbell, *op. cit.*, Chapter 3.

111. Brzezinski, *op. cit.*, p. 207.

112. *Ibid.*, p. 208.

113. Address by Marshal Tito to a meeting of the Yugoslav League of Communists at Tula, November 11, 1956 (translated in *The Soviet-Yugoslav Controversy*, p. 69).

114. *Pravda*, November 23, 1956 (translated in *The Soviet-Yugoslav Controversy*, p. 81).

115. Andrija Partonic, "The USSR Government's One-Sided Acts," *Review of International Affairs*, Vol. 9, No. 187 (June 16, 1958), p. 3.

116. For a listing of the Soviet aid disbursements, see Marshall I. Goldman, *Soviet Foreign Aid* (New York: Frederick A. Praeger, 1967), pp. 32-37.

117. Partonic, *loc. cit.*

118. For a discussion of the events of the conference, see Brzezinski, *op. cit.*, pp. 317-20.

119. *Kommunist*, Vol. 34, No. 6 (April 19, 1958) (translated in *The Soviet-Yugoslav Controversy*, p. 159).

120. *Pravda*, May 9, 1958 (translated in *The Soviet-Yugoslav Controversy*, p. 187).

121. Speech by Nikita Khrushchev at the 7th Congress of the Bulgarian Communist Party, June 3, 1958 (translated in *The Soviet-Yugoslav Controversy*, p. 196.)

122. Speech by Foreign Minister Koca Popovic, November 26, 1958, cited in *East Europe*, Vol. 8, No. 1 (January, 1969), p. 43.

123. M. Pericic, "Trade with the Countries of Eastern Europe," *Review of International Affairs* (Belgrade), Vol. 10, No. 216 (April 1, 1959), p. 5.

124. *Vesnik Jugoslavenske Investicione Banke*, January, 1959, cited in *Radio Free Europe Research Report: Yugoslavia*, March 14, 1959.

125. *Christian Science Monitor*, May 4, 1959.

126. *Pravda*, November 11, 1958 (translated in *Current Digest of the Soviet Press*, Vol. 10, No. 45 [December 17, 1958], p. 10). Another possible reason for Khrushchev's interest in continuing trade was the Soviet bloc's need

for Yugoslavia's raw materials because of the raw material shortage that plagued the bloc in the mid-1950's. On this point, see Stanley J. Zyzniewski, "Industry and Labor in East Europe," *Eastern Europe in the Sixties,* ed. Stephen Fischer-Galati (New York: Frederick A. Praeger, 1963), pp. 90-91.

127. *Radio Belgrade,* April 25, 1959.

128. *Vneshniaia Torgovlia SSSR za 1965* (Moscow: Mezhdunarodnye Otnosheniia, 1966), p. 12.

129. Campbell, *op. cit.,* pp. 51-52.

130. *Ibid.,* p. 109.

131. Brzezinski, *op. cit.,* p. 332.

132. Michael Kaser, *Comecon* (London: Oxford University Press, 1967), pp. 102-4.

133. *East Europe,* Vol. 16, No. 11 (November, 1967), p. 34.

134. *East Europe,* Vol. 16, No. 4 (April, 1967), p. 9.

135. *Radio Belgrade,* January 4, 1970. For an analysis of Soviet-Yugoslav relations since the invasion of Czechoslovakia, see Dennison I. Rusinow, *Yugoslavia and Stalin's Successors 1968-69* (Hanover: American Universities Field Staff Report, 1969).

136. Khrushchev recognized this point in discussing Yugoslavia in his secret speech to the 20th Congress of the CPSU (translated in *The Anti-Stalin Campaign and International Communism* [New York: Columbia University Press, 1956], pp. 62-63).

CHAPTER 3

SOVIET USE OF ECONOMIC PRESSURE AGAINST ALBANIA

The employment of Soviet economic pressure against Albania was in many ways quite similar to its utilization against Yugoslavia in the 1948-49 period. Thus within one and one-half years of the first open conflict between the two nations, a total trade embargo was imposed. Similarly, the early stages of economic pressure were followed by an attempt to split the Albanian party. There were also, however, some significant differences. Stalin ordered the other communist nations of Eastern Europe to cease all trade with Yugoslavia, but under Khrushchev the nations of Eastern Europe continued trading with Albania despite the Soviet embargo. In addition, whereas Yugoslavia turned to the Western nations for aid during Stalin's blockade, Albania received most of its alternate supplies from Communist China. Albania, in fact, played a large role in the early stages of the Sino-Soviet conflict.[1]

THE POLITICAL BACKGROUND OF THE CONFLICT

In order to understand the reasons behind the Albanian leadership's decision to ally itself with the Chinese Communists at the Bucharest Conference, it is necessary to first examine the salient points of Albania's brief national history.[2] Weak and surrounded by enemies coveting its territory, Albania has faced the prospect of partition almost since its establishment as a nation-state in 1912.

Yugoslavia, to the north and northeast of Albania, has sought her northern section since World War I and has twice dominated the entire country (1924-26 and 1945-48). In 1947, Tito seemed to have Stalin's permission to "swallow" Albania and make it a province of Yugoslavia.[3] Today, more than one million Albanians live in the "Kosmet" province of Yugoslavia, which lies along the northeast border of Albania. To the south lies Greece, which covets Albania's southernmost province. In this region, which Greece refers to as "Northern Epirus," lives a large Greek minority. Thus a primary objective of Albanian foreign policy, both before and after the communists took control, has been of necessity the preservation of the nation against the constant threat of partition by its more powerful neighbors.

Communist rule came to Albania in the latter stages of World War II. The Albanian communists, together with Yugoslav partisans who had organized them, seized control of the country following the withdrawal of German troops who had been occupying it. Yugoslavia then dominated the economic and political life of Albania and seemed well on its way toward annexing the tiny Balkan nation when the Cominform Resolution expelling Yugoslavia provided one faction of the Albanian leadership with the opportunity to gain a more independent position for their nation by siding with the Soviet Union against Tito.[4]

This faction, led by Enver Hoxha, who was the party's first secretary, had since 1945 been contending for party leadership with another faction whose leader was Koci Xoxe, the Minister of Interior. Xoxe was pro-Yugoslav; Hoxha preferred to have Albania independent of Yugoslavia.

Hoxha tried immediately after the war to lessen dependence on Yugoslavia by resuming relations with Italy (Yugoslavia's bitter foe over Trieste), even sending Albanian students to Italy to study.[5] In 1947, he sought to lessen Albania's increasing economic dependence on Yugoslavia by going to Moscow in search of economic aid. In this quest, Hoxha met with success and on July 27 a Soviet-Albanian communique stated:

> Taking into account the great and heavy losses suffered by Albania during the war and in answer to a request of the Albanian government for economic aid, the Soviet Union will furnish Albania, on credit, equipment for light industry and agricultural machinery.[6]

By this time, relations between the USSR and Yugoslavia had already grown tense, and Stalin, as he was to show later, was interested in weakening Tito's hold over Albania. Indeed, an article on the Albanian economy appearing in *Vneshniaia Torgovlia* several months later did not even mention the large amount of aid given by Yugoslavia (approximately 50 per cent of Albania's government revenues were provided by Yugoslavia in 1947 and 1948), but instead stressed the role of Soviet aid.[7]

In his domestic contest with Xoxe for control of the Albanian Communist Party, Hoxha fared less well. From 1945 on, Xoxe steadily gained ground and weakened Hoxha's position. In 1947, Nako Spiro, one of Hoxha's allies, was forced to commit suicide for opposing the economic agreements between Yugoslavia and Albania and for favoring Albanian self-sufficiency and economic development without Yugoslavia. But when Yugoslavia was expelled from the Cominform, Hoxha was able, with Soviet help, to depose Xoxe and have him executed.

Hoxha wasted no time in breaking Albania's economic and political bonds to Yugoslavia. On July 1, 1948, Albania became the first communist nation to break its trade agreements with Yugoslavia. Yugoslav economic aid, which less than a year before had been effusively praised, now received a new description:

> The Yugoslav Government brutally pursued a policy of domination in our country, an economic policy of colonial exploitation. It

threatened the sovereignty and the independence of the Albanian state, trampled down the principle of equality and reciprocity of rights, and constantly strove to force its point of view upon Albania in open contradiction with the interests of our country. *The Yugoslav Government has prevented our economy from developing and advancing toward socialism* [emphasis added].[8]

A short time later, Hoxha dispatched an economic delegation to Moscow to ask for aid, and the Soviet Union wasted little time in moving to replace Yugoslavia as Albania's economic and political protector. On September 28, 1948, the USSR agreed to accept all Albanian exports originally intended for Yugoslavia and to provide Albania with the products Yugoslavia had contracted to deliver.[9]

In March, 1949, Hoxha himself went to the USSR to arrange for developmental aid for his nation's backward agrarian economy, which at the time possessed virtually no industry or skilled workers. Albania had just begun a "two-year plan," and Soviet aid was destined to play a major role in giving Albania a light industrial base. Hoxha was not disappointed in his quest, as the USSR promised Albania a number of factories to assist it in "building Socialism"—on credit.[10] In addition, probably under Stalin's prodding, other nations of Eastern Europe also signed aid agreements with Albania in 1949.[11]

In February, 1951, the year in which the USSR accounted for 57 per cent of Albania's trade, the two countries signed a long-term trade agreement (to coincide with Albania's first five-year plan), another credit agreement, and a technical assistance agreement.[12] The training of an Albanian technical intelligentsia received its start in 1952 when an agreement was concluded on "reciprocal study of students" and Russia began to educate large numbers of Albanian students.[13]

Relations between Albania and the Soviet Union continued to be extremely cordial during the remaining years of Stalin's life. While the USSR was extracting resources from the other East European nations in the form of raw materials and machinery, it was extending economic assistance to Albania and compelling its satellites to do so as well. Stalin's motives in helping Albania seem clear. First, Hoxha was a bitter opponent of Tito and hence a useful tool in the anti-Tito movement. Second, the rapid development of the Albanian economy provided Stalin with an excellent contrast to Yugoslavia's economy which was floundering during this period. In an article in the October, 1952, *Vneshniaia Torgovlia* describing the gains of the Albanian economy, F. Gormunov stated:

The successes in the political and economic life of Albania are in clear contrast to the progressive degradation of Yugoslavia which as a result of the perfidious bourgeois nationalist policy of the Titoist Fascist clique has degenerated into the worst type of capitalist state with a dictatorial regime, which has lost its independence and turned into an American colony.... At the same time that Albania is progressing along the path of progress, of economic prosperity, on the path of constructing the foundations of socialism, Yugoslavia is heading for an economic catastrophe.[14]

The accession of Khrushchev to power, however, ended the rather halcyon economic and political relations between the two countries. Khrushchev's moves toward a rapprochement with Yugoslavia brought on a lessened interest in economic assistance for Albania. The rapid development of the Albanian economy, which had been so warmly praised in Stalin's day by the Soviet economic press, now began to be questioned. In particular, by 1956, the USSR was telling Albania it would have to depend to a much greater degree on its own efforts for the second Albanian five-year plan. The Soviet economist K. Danilov, writing in the November, 1956, *Voprosy Ekonomiki,* bluntly stated:

One of the most important tasks in the area of the further development of Albania's economy and the growth of the welfare of its people lies in the uncovering and thorough utilization of the *existing internal resources* of the state [emphasis added].[15]

Even worse, from the point of view of Hoxha, were the political dangers of the rapprochement. Suspecting that among Tito's prices for the rapprochement was the rehabilitation of Xoxe, who had been purged as a Titoist, and his own ouster, Hoxha refused to rehabilitate his former opponent despite heavy Soviet pressure (Suslov and Pospelov visited Albania in April, 1956).[16]

Indeed, there were certain elements in the Albanian party who were "opportunists," as Hoxha later was to call them, and wanted to jump aboard the Yugoslav bandwagon and dump Hoxha. Unfortunately for them, they jumped too soon; and thanks to his own ruthlessness, his nation's renewed fear of Yugoslav domination, and the bloc-wide anti-Yugoslav feeling following the Hungarian Revolution, Hoxha remained in control. But no longer would Hoxha trust Khrushchev, whose rapprochement with Tito had almost meant his own ouster.

Hoxha's deep hatred and fear of Yugoslavia, and particularly of Tito, was to be the central factor in his relations with the Soviet Union until the rupture of diplomatic relations in 1961. The nature of his feelings toward the Yugoslavs and the relationship between his ideological and nationalist opposition to Tito are well reflected in the following excerpt from an article that appeared in *Zeri i Popullit* on July 17, 1960:

The history of relations between our country and Titoist Yugoslavia is a history of plots aimed at liquidating our independence and transforming Albania into a part of the Titoist Hell. . . . He who does not know the history of relations between our country and Yugoslavia cannot fully and precisely appreciate the danger the Yugoslav revisionists represent.[17]

Following the Hungarian Revolution, there was a temporary improvement in relations between the USSR and Albania. On November 7, *Pravda* printed a bitter attack on Tito, which was written by Hoxha, and less than two months later on January 1, 1957, Albania obtained an $18.5 million credit from the Soviet Union.[18] Further Soviet economic aid followed three months later. In an agreement signed on April 17, 1957, the Soviet Union not only freed Albania from all previous debts (including the one incurred on January 1)—a total of $105 million—but also agreed to grant technical assistance in increasing agricultural production and mineral extraction.[19] In addition, Albania obtained a $7.75 million credit for the purchase of wheat, rice, and vegetable oil. In an effort to put the relations of the two nations on a more equal basis, the USSR also agreed to conclude with Albania agreements on trade and sea navigation, citizenship, mutual legal aid in criminal and civil court cases, and a convention on consular questions.[20]

Nonetheless, Albania was no longer the docile satellite of Stalinist days. On August 27, 1957, in an interview with Harrison Salisbury of *The New York Times,* the Albanian Premier Mehmet Shehu announced that Albania was now ready not only for diplomatic relations with the United States, but for trade relations and tourists as well.[21] In early 1958, the Albanian government sharply increased its goals for the second five-year plan in the area of increased investment and capital goods production, an action that did not meet with the full approval of the USSR.[22] By 1958, Hoxha was casting around for another ally in the Communist Camp who could protect him against the intrigues of both Tito and Khrushchev. The ally he found was Communist China which, for reasons of its own, had become strongly anti-revisionist—and hence anti-Tito—by the end of 1957.[23]

The draft program of the Yugoslav Communist Party, which appeared in the spring of 1958, precipitated a major round of polemics in the international communist movement. Although the Soviet Union's critical comments on the draft program were relatively mild in nature, those of Communist China and Albania were extremely harsh.[24] Relations between the two leading anti-Tito nations grew warmer in September when Beqir Balluku, Albania's Minister of Defense, visited China. In January, 1959, the Chinese who had been granting Albania economic assistance since 1954, offered a $13.75 million loan for Albania's third five-year plan (1961-65).[25] It was perhaps to counter this that Khrushchev gave Albania a $75 million developmental credit for the five-year plan and, at the same time, also promised the Albanians an $8.75 million loan for the development of the Albanian oil industry.[26] In addition, Albania obtained a $25 million loan from Czechoslovakia and a $10 million credit from East Germany. The Soviet leaders also promised in January to build a large "Palace of Culture" in Albania as a gift of the Russian people.[27]

Despite the economic largesse, relations were not particularly warm between the Russian and Albanian leaders in the spring of 1959 because Khrushchev had again begun to work for a rapprochement with Yugoslavia. Khrushchev's trip to Albania in May, 1959, neither improved relations between the two nations nor impeded the growing friendship between

Albania and China. Indeed, Khrushchev cast a pall on his visit even before he arrived by radioing "warm congratulations" to Tito on the occasion of the Yugoslav leader's birthday while he was flying over Yugoslavia en route to Albania.[28] While in Albania, Khrushchev paid tribute to the late American Secretary of State John Foster Dulles who, Khrushchev stated, had displayed a "more sober understanding of the international situation" in the last months of his life.[29] This too was not well received by the Albanians, who had already begun to echo the Chinese refrain about the "nature of imperialism." Khrushchev also came into conflict with his hosts in the economic sphere. According to later Albanian reports, Khrushchev is supposed to have attempted to convince the Albanians that they should become an "orchard" of socialism where "oranges, lemons and perhaps even bananas" would grow for the benefit of all the socialist peoples.[30] This remark did not endear him to his industrialization-minded hosts who had the vision of transforming their still largely agrarian country into an industrial one.

Relations between the two nations continued to deteriorate until the Bucharest Conference in June, 1960. In January, the Russians reportedly were unsuccessful in an attempt to persuade the Albanians to end their close friendship with China, and the failure of Hoxha and Shehu to attend the Warsaw Pact Consultative Conference in March was indicative of the strained relations between the two countries.[31] In April, the Chinese Communists openly polemicized against the Soviet Union with their "Lenin Birthday Theses," and two months later there was an open confrontation between the two leading communist states at the Bucharest Conference where Albania chose to back China on the most important issues. But before an examination is made of the economic penalties incurred by Albania for its pro-Chinese stand, it is necessary to examine Albania's vulnerability to Soviet economic pressure.

ALBANIA'S ECONOMIC VULNERABILITY

Albania's vulnerability to Soviet economic pressure was in many ways similar to Yugoslavia's twelve years earlier. It was almost completely dependent for its imports on the USSR and the nations the Russians controlled, and its economic development was contingent on supplies of capital equipment and technical assistance from the same countries. In one respect, however, Albania had a clear advantage over the Yugoslavs in 1948; by 1960, its economy had recovered from the destruction wrought by World War II and the Albanian leaders had none of the reconstruction problems that plagued Yugoslavia.

Prior to World War II, Albania was economically the most backward nation in Europe. The vast majority of its population were farmers, and the small amount of industry that existed in the country produced primarily consumer goods such as flour, hides, macaroni, and cigarettes.[32] Its mines produced chrome and copper, and a small number of oil wells were also in operation.[33] As in Yugoslavia, the war caused a great deal of destruction, and when the Italians departed at the end of the conflict, the Albanian leaders faced the problem of rebuilding destroyed homes, factories, and mines. They also had the problem of acquiring the necessary technical specialists to run their economy, because in the inter-war period almost all of the technical jobs in Albania's economy were held by Italians.[34]

During the period of Yugoslav hegemony over Albania immediately following the war, Tito provided the Albanians with economic aid and technical assistance from his own meager resources. Tito's aim during this period seems to have been the incorporation of Albania into Yugoslavia, and the economic agreements signed with the Albanians offer evidence in support of this thesis. Thus in July, 1946, an agreement was signed which contained the following provisions: (1) the establishment of an agency to coordinate the economic plans of the two countries; (2) the equalization of the Albanian lek with the Yugoslav dinar on a one-to-one basis; (3) the introduction into Albania of the Yugoslav price system; and (4) the abolition of all tariffs and customs duties between the two countries and the establishment of a joint Albanian-Yugoslav Customs Commission to supervise the single customs area.[35]

The two countries were even more closely bound together by the treaty of November 28, 1946. The key provisions of this treaty called for the establishment of joint-stock companies in petroleum mining, ore prospecting and exploitation, electrification, foreign trade, and banking.[36] In addition, the Yugoslavs claim that their credits to the Albanian economy accounted for 57 per cent of Albania's state revenue in 1947 and 48 per cent in 1948.[37]

Albania's break with Yugoslavia in 1948 proved advantageous for Hoxha economically as well as politically. Not only did the Soviet Union have no territorial claims against Albania, it could also provide the tiny Balkan nation with far more economic aid and more and far better trained technicians to aid in its economic development than could Yugoslavia. The Soviet Union had given economic assistance in the form of grain shipments to Albania as early as 1946 and in 1947 delivered light industrial machinery and agricultural equipment on credit.[38] When the Cominform break occurred, the Soviet Union not only provided Albania with the imports previously acquired from Yugoslavia, but also offered technical assistance and capital goods aid as well. This coincided exactly with the Albanian leaders' desire to transform their backward agricultural state into an "agrarian-industrial" country.

Albania's first five-year plan (1951-55) was directed primarily at establishing a light industrial base for the country. With the aid of Soviet and satellite economic assistance, the Stalin textile mill (with a capacity of 20 million meters of cloth per year), the Lenin hydroelectric plant, a sugar refinery, a cement factory, woodworking plants, cotton and rice gins, a tobacco curing plant, and a tannery were built, along with a number of smaller installations.[39] At the completion of the five-year plan, the Albanians claimed that total industrial production had increased elevenfold compared with 1938 and that Albania had been transformed from "a backward agricultural to an agrarian-industrial nation."[40]

At the start of the second five-year plan (1956-60), as we have already seen, the Albanian leaders were told by the Russians that they would have to depend more on their own resources and less on Soviet aid for their economic development. Consequently, the major effort made during the second five-year plan was on increasing the output of Albania's mines and oil wells so that these products could be exported in exchange for industrial equipment. Due to the raw material shortage in Eastern Europe at that time, the Soviet Union was willing to extend technical assistance to develop Albania's copper and chromium mines, and Czechoslovakia invested in its nickel mines.[41] During this period, another major hydroelectric plant was constructed and Albania's oil production rapidly increased—a matter of great pride for the Albanians. By 1959, extraction of copper, chrome, and nickel ore had increased sharply, oil extraction had more than doubled, production of electric energy had tripled, and the production of building materials (cement, bricks, and lumber) had increased by 40 per cent as compared with 1954.[42]

By the end of 1959, the Albanian leaders had completed detailed planning for their third five-year plan (1961-65). Writing in the November, 1959, issue of *Voprosy Ekonomiki*, Kocho Teodosi, a member of Albania's Council of Ministers, had the following vision of the development of the Albanian economy.

Great prospects have opened before Albania. At the present time the Albanian Party of Labor and the government of the Albanian People's Republic have prepared a preliminary perspective plan for the development of the state from 1961-75. On the basis of materials of this plan, the draft five year economic and cultural plan (1961-65) has been put together. In the course of this period Albania will follow the road of transformation from an agrarian-industrial to an industrial-agrarian state. The draft of the third five year plan has been worked out taking into consideration the calculations of the Council for Mutual Economic Assistance which assures the coordination of the economic plans of the states of the socialist camp. *Our state has concluded agreements on economic cooperation with states who are members of the Council for Mutual Economic Assistance. These agreements assure the necessary material-technical aid for the fulfillment of the third five year plan.*

It is foreseen that industrial production will increase almost 110% at the end of the third five year plan in comparison with 1958. The mining industry will rapidly develop. New branches of industry will be created: the chemical, ferro-chrome, copper, smelting, the production of superphosphate fertilizer, etc. The (electric) energy base will be expanded. The production of electricity by the end of the third five year plan will be three times greater than 1960. A large number of enterprises will also be constructed in the textile industry, the construction materials industry, and the food industry [emphasis added].[43]

The successful completion of this rather ambitious plan was, as Teodosi himself pointed out, dependent on the "necessary material-technical aid" granted Albania by the members of CMEA. Chief among the CMEA aid donors was the Soviet Union. Soviet aid, although not as extensive as the Albanians might have wished, had nonetheless provided the basis for Albania's economic advancement up to 1959. Nesti Nase, then Albanian ambassador to the Soviet Union, in an article in the June, 1959, issue of *International Affairs,* expressed his appreciation for Soviet aid in these terms:

> It is difficult to overestimate the importance of Soviet-Albanian friendship in the building of Socialism in our country. The People's Republic of Albania has received from the USSR the most up-to-date equipment for the numerous plants built in our country since liberation, thousands of agricultural machines and plant and equipment for mines, transport, communications and the health services. Hundreds of highly qualified Soviet experts have helped us in building factories and mills, in our agricultural, scientific and cultural development. . . .
>
> The Albanian people rightly consider the invaluable assistance and support of the first Socialist Power—the USSR—as the source of all their victories. Our people owes its life, freedom, independence and outstanding successes in the Socialist transformation of their country to friendship with the Soviet Union and its tremendous disinterested aid.[44]

In January, 1959, probably to match Chinese competition, the Soviet Union had agreed to provide Albania with a $75 million credit for the construction of a number of enterprises during the third five-year plan, and had also granted the Albanians an $8.75 million loan for the development of their oil industry in the 1959-60 period. Economic credits for Albania's five-year plan were also provided by Czechoslovakia ($25 million) and East Germany ($10 million).

Soviet technical assistance was to play a major role in Albania's third five-year plan. The shortage of skilled workers and technicians had been a continual problem. Near the end of the first Albanian five-year plan, Albanian Premier Mehmet Shehu stated:

> We have created a light industry with modern equipment granted to us by the Soviet Union and the Peoples Democracies. Our task is to strive for a rational exploitation of existing industry and to extend development of industrial production. *In order to insure a*

*rational exploitation of our industrial equipment we must devote
particular attention to the preparation of technical cadres*
[emphasis added].[45]

By 1959, a number of Albanian technicians had been trained in the
Soviet Union, but the Albanians were still dependent on Soviet technical
assistance for the construction and operation of their major industries. On
July 4, 1959, Radio Tirana reported that the USSR had agreed to provide
Albania with assistance in the following areas in the last years of its second
five-year plan and for its third five-year plan:

Construction of industrial chemical enterprises; the metal construction industry; the food industry; thermo-electric stations; high
power lines; the expansion and reconstruction of transport; and the
reconstruction and tubing of the petroleum and gas projects.[46]

In this agreement, the Russians also promised to aid other industrial projects
and complete geological prospecting activities aimed at discovering mineral
raw materials for the construction materials industry.[47] The extent of Soviet
technical assistance was described in these words by Radio Tirana:

[Soviet] technical aid [will be provided] for prospecting and
planning, providing equipment, assisting in construction, consulting,
and in assembling, putting into operation and exploiting machinery
as well as in assisting in the training of local cadres who will work
in these enterprises which will be constructed in full cooperation
with the Soviet Union.[48]

In agreeing to provide technical assistance of this nature, the Soviet Union
had also prepared (although perhaps not intentionally) a major weapon of
economic pressure—the abrupt withdrawal of the technicians. Indeed, less
than two years after the agreements on technical assistance were signed, all
the Soviet technicians had left Albania.

In the case of Albania, it is difficult to separate economic assistance
from trade relations, for the Albanians continually ran a large deficit in trade
with the Soviet Union (see Table 3). The trade statistics for the year
1959—the year before the USSR began to exert economic pressure—offer an
indication of the vulnerability of the Albanian economy to a sudden
disruption of trade with the USSR. In 1959, no less than 56 per cent of
Albania's imports came from the Soviet Union; another 12 per cent came
from Czechoslovakia and 8 per cent from East Germany.[49] Almost half of
the commodities Albania imported from the Soviet Union in 1959 were in
the category "machinery and equipment," and another 15 per cent consisted
of wheat (94,300 tons). Machinery and materials for complete factories
accounted for 11 per cent of Albania's imports, oil-drilling equipment

TABLE 3

Soviet-Albanian Commodity Trade, 1955-62
(in millions of new rubles)

	1955	1956	1957	1958	1959	1960	1961	1962
Soviet Exports	15.1	18.2	32.7	44.3	44.0	39.2	18.3	0
Albanian Exports	5.5	8.2	14.1	14.1	13.3	21.8	19.6	0
Soviet Balance	9.6	10.0	18.6	30.2	30.7	17.4	−1.3	
Soviet Exports (Commodity)								
1. Machinery and Equipment	8.445	9.370	13.270	26.234	21.71	22.12	8.21	
2. Oil Machinery	1.270	1.724	2.435	6.260	4.173	1.801	1.010	
3. Complete Factories	1.380	2.480	2.480	1.800	4.675	11.539	2.960	
4. Tractors and Agricultural Machinery	2.419	.982	2.680	3.295	3.072	3.401	1.843	
(a) tractors (number)	248	1	242	268	361	401	155	
5. Auto Transport and Garage Equipment	1.232	1.643	2.211	4.620	4.600	2.055	.975	
(a) heavy trucks (number)	232	273	445	829	1,058	291	128	
6. Pipes	1.392	.780	1.720	2.674	4.094	2.118	1.534	
(a) oil pipes	1.040	.513	1.120	1.742	2.941	1.531	.994	
7. Wheat (ruble value)	.848	1.520	7.691	3.690	6.682	6.570	3.545	
Wheat (thousand tons)	10	17.3	81.4	49.1	94,300	96,300	53,700	
8. Spare Parts	.995	1.245	1.327	1.944	2.585	3.176	2.110	

Albanian Exports (Commodity)	1955	1956	1957	1958	1959	1960	1961	1962
1. Crude Oil								
(a) ruble value	1.670	2.087	3.214	1.141	.989	2.274	1.605	
(b) thousand metric tons	107.7	134.7	207.3	73.6	70.9	163.0	115.0	
2. Bitumen	2.201	1.596	4.070	3.351	3.888	4.485	3.864	
3. Raw Tobacco	1.172	2.230	4.425	4.134	1.832	4.639	1.843	
4. Cigarettes	---	---	.348	3.226	4.071	6.316	7.558	
5. Wood Products and Cellulose	.403	.535	.411	.616	.630	1.157	1.066	

Sources: Vneshniaia Torgovlia SSSR za 1956 god (Moscow: Vneshtorgizdat, 1957), pp. 38-41; *Vneshniaia Torgovlia SSSR za 1958 god* (Moscow: Vneshtorgizdat, 1959), pp. 39-43; *Vneshniaia Torgovlia SSSR za 1960 god* (Moscow: Vneshtorgizdat, 1961), pp. 61-65; *Vneshniaia Torgovlia SSSR za 1961 god* (Moscow: Vneshtorgizdat, 1962), pp. 73-78.

accounted for 10 per cent, tractors and agricultural equipment for 7 per cent, heavy trucks for 5 per cent, oil pipelines for 5 per cent, and electric power equipment for 2.5 per cent. Significantly, 5 per cent of Albania's imports came in the form of spare parts for Soviet-supplied equipment and agricultural machinery.[50] The role of wheat imports is worthy of note; Albania's agricultural production had not grown as rapidly as industrial production and in some years had actually decreased. (Thus in 1957, 121,168 tons of wheat were produced, but this dropped to 96,678 tons in 1958 and rose only to 101,666 tons in 1959.[51])

The Soviet Union also took the bulk of Albania's exports in 1959 (45 per cent), and Czechoslovakia accounted for 19 per cent, East Germany 14 per cent, and Hungary 7 per cent.[52] Albania's exports to the USSR consisted primarily of cigarettes (31 per cent), bitumen (29 per cent), raw tobacco (14 per cent), and crude oil (7 per cent).[53] Only bitumen was an import of real value to the Soviet economy, with Albania supplying 70 per cent of total Soviet imports of the commodity.[54] Total Albanian exports to the USSR in 1959 accounted for less than .3 per cent of Soviet imports in that year. The dependency of Albania on trade with nations of the Soviet bloc (the USSR and Eastern Europe, excluding Yugoslavia) can perhaps best be seen from the following figures. These nations accounted for no less than 94 per cent of Albania's exports and 93 per cent of its imports in 1959. By contrast, China provided only 3 per cent of Albania's imports and absorbed only 2.5 per cent of its exports in the same year.[55] The situation was, however, to reverse itself several years later.

The Soviet Union, through its economic advisors and embassy in Tirana, was well aware of the economic vulnerability of the Albanian economy. In an article in the October, 1958, issue of *Vneshniaia Torgovlia,* A. Poliakova described in considerable detail the role of foreign trade and economic assistance in developing the Albanian economy. She concluded her article with these words:

> The Plenum of the Central Committee of the Albanian Party of Labor which convened in February 1958 laid forth before the Albanian people large tasks in the development of the economy and culture of the people. Albania's foreign trade should play a major role in the fulfillment of these tasks.[56]

Thus by 1959, although its economy had made significant advances since World War II, Albania was extremely vulnerable to Soviet economic pressure. The overwhelming share of its imports came from nations in the Soviet bloc, and its third five-year plan was dependent on capital and technical assistance from the same nations. The next section will illustrate how Khrushchev attempted to exploit Albania's economic weakness to force the tiny Balkan nation to follow the Soviet line against China.

IMPLEMENTATION OF SOVIET ECONOMIC PRESSURE

As in the case of Yugoslavia in the 1948-49 period, the Soviet leaders orchestrated a number of different pressures—economic, political, and military—in an effort to force Albania to accede to Russian demands. This section will concentrate primarily on the economic pressures but will also describe the major political and military pressures employed by the Soviet leaders in order to relate them to the economic pressures. Whereas the ideological disputes that played a major role in the conflict have been dealt with in considerable detail elsewhere, ideological issues will be mentioned here only insofar as they relate directly to an economic, political, or military pressure.[57]

Soviet economic pressure against Albania began in March, 1960. On March 16, possibly in reprisal for the failure of Hoxha or Shehu to attend the special Warsaw Pact Consultative Conference held that month, the Soviet government informed the Albanians of its intentions to alter a 1952 scholarship agreement whereby the Russians paid 60 per cent of the cost of tuition and upkeep for Albanian students studying in the USSR. Although the Albanians have not indicated the nature of the proposed changes—they have said only that the USSR wanted the conclusion of a "new agreement on different bases and conditions than 1952"—it would appear that the Soviets planned to cancel the Albanian scholarships and require the Albanians to pay all tuition and upkeep costs themselves.[58] The Albanians, citing "the concrete situation existing in Albania, the urgent need for trained cadres and the financial burden that would follow from a change in the conditions of study," then appealed to the Russians for a cancellation of the proposed change.[59] The Russians did not reply to the Albanian appeal until June 6, although they took no unilateral action to alter the agreement in the meantime. At this point, with an Albanian delegation in China and the Bucharest Conference looming on the horizon, the Albanians got a verbal assurance from Soviet Deputy Minister of Foreign Affairs N. P. Firyubin that their appeal had been taken into consideration and that a decision had been made "that the conditions of the 1952 agreement should remain in force."[60] In making this decision, Khrushchev may have hoped either to avert a situation whereby Albania might be forced prematurely into the arms of China, or he may have tried to strengthen the hand of such pro-Soviet members of the Albanian Politburo as Liri Belishova who was then touring China.

In any case, Khrushchev simultaneously applied another form of pressure, this time to make the Albanians aware of their international political vulnerability. On June 5, Khrushchev met with Sophokles Venizelos, a left-wing political leader in Greece. Venizelos, who was an advocate of Greece's withdrawal from NATO, had come to Moscow to complain about Albanian treatment of the Greek minority in Southern Albania. Khrushchev told him:

The communist parties salute the idea that every minority should be
autonomous in order to be able to develop its language and
civilization in accordance with its wishes. . . . I can assure you I will
communicate these things to Comrade Enver Hoxha when I meet
him in Bucharest [emphasis added].[61]

The meaning of the statement was not lost on the partition-fearing Albanian
leader.[62]

Following the Bucharest Conference, in which the Albanian representatives openly sided with the Chinese on key issues (neither Hoxha nor Shehu
attended this conference either), Khrushchev began to step up Soviet pressure.
During the summer, he made an attempt to split the Albanian leadership and
oust Hoxha from power. The Albanians were later to claim that during the
summer of 1960 the Russians had:

. . . launched a feverish attack on the Marxist-Leninist line of the
PPSh (the Albanian Communist Party), had tried to split our party
and sow panic and confusion in its ranks, and had tried to separate
the leaders from the party and to incite against them the army cadres
and other cadres who had studied in the Soviet Union.[63]

Concurrent with his attempts to split the Albanian leadership, Khrushchev
exercised Soviet economic leverage over Albania to bring added pressure upon
it. Albania had obtained 94,000 tons of wheat from the USSR in 1959 while
producing 101,666 tons of wheat and 208,617 tons of corn domestically.[64]
Due to a drought in 1960, the Albanian domestic production of grain went
down and the Albanian government had to turn to the USSR for a special
shipment of 50,000 tons of grain to help alleviate the crisis. According to one
Albanian account of what then transpired, "Khrushchev refused and, what is
more, remained silent for a long time before replying."[65] The Albanian
account is, however, somewhat contradictory. In another account, Hoxha
reportedly stated that after a 45-day delay the Russians offered to sell 10,000
tons of wheat for gold (which the Albanians obviously did not have) instead of
selling it on credit as had earlier been the custom.[66] Even if the latter account
is correct, there is no question but that this was a severe pressure to place on
the Albanian leadership, and one calculated to break its alliance with China,
which at the time was undergoing a major grain crisis itself.

It was in an attempt to capitalize on the vulnerable position of the
Albanian leadership, faced with both a grain shortage and threats from
pro-Soviet elements within the party, that on August 13 Khrushchev proposed
a meeting with Hoxha which, in the Albanian leader's words, was:

. . . not for the purpose of settling the differences between the PPSh
and the Soviet leadership, but in order to place the PPSh in the same
ranks as the Khrushchev group against a 3rd party (China) and thus
to split the socialist camp.[67]

According to Hoxha, the Soviet letter made the following proposal:

> We feel it is important that the PPSh and the CPSU go to the forthcoming November Conference with absolute unity of views. The CPSU Central Committee believes that with this in mind it would be reasonable to organize a meeting of representatives of our two parties before the Conference.[68]

This letter, coming at a time of strong Soviet pressure on the Albanian leadership, was in many respects similar to Stalin's letter of March 27, 1948, to Tito. Khrushchev's efforts to split the Albanian party and oust Hoxha, however, were no more successful than Stalin's earlier efforts to oust Tito. Despite their own serious famine caused both by natural disasters and the follies of the "Great Leap Forward," the Chinese Communists spent some of their scarce foreign exchange to provide Albania with the needed wheat. In addition, Hoxha succeeded in purging the pro-Soviet elements of the Albanian party, led by Liri Belishova and Koco Tashko. Thus a united Albanian leadership, strengthened by the knowledge that the Chinese would give it concrete assistance, was able to stand up to Khrushchev. An immediate result was the August 23 Radio Tirana broadcast that denounced Venizelos (and indirectly Khrushchev) as well as any possibility of "autonomy" for the Greek inhabitants of Albania:

> Recently Sophokles Venizelos trumpeted the well-known reactionary slogan of the Greek Chauvinists about the autonomy of the so-called Northern Epirus. This slogan is taken from the reactionary arsenal of his father Eleftherios Venizelos, who in 1914 incited Zographos gangs to satisfy the cupidity of Greek chauvinists. Since 1914 the Albanian people have defended with their blood the territorial integrity of Albania.[69]

Several days later, on August 27, the Albanian Central Committee in a letter to the Central Committee of the CPSU announced its refusal to meet with the Soviet body on the conditions laid down by Khrushchev.[70]

Khrushchev, who was preparing to go to the United Nations at this time, did not take any overt action against the Albanians until he returned to the USSR, although the head of the Albanian delegation to the United Nations, Mehmet Shehu, received the "cold-shoulder" treatment from his communist colleagues while he was in New York.[71] The Albanians, however, were not idle during this period. In September, an Albanian-Chinese friendship delegation led by Albania's Minister of Heavy Industry Abdul Kellexi began a long visit in China which was to culminate not only in warm pledges of mutual admiration and mutual support but also in a number of economic agreements between the two countries. Confident of Chinese aid, the Albanian Central Committee on October 11, 1960, published the directives for Albania's third five-year plan.[72] One day earlier, the Albanian radio had announced the arrival of 9,100 tons of grain from China.[73]

Thus upon his return from the United Nations, Khrushchev was faced by an Albanian leadership that had weathered a number of Soviet pressures and was now even more firmly aligned with China than before. The Albanian five-year plan was, however, heavily dependent on Soviet supplies of equipment and technical assistance, and it was in this area that Khrushchev now began to apply pressure. An Albanian trade delegation had come to Moscow in mid-October to negotiate the all-important trade agreement for the 1961-65 five-year plan period, but the delegation was kept waiting by Khrushchev who, in delaying trade talks, was exerting a pressure similar to the one exerted on Tito by Stalin in December, 1947.[74]

Then, on November 10, the day of the opening of the Conference of the Eighty-One Communist Parties, the Russians once again reminded the Albanians of their possible isolation in Europe in the absence of Soviet support. A Radio Moscow broadcast beamed to Albania in Albanian stated:

> From the first days of its existence Soviet Russia has raised its voice for Albania's independence and sovereignty.... A wise Albanian saying runs: "a true friend proves himself in time of need." When Fascist Italy occupied Albania, the Soviet Union . . . raised its powerful voice in defense of the rights of the Albanian people.[75]

The broadcast went on to describe the Tirana Palace of Culture which the Russians were building in Tirana as a gift to the Albanian people:

> The Palace of Culture, a gift of the USSR will be a monumental symbol of the beautiful love and friendship of the Soviet People for the Albanian People.[76]

The Palace of Culture was to be an early victim of the growing conflict between the two nations, and it is perhaps for this reason that the radio broadcast emphasized the symbolic nature of the building.

On November 12, Khrushchev had a face-to-face meeting with Hoxha, but the circulation of an anti-Hoxha draft letter to each of the 81 parties prior to the meeting doomed the already dim chances such a conference might have had for bringing about a rapprochement between the two leaders. Indeed, Hoxha later stated that Khrushchev had said at the time that he could reach a "better understanding with Macmillan than he could with the Albanians."[77] One week after the abortive confrontation between Khrushchev and Hoxha, the Albanian ambassador to Communist China held a press conference in Peking during which he discussed the achievements of the Albanian Peoples Republic since its liberation. Included among his remarks, which the Chinese radio broadcast on November 23, was the statement: "Albania is no longer isolated and without assistance."[78] Two days later, the Albanian delegation angrily left Moscow.

Following the departure of the Albanian delegation, Soviet pressure was increased in a number of areas. In the economic sphere, veiled threats were made to cut off Soviet credits. On November 29, 1960, a Bulgarian official, Rayko Damayanov, who was almost certainly following Soviet instructions, made the following comment in a speech at an Albanian Embassy reception commemorating Albanian National Day:

> Following the victory over fascism, friendship and cooperation between the Bulgarian and Albanian peoples have been growing steadily and developing *on the basis of their common friendship with the peoples of the great Soviet Union.* Thanks to this friendship, which is sacred to our peoples and thanks to the great and selfless assistance of the Soviet Union, our peoples have preserved their national independence and have achieved remarkable economic and cultural successes. *We are convinced that the consolidation of our peoples' friendship with the fraternal Soviet people will guarantee the further development of Bulgaria and Albania as independent socialist states and will guarantee new successes in the joint struggle for the construction of socialist society* [emphasis added].[79]

On the same day, Radio Moscow, in sending "greetings" to Albania, stated pointedly:

> During the years of socialist building, the working class, peasantry, and intelligentsia of the Albanian Peoples Republic *with the aid given by the fraternal socialist camp,* have achieved great success [emphasis added].[80]

In addition to subtle threats of ending economic assistance, the Russians also began to increase the political pressure on Albania by making a determined effort to improve relations with Yugoslavia. On November 29, Radio Moscow in a broadcast to Western Europe stated:

> On the international scene the Soviet Union and Yugoslavia are brought together on a number of issues by the common striving of both countries as well as other peace loving nations to secure the triumph of the principles of peaceful coexistence to ensure world peace. In the future, too, the Soviet Union will strive to develop good relations with Yugoslavia, *to extend trade and cultural relations with it in the interests of strengthening international friendship* [emphasis added].[81]

As the Soviet Union increased pressure on Albania, the Balkan nation was consolidating its alliance with China still further. On November 29, Mao Tse-tung, Chou En-lai, and Chu Teh attended a reception given by the Albanian ambassador.[82] In a speech delivered at the reception, Chou En-lai assured the Albanians that they could expect to receive aid from China, and he expressed appreciation for the "powerful support" China had received from the Albanian people.[83]

Interestingly enough, despite the delay in trade negotiations which had lasted two months by mid-December, the Albanian government made an official request for Soviet technical assistance for the year 1961 on December 14. At the same time, it requested that the term of Soviet specialists working in the Albanian oil industry be extended.[84] Khrushchev, however, had apparently already decided that he would exploit Albania's economic vulnerability in an attempt to force the Albanian leaders into concessions. Consequently, sometime in December, the Russians suggested "high level discussions on economic matters" to the Albanian party,[85] and on December 21 Soviet Deputy Foreign Trade Minister Vladimir Semichastny told the members of the Albanian trade delegation who had been waiting in Moscow for some 64 days for negotiations to begin that "it would be advisable to postpone the matter of signing a long-term commercial agreement for 1961-65 and the agreement on credits to Albania in view of the need to discuss this question on a higher level."[86] In the words of the Albanians:

> In practice this meant that the Soviet government was linking negotiations on economic questions and the conclusion of the agreements to its efforts to make our party submit to the views of N. Khrushchev's group.... *It is clear that the Soviet leadership was exploiting the question of economic aid as a means of exerting pressure on the PPSh* on the eve of its Fourth Congress, which was to be held in February 1961 in order to force it to renounce its Marxist-Leninist positions [emphasis added].[87]

On January 4, the USSR signed a trade agreement with Albania, but only for the year 1961, and no mention was made of Soviet credits. The TASS announcement was curt in the extreme and, when it was republished in *Vneshniaia Torgovlia,* it appeared on the same page on which a major increase in trade with the Sudan was described.[88] Although the details of the Soviet-Albanian trade agreement were not announced, later trade statistics issued by both countries indicated that it was a straight barter agreement with Albania exporting to the Soviet Union approximately as much as it received from it. Soviet exports dropped more than 50 per cent compared to 1960, but Albanian exports dropped only 10 per cent (see Table 3).

Soviet exports to Albania had already begun to contract in 1960, but only by 10 per cent. Soviet shipments of tractors and complete factories actually increased over 1959, and most other products were sent in approximately the same amounts. The only commodities showing significant decreases were heavy trucks (1,058 to 291) and oil industry equipment (4.17 million rubles to 1.8 million). Whereas the Albanians had taken great pride in the expansion of their oil industry, this was probably more than an arbitrarily chosen decrease.* The Soviet decision to withdraw oil specialists in late January, 1961, adds credence to this view.

Indeed, on January 20, 1961, as a foretaste of what was to come, A. Pikalov, acting economic attache in the Soviet Embassy in Tirana, told the

---

*The Albanian press up to 1961 had often reported with pride the achievements of the Albanian oil industry.

Albanian Minister of Mining that all Soviet oil specialists would be withdrawn in a 7-10 day period because "the agreement of 22 November 1957 had been fulfilled."[89] Despite Albanian requests for them to stay, the Soviet specialists left Albania by the end of the month and, according to information recently made public by the Albanians, they allegedly sabotaged Albania's oil installations before they departed.[90] This appears to have been the final Soviet attempt to persuade the Albanian leaders to change their policies prior to the Albanian Party Congress.

This attempt, however, had little effect on the Albanians, whose position was considerably strengthened at the beginning of February when a long-term trade and assistance agreement was signed with China.[91]

Two weeks after the Soviet oil specialists were withdrawn, the Fourth Albanian Party Congress began. The Albanian leaders made no ideological concessions to the Soviet Union during the Congress; and, according to a later report by the chief Soviet delegate to the Congress, Petr Pospelov:

> During the last Congress of the Albanian Party of Labor we encountered a number of glaring instances of direct anti-Soviet attacks by prominent Albanian officials, instances of a humiliating, hostile attitude toward our specialists, geologists and Soviet seamen. On behalf of the Central Committee, we handed the Albanian leaders the following protest and warning on February 20, 1961:
>
> The Central Committee of our party considers that such instances not only impede the development and strengthening of Albanian-Soviet friendship but also run counter to the interests of the entire Socialist Camp. If these abnormal phenomena are not stopped in good time, they may entail serious consequences.[92]

Apparently, they were not "stopped in good time," for at the end of March Khrushchev and Novotny announced that "they would cut off all assistance to Albania."[93] At the same time, in what could well be interpreted as a slap at Albania, a long-term trade agreement was signed between the Soviet Union and Yugoslavia which called for a doubling of Soviet-Yugoslav trade by 1965 compared to the 1960 level.[94]

The Albanians, however, had already acquired an alternate supplier of both investment credits and imports. On April 23, the details of the Sino-Albanian trade-and-aid agreement were announced, according to which the Chinese agreed to supply Albania with a $123 million credit for the construction of 25 major industrial projects during the third five-year plan.[95] This amount exceeded the $118 million promised by the USSR and the nations of Eastern Europe for the same period. As an added bonus, the Chinese purchased 2,200,000 bushels (60,000 tons) of wheat from Canada in April and had it shipped to their Balkan ally.[96]

Five days after the announcement of the Sino-Albanian agreement came the formal cancellation of Soviet aid. In a letter to the Albanian party, Soviet First Deputy Premier Aleksei Kosygin stated:

After weighing all the circumstances, the Soviet Government is obliged to re-examine the question of future relations with the Albanian People's Republic. . . . The Soviet People and the peoples of the other socialist countries would not understand us if we, while depriving our country of material resources, should continue to satisfy the demands of the Albanian leaders who, to the detriment of the interests of the Albanian people have trampled on elementary norms in relations with the USSR and its government. . . . It is understandable that the Albanian leadership cannot expect in the future that the USSR will help it as it has in the past, with aid from which only true friends and brothers have a right to benefit. The Soviet Union deems it necessary henceforth to establish its relations with Albania on a new basis, taking into account the unfriendly policy of its leadership toward the Soviet Union and the other socialist countries. . . . As concerns future relations between our countries, and USSR aid to Albania, these will depend entirely on the attitude adopted by the Albanian party.[97]

This letter is quite similar to the Soviet note to the Yugoslavs in 1948, which, as we have already seen, stated that "the Soviet Union can only offer aid to friends."

On the same day as the announcement of the abrogation of the trade agreements came another announcement perhaps equally as distasteful to the Albanian leaders. This was the announcement that an exchange of visits between the Yugoslav and Russian foreign ministers had been agreed to.[98] Fifty Soviet specialists left Albania the next day, and the rest, including those working on the Palace of Culture, left shortly thereafter.[99]

Relations between Albania and the USSR deteriorated very sharply following the abrogation of aid agreements. In May, Hoxha placed on trial a number of pro-Russian Albanian leaders who were allegedly involved in the "plot" of the Yugoslavs, Greeks, and U.S. Sixth Fleet to overthrow his regime. It was also in May that Russian submarines were withdrawn from their Albanian base in Vlores. This removed the Soviet military presence from Albania, thus leaving the Albanians considerably more vulnerable to attack from their neighbors.[100] It was perhaps in response to this form of pressure that the Albanian leaders decided to improve relations with the less powerful of their two dangerous neighbors, Greece, and on June 23, 1961, forty-one Greek peasants who had been taken as hostages to Albania by the Greek communist guerrillas were returned to Greece.[101]

By July 1 it had become apparent that the Soviet Union had not only terminated its credits to Albania, but that it had also severely cut its exports to that country as well. On this date, the Albanian Central Committee approved an intensive "policy of savings" and called for efforts to cut imports "on the basis that the necessary conditions have been created to produce many articles which in the past had to be imported."[102] The Albanians were beginning to tighten their already taut belts even further. The extent of belt-tightening needed was indicated by the remarks of the Albanian ambassador to China, who stated in a press conference in November, 1960, that Albania produced domestically only 40 per cent of the machine parts that it utilized.[103]

On August 19, 1961, the Soviet ambassador to Albania, Josef Shikin, left Tirana and was never to return. Then, on August 26, only five days before the beginning of the fall semester, the Soviet Union abruptly canceled the scholarships of the Albanian students studying in the USSR. At the same time, the Albanian ambassador was handed a note describing the "slanderous anti-Soviet" activities carried on by Albanian students attending Soviet institutions of higher learning and warned that "in the event of anti-Soviet outbursts on the part of Albanian students they will be asked to leave the USSR."[104] By the end of the 22nd CPSU Party Congress several months later, all Albanian students had in fact left the USSR.

During the 22nd Congress, Khrushchev delivered a number of vituperative attacks against the Hoxha regime. Not only did Khrushchev denounce Hoxha as a "leftist nationalist deviationist,"[105] but he also called for Hoxha's overthrow. In a speech in many ways similar to the Cominform resolution excommunicating Yugoslavia in 1948, Khrushchev stated:

> We are certain the time will come when the Albanian communists and the Albanian people will have their say, and then the Albanian leaders will have to answer for the harm they have done their country, their people and the *cause of socialist construction in Albania* [emphasis added].[106]

Diplomatic relations between the two countries were broken off on December 3, 1961, after the USSR had rejected an Albanian demand to reduce the size of its embassy in Tirana as "an unprecedented step in relations between states, especially between socialist states."[107] Trade relations also came to an end, according to the Russians because the Albanians had failed to make deliveries to the USSR:

> In Albania, measures were taken which impeded normal trade with the Soviet Union. In particular, Albanian organizations began to delay shipments of goods to the USSR and even unloaded ships which had been prepared for shipment.[108]

In addition to terminating trade and diplomatic relations, the Russians also took measures to exclude Albania from CMEA, the intra-Camp economic organization. On December 17, *Pravda* reprinted the comments of P. Jaroszewicz, Poland's representative to CMEA, who in discussing the 15th Session which had just been concluded in Warsaw, stated:

> In our work we referred to the materials of the (22nd CPSU) Congress, and were guided by its directives. . . . As far as the last session is concerned, Albania did not come to Warsaw at all. One is forced to conclude that the Albanian leaders, in shunning coopera- tion with the CMEA, are pursuing a course of worsening relations

with the socialist countries which will harm only the Albanian people.[109]

Thus by the end of 1961, not only had the USSR severed diplomatic relations and economic intercourse, it had also excluded Albania from participation in CMEA. Nonetheless, although some East European nations followed the Soviet lead in severing diplomatic relations with Albania, none of them took the additional step of severing trade relations. An explanation for this phenomenon, so unlike Soviet policy toward Yugoslavia in 1949, will be given below, along with an examination of the effect of the Soviet trade-and-aid embargo on Albania and the changing nature of Soviet strategy toward the tiny Balkan nation.

In determining the effect of the Soviet embargo on the Albanian economy, it is necessary first to review the actions taken by the Soviet Union against Albania. In addition to cutting off all trade, the USSR expelled the Albanian students from the USSR (and had them expelled from the East European nations as well), withdrew professors and instructors from Albanian schools and universities, withdrew all specialists giving technical assistance to the Albanian economy, canceled all grants for Albania's third five-year plan, eliminated all shipments of military equipment to the Albanian army, and effectively excluded Albania from participation in CMEA.

Despite these pressures, the Soviet Union did not compel the Eastern European communist nations to eliminate trade with Albania. Exports from these nations dropped in 1962 (see Table 4), but they rose again in 1963. Hence there was no economic blockade of Albania similar to the one imposed on Yugoslavia in 1949-53. Although China provided the bulk of Albania's trade during the 1962-64 period, the nations of Eastern Europe provided approximately 25 per cent, including certain kinds of machinery and equipment that the Chinese were unable to supply.[110] Although Albania no longer obtained credits from the region, the trade relations it continued to maintain were a valuable aid to its strained economy.

In analyzing the reasons why the nations of Eastern Europe maintained trade relations with Albania, one is confronted with several possibilities. William Griffith suggests that this might indicate "a preference on the part of some of the East European leaderships (in particular, the Polish) to encourage a continuation of Albania's defiance whereby they would gain increased maneuverability vis-a-vis Moscow."[111] This possibility, however, does not seem too likely. It is doubtful whether such nations as East Germany or Czechoslovakia, or even Poland, would take the risk of incurring the displeasure of the Soviet Union on the relatively minor issue (to them) of trade with Albania. Indeed, the reverse seems to be the case. It would appear that Khrushchev deliberately kept some lines of contact open with Albania for two reasons. The first was to prevent that nation from "pulling a Yugoslavia," that is, turning to the West for goods China could not supply. The fact that Albania signed a major trade agreement with Italy on December 6, 1961, may have played some role in this decision.[112]

TABLE 4

Eastern European Trade with Albania, 1961-64
(in million leks)

	Exports to Albania				Imports from Albania			
	1961	1962	1963	1964	1961	1962	1962	1964
Bulgaria	93.3	23.7	30.3	40.1	84.5	102.7	114.9	38.9
Czechoslovakia	515.9	435.7	505.6	472.2	482.7	522.1	294.8	571.0
East Germany	201.8	121.0	180.8	259.1	230.5	242.3	156.9	303.8
Hungary	165.5	83.0	104.3	112.9	127.3	76.2	123.9	81.7
Poland	199.1	158.3	226.2	369.0	199.0	245.1	202.4	290.7
Rumania	64.8	45.7	80.7	118.4	18.5	58.1	91.1	120.1

Source: U.N. Yearbook of International Trade Statistics, 1965, p. 42.

A second reason probably stems from Khrushchev's hope that a change in the leadership of the PPSh would occur. By maintaining a certain degree of economic pressure on the country, he probably hoped that the existing leadership might yet crack and a new ruling clique more friendly to the USSR might come to power. Were this in fact to take place, a rapprochement would occur without Albania having been as excluded from the Soviet bloc as Yugoslavia had been. Indeed, according to a "high ranking Bulgarian official" interviewed by an Associated Press reporter on December 27, 1961, relations between his country and Albania were maintained in order to make it easier one day "for Albania to return to the Socialist family."[113] An additional advantage of the maintenance of diplomatic and trade relations by Eastern European nations close to the USSR lay in the fact that they could provide the CPSU with a major source of intelligence on developments within Albania.

The Albanian leaders, like the Yugoslav leaders, attempted to make domestic political capital over the fact that the USSR had cut off trade and aid and was thus committing the unpardonable sin of impeding the "building of Socialism" in Albania. In a *Zeri i Popullit* article, they vilified Khrushchev who:

. . . unilaterally and with the sole aim of obstructing the building of socialism in Albania canceled the credits granted by normal agreement to the Albanian People's Republic by the Soviet Union for the third five year plan, 1961-1965, arbitrarily violated and annulled the 1961 trade agreement, unilaterally withdrew Soviet technicians, liquidated in fact the agreements on cultural cooperation, expelled on false grounds a number of Albanian students and cadets from the Soviet Union, canceled the agreement on the granting of scholarships to Albanian cadets and students studying in the Soviet Union, violated the military agreements, and organized a strict economic, political and military blockade of the Albanian People's Republic.[114]

Then in an attempt to rally the Albanian people and further discredit Khrushchev, the Albanian leaders went on to say:

The Albanian people and the Party of Labor of Albania will firmly march along the correct road of Socialist construction and defense of our socialist homeland. Temporary difficulties will not stop us on our road. We are sure of our future. The tasks of the third five year plan will be fulfilled and overfulfilled regardless of the obstacles that N. Khrushchev and his followers are trying to raise before us.[115]

The Russians, for their part, attempted to discredit the Albanian leaders on ideological grounds by accusing them of turning to the "imperialists" for aid.[116] When this proved not to be the case, the Russians switched their propaganda line to assert that the Albanians could have "constructed Socialism" more easily if they had the aid of the Soviet Union. This propaganda line was to continue until the fall of Khrushchev and, after a brief interlude, to begin once again as new leaders of the USSR found they could not deal with the Albanians either.

There is no question but that in the first several years of the Soviet embargo "the construction of Socialism" in Albania was impeded. Although the presence of Chinese technicians and credits succeeded in keeping the Albanian economy afloat, neither the quality of the goods China supplied nor the level of expertise of the Chinese technical assistance personnel could be compared to the Russian. Yugoslavia, in turning to the United States despite ideological differences, found its new benefactor both richer and on a higher technological level than the Soviet Union; Albania, despite ideological affinity, found China to be both poorer and on a far lower technological level than the USSR.

The year 1962 was a particularly difficult one for the Albanians. Chinese aid was slow in coming, and there were frequent reports in the Albanian press of the need to fabricate spare parts.[117] The situation got so bad that on April 26, 1962, *Zeri i Popullit* praised a worker in a mechanical enterprise at Durres who utilized in his work 50 per cent of the old nails he succeeded in extracting from old armatures.[118] Albania's problems with agricultural production, serious even in the days of good relations with the USSR, now took on even more alarming dimensions. A Central Committee Plenum in 1962 issued the following statement:

Under the newly created conditions, the growth in farm and dairy production, *and primarily in bread grain production,* constitute the principal duty of the country's economy [original emphasis].[119]

Another serious problem lay in Albania's military establishment, which had previously obtained the bulk of its equipment from the USSR. In a *Zeri i Popullit* article on August 16, 1966, Hito Cako, chief of the political directorate of the army, described how the military had attempted to conserve funds during the period of the third five-year plan.

The extension of wearing clothes, of the material basis for training, of the means of living, of the introduction of inventorying in the canteens and messhalls, the lowering of expenditures of raw materials, the re-examination of the cost of fuels, the lowering of costs by military economic enterprises, the replacement of costly items by less costly materials, the further utilization of old spare parts, etc., amounted to savings of 100 million lek during the third five year period.[120]

He went on to praise such unit slogans as:

Hit the bull's eye with the first bullet; learn to organize a way of life and other activities in the open without capital investments but with the most adaptable material circumstances, and open more arable land than suggested and plant more than the plans call for.[121]

To compensate for the absence of Soviet supplies, there was a major change in the nature of Albanian imports. Instead of having a large percentage of its imports in the form of machinery and equipment, the Albanians now began to concentrate on the import of semi-manufactures such as rolled steel for conversion into finished products in Albania.[122] The *Albanian Statistical Yearbook* for 1963, of which an excerpt is reproduced as Table 5, illustrates the nature of the change in Albania's foreign trade.

The absence of Soviet and East European credits also created the need for Albania to expand its exports to pay for imports from Eastern Europe and capitalist states. In striving to increase exports, the Albanians found themselves in the somewhat ironic position of trying to develop their garden vegetable industries—the very ones that Khrushchev told them to concentrate on in 1959. The June, 1964, issue of *Socialist Agriculture* carried the following exhortation:

> Every worker in the farm enterprise and every collective farmer should be aware of the motto: *without exports there can be no imports.* It must be also remembered that to increase exports means to increase the efforts against . . . the devilish plots of the modern revisionists. It also means to destroy their means of obliterating our country through slanders and blockade [original emphasis].[123]

A key problem faced by the Albanians in trying to expand their exports, particularly to Western nations, was the problem of quality. In the March-April, 1964, issue of *Ekonomia Popullore,* there appeared an article by Kico Ngjela entitled "The Improvement of the Quality of Exports Is a State Duty of Greatest Importance." In the article, Ngjela stated:

> The production enterprises are faced with no problems regarding the question of quantity. However, the same cannot be said about the quality, packaging, wrapping and labeling of export products. In this respect there are many shortcomings which in the final analysis harm the profits of Albanian exports, i.e., they lower their value.[124]

Ngjela also announced that a special branch of the Trade Ministry had been set up "to approve, prior to final shipment only products which met the standards set by the buyer or distributor."[125]

One of the heaviest blows to the Albanian five-year plan was the departure of the Russian and East European technicians whom the Albanians say they "greatly needed."[126] There are serious language difficulties between the Albanians and the Chinese specialists, as few Albanians or Chinese know each other's language.[127] The main language of communication has been Russian, but knowledge of even this language is extremely limited in Albania. The Albanians themselves have disclosed the problems caused their economy by the lack of trained personnel. Albanian Minister of Education Manush Myftui stated on July 21, 1962, that out of a labor force of 210,000 only 95,000 were "skilled workers." In addition, Myftui stated that twenty industrial enterprises

TABLE 5

Albanian Commodity Imports, 1960-62

Products	Unit	1960	1961	1962
a. Diesel Motors	ea.	43	39	21
Electronic Equipment	ea.	70	115	68
Electromotors	ea.	631	128	264
Generators	ea.	57	1	---
Power Transformers	ea.	159	68	31
Pneumatic Hammers	ea.	200	50	110
Cranes	ea.	15	1	3
Excavators	ea.	2	3	---
Bulldozers	ea.	21	5	---
Pumps	ea.	205	123	114
Laboratory Equipment	1,000 lek	19,244	11,449	5,660
Medical Equipment	1,000 lek	11,229	7,477	8,214
b. Coke	ton	8,323	5,954	17,960
Rolled Metal	ton	981	1,301	2,257
Construction Steel	ton	7,623	11,042	19,317
Castings	ton	1,866	2,220	5,040
Sheet Metal	ton	9,061	12,337	17,836
Assorted Steel	ton	2,107	2,602	3,466
Nails and Bolts	ton	1,546	1,824	4,154
Sulphuric Acid	ton	317	472	1,229
c. Tractors	ea.	505	197	538[a]
Trucks	ea.	435	434	92
Trailers	ea.	217	24	34
Cars	ea.	158	---	1
Buses	ea.	9	15	5
Bicycles	ea.	6,754	2,334	3,770
Motorcycles	ea.	85	1	21
Spare Parts	1,000 lek	263,318	213,310	215,379
Radios	ea.	8,041	6,827	5,283
d. Caustic Soda	ton	922	655	1,300
Calcinated Soda	ton	1,326	774	4,445
Zinc Oxide	ton	88	145	283
Calcium Carbide	ton	170	450	902
Rubber	ton	295	323	357
Industrial Oil	ton	493	659	1,249
Paper	ton	4,520	4,423	5,086

[a]Of which 522 were from China, the remaining 16 from East Germany.

Source: Albanian Statistical Yearbook, 1963 (Tirana, 1964) (translated in Radio Free Europe Research Report: Albania, September 17, 1964).

and four communication centers were without highly specialized personnel and attributed deficiencies in Albanian education to "the inexperience of instructors, the inability of instructors to read foreign literature and the lack of translated materials." He concluded by stating: "Especially today, when cooperation with specialists and scientists from the Socialist countries has been reduced to a minimum, our people are faced with great tasks."[128]

The departure of Soviet bloc professors from the University of Tirana and the expulsion of Albanian students from Soviet and East European universities and institutes was another negative consequence of the Soviet-Albanian conflict for the Albanian economy. According to Soviet statistics, between 1952 and 1961, "663 Albanian students received diplomas from Soviet higher education establishments and an additional 12 Albanian scientists completed post-graduate studies."[129] Since most of the Albanian students (numbering approximately 4,500) who were studying in Soviet bloc schools were preparing themselves to be scientists and engineers,[130] the cancellation of their scholarships and their abrupt return to Albania (some were not even allowed to bring their textbooks) has unquestionably hurt Albania's economic development.

As a result of all the Soviet pressures and the slowness in Chinese deliveries, as well as attempts to conserve raw materials and limit imports, the growth rate of the Albanian economy was minimal for the first two and a half years of the third five-year plan. Indeed, during the first half of the plan, the only installations constructed were a furniture plant, five cold storage plants, a power dam, and a 30-kilometer railroad from Vore to Lac.[131] An editorial in the June, 1963, party journal *Rruga e Partise* summed up the situation in these terms:

> Building enterprises should realize that industrial construction during 1961-62 experienced a definite slowdown as a result of the economic blockade instituted by N. Khrushchev and his group. Consequently, 1963-65 represents years heavily burdened with industrial projects. The nature of the projects which are being constructed with the fraternal and internationalist aid of the People's Republic of China, is such that any initial mistakes will have adverse effects on the future. Their proper handling is of utmost importance to the further development of the country. These projects are technically very complicated, of a nature never before encountered in our country.[132]

The first description in percentage terms of Albanian industrial growth during the third five-year plan came on November 26, 1963, in an interview with Adil Carcani, Albania's Minister of Mines, broadcast by Radio Tirana. Carcani stated that "despite the difficulties and obstacles created by the strict economic blockade of the modern revisionists, led by the N. Khrushchev group, mineral production during the first ten months of 1963 (compared to 1960), increased by 2.5%."[133] This meant that due to the blockade the growth of Albania's mineral production had averaged less than 1 per cent per year, even if one accepts the Albanian figures.

By the middle of 1964, the Albanian leaders were already willing to backtrack on their ambitious plans for the third five-year plan. In an article in the July, 1964, issue of *Rruga e Partise,* Albanian economist Hekuran Mara conceded:

Under the present level of development of productive forces the creation of a complex heavy industry has not been possible *nor was it necessary for Albania.* If we regarded the possibility of exploiting our resources only by means of the creation of heavy industry, this would have been unrealistic and wrong. Furthermore, if through the creation of heavy industry the concrete conditions of our country had not been taken into consideration, then the results would have been negative [emphasis added].[134]

Mara went on to admit that the creation of the chemical industry, envisioned by Teodosi in 1959, was beyond Albania's capabilities:

The establishment of a complex chemical industry under the present conditions through reliance on domestic forces would be a very difficult proposition. The country lacks the financial means and the capacity to train highly educated cadres for this industrial sector.[135]

By implication, Mara also admitted that the Chinese would not be able to help the Albanians establish a chemical industry either.

In an attempt to increase production through administrative measures, particularly the production of consumer goods, the Albanian economy was partially decentralized in 1965.* In describing the reasons for the decentralization, the Albanian economist Sadik Shkembi, writing in the May-June, 1965, issue of *Ekonomia Popullore,* stated:

The more local industry depends upon local raw material resources and the less it depends for these materials upon the state in a centralized manner, the more the people's economy will benefit and the more proud we can be of the local industry and artisan cooperatives.[136]

Nonetheless, despite all the efforts of the Albanians, the third five-year plan was not fulfilled. Although in a speech in Peking in 1966 Hoxha stated that "far from being a failure, the third five year plan was *in the main* successfully fulfilled" (emphasis added), the statistics he went on to list were below the goals of the plan. Thus, according to Hoxha, industrial output increased by 39 per cent over 1960 whereas in 1961 he had predicted a 52 per cent increase.[137] Nonetheless, even a 39 per cent increase was a major accomplishment (assuming Hoxha's figures are correct), considering the pressures under which the Albanian economy labored during the period.

---

*Note the similarity to the Yugoslav policy of the early 1950's (see Chapter 2).

Soviet strategy toward Albania remained constant during the period from the 22nd CPSU Congress to Khrushchev's ouster. Although permitting the Eastern European nations to continue trade relations with Albania, the Russians kept up a steady drumfire of propaganda about the successes in "building Socialism" the Albanians *might have achieved* had they continued friendly relations with the USSR. Thus on January 8, 1963, Moscow Radio stated:

> The Albanian propaganda machine recently made a big hullabaloo about the start of construction of three factories. This, when only three to four years ago, if one reads the Albanian press of those times, he will notice that practically each week announcements were made to the effect that production had started in some new factory or that construction had started on another.[138]

More than a year and a half later, on September 12, 1964, Moscow Radio's message was very much the same.

> The successes (of the past twenty years) would have been still greater had the leadership of the Albanian Workers Party not betrayed Marxism-Leninism and Proletarian Internationalism in 1960; had it not pursued a conspiratorial line against political, economic and cultural cooperation with the Soviet Union and other socialist countries. . . .
>
> Forgotten are the promises which Enver Hoxha made at the Fourth Party Congress to raise the real income of the workers and clerks by 30% and that of the farmers by 35% during the third five year plan. Between 1956 and 1961 there were seven price reductions whereas between 1961 and 1964 there have been none. All these data convincingly show the difficult situation into which the Albanian leaders have put the population through their anti-national policies.[139]

Following the fall of Khrushchev, however, the new Russian leadership attempted a rapprochement with Albania. On November 10, 1964, Moscow Radio broadcast the following message to Albania:

> The Soviet Union and the other Socialist states have helped Albania to assume its place in the international arena and to increase its influence. Soviet citizens wholeheartedly wish the workers of the Albanian Peoples Republic new successes.[140]

Any hope the Russian leaders might have entertained of a rapprochement were dashed on November 13, however, when Radio Tirana, after stating that *Zeri i Popullit* had held up publication of an article denouncing "modern revisionism" for three weeks (since Khrushchev was overthrown), stated:

Meanwhile, the present Soviet leaders have declared more than once that they will continue the revisionist policy of the 20th, 21st, and 22nd Congresses of the Soviet Communist Party.[141]

Of particular irritation to the Albanians was the inclusion of Yugoslavia in CMEA as an associate member on November 17—an overt sign that the new Soviet leaders would continue the Khrushchevian policy of close friendship with Yugoslavia.[142]

Nonetheless, the Russian leaders, exercising more patience with Albania than had Khrushchev, pressed on with their attempt to improve relations. On November 27, *Izvestia* stated that Soviet relations with Albania, as with the other communist countries, were based "on the principles of proletarian internationalism, equality and respect for national independence, non-interference in internal affairs, and close *cooperation and mutual assistance*" (emphasis added).[143] If the last statement contained a hint of resumed economic aid, it received an insulting reply from the Albanians. On November 29, 1964, in a speech to a gathering of "Marxist-Leninist" forces who had come to Tirana for Albania's 20th anniversary celebrations, Enver Hoxha stated Albanian terms for a reconciliation with the Soviet Union. He demanded, among other things, that the new Soviet leaders "apologize" to Albania and also pay for all the damages inflicted on Albania in the economic, military, and cultural fields.[144] Although the Russians did not accede to the humiliating Albanian demands, they nonetheless were to continue to strive for improved relations over the next two years despite continual rejections from Tirana.

In January, 1965, the Polish Communist Party (almost certainly under instructions from the USSR) officially invited the Albanian party to participate in a Warsaw Pact meeting which was to take place in the Polish capital, but the invitation was refused.[145] One year later, on Polish initiative, the two nations agreed to raise their diplomatic relations to the ambassadorial level. Soon after the Albanian ambassador arrived in Poland, however, he was expelled for allegedly helping some anti-Gomulka Poles to leave the country.[146] Nonetheless, the Russians kept trying. In March, 1966, they invited Albania to send a delegation to the 23rd CPSU Congress and, perhaps to add some incentive for the Albanians to attend, they also offered to resume trade relations. The Albanians, who were to sign a second major economic agreement with China two months later, ignored the offer of a resumption in trade and described the invitation to the CPSU Congress in these terms:

> The Khrushchevite leadership in recent days had the insolence to invite our party to send a delegation to the 23rd CPSU Congress. But, rightly, the Albanian Workers Party Central Committee has refused with contempt to accept the letter containing the invitation since now there are no ties between the Albanian Workers Party and the treacherous Soviet Revisionist leadership either through the party or through the state.

> The Albanian Workers Party has not established and does not intend to establish relations with traitors of Communism, renegades of Marxism-Leninism.[147]

One year later, the Soviets invited the Albanians to participate in the 50th anniversary celebrations of the October Revolution, but they were again met by a negative reply:

> The Moscow renegades had the impudence to invite our party to participate in "festivities" for the 50th Anniversary of the great socialist October Revolution which they are organizing in Moscow. Our party has rejected with contempt this dirty invitation of the Soviet Revisionists. We are going to celebrate the great October Revolution in our fatherland in the midst of happiness.[148]

Then, on November 29, 1967, Radio Moscow returned to its earlier propaganda refrain in commemorating the 23rd anniversary of Albania's liberation: "The building of socialism in Albania would have been easier if the country had relied on the help of the other socialist countries."[149]

Relations between Albania and the Soviet Union hit a new low after the Soviet invasion of Czechoslovakia. Albania reacted to the invasion not only by denouncing the Soviet Union, but also by announcing its official withdrawal from the Warsaw Pact, an organization in which it had not participated since 1961. Nonetheless, the Brezhnev-Kosygin leadership evidently continued to hope, as had Khrushchev, that eventually a new leadership would come to power in Albania, and in the meantime it continued to remind the Albanians of the possibilities awaiting their country if good relations were again restored. Thus, on November 28, 1969, *Pravda* carried the following article commemorating the 25th anniversary of Albania's liberation:

> Relying on assistance and support from the Soviet Union and other socialist countries, the Albanian people rapidly changed the face of their country. The power, oil, mining, woodworking, textile, food and other branches of industry were essentially created anew. Agriculture, science and culture developed substantially. There was improvement in the living standard of the working people. From being a country of horse-drawn plows and cottage industry, Albania became an agrarian-industrial state with a developed industry and a cooperative system of agriculture.
>
> *The successes of the Albanian working people in building a new life would now be even greater, had the country's development proceeded along the path of strengthened friendship and cooperation among the countries of socialism, the path of unity and solidarity of the world Communist and workers' movement.* Unfortunately, the policy chosen by the Albanian leadership placed the A.P.R. in a state of self-imposed isolation and hurt the cause of socialism in that country and the general struggle of the people against imperialism. . . .

The C.P.S.U. Central Committee and the Soviet Government have favored and continue to favor normalization of Soviet-Albanian relations on a foundation of equality, mutual respect and non-intervention in each others' internal affairs, on the foundation of the principles of Marxism-Leninism. This would accord with the interests of the peoples of the entire socialist commonwealth and of the Albanian people themselves first of all [emphasis added].[150]

In assessing the use of Soviet economic pressure against Albania, it becomes apparent that there are some similarities with the Yugoslav case of 1948-53. In both instances, economic pressures were utilized to "soften up" the target party prior to a Soviet attempt to split it. These, in the case of Albania, were the threat to cut off scholarships to Albanian students and the refusal to deliver needed grain. These pressures were, however, more limited than the ones employed against Yugoslavia, where the Soviet specialists were withdrawn prior to the attempts at a coup. Once the attempted split of the party had failed, events took their course in much the same way. There was a gradual increase in the level of economic pressure until trade relations were cut off. The gradualness of the increase not only provided the Albanians with time to readjust their economy; from the Soviet point of view, it also gave time for an Albanian change in policy. In the Albanian case, geopolitical considerations also played a role as Soviet overtures to Yugoslavia, the interview with Venizelos, and the withdrawal of Soviet submarines all added to the pressure on the Hoxha regime. This was a more orchestrated form of pressure than that used against Yugoslavia, where military maneuvers on Yugoslavia's borders did not start until after the blockade was imposed.

A major difference in the two cases, and perhaps a lesson drawn from the Yugoslav experience, was the decision by Khrushchev not to sever all relations between Albania and the nations controlled by the Soviet Union. By breaking trade relations but allowing the other East European nations to continue trading with Albania, Khrushchev kept the pressure on the Albanian leadership and yet did not fully exclude that nation from the Soviet bloc. By maintaining a constant stream of propaganda to Albania about the benefits of a good relationship with the USSR, Khrushchev kept open the possibility of an eventual rapprochement.

Following the fall of Khrushchev, the new Soviet leaders attempted to improve relations with Albania. Unlike the case of Yugoslavia where Stalin's successors, through certain ideological concessions and the agreement to resume trade, had effected a rapprochement, the new Soviet leaders were unwilling to make major ideological concessions although they were willing to resume trade relations in an attempt to improve state relations with Albania. The Albanians, despite economic problems of their own, refused the offer. They were, in fact, more interested in national independence than in "building Socialism."

NOTES

1. Many of the documents pertaining to the Soviet-Albanian conflict have been translated into English and are found in the second section of William E. Griffith's book *Albania and the Sino-Soviet Rift* (Cambridge: MIT Press, 1963), and in the documentary collection edited by Alexander Dallin, *Diversity in International Communism: A Documentary Record 1961-1963* (New York: Columbia University Press, 1963). Additional documents are found in a documentary collection published by the Albanian government, *The Facts About Soviet-Albanian Relations* (Tirana: Naim Frasheri State Publishing House, 1964). This book will hereafter be cited as *Facts*.

2. For a brief review of Albania's history, see Stavro Skendi, *Albania* (New York: Frederick A. Praeger, 1956), Chapter 1.

3. Milovan Djilas, *Conversations with Stalin* (New York: Harcourt Brace and World, 1962), p. 134.

4. For a detailed history of this period, see Robert Lee Wolff, *The Balkans in Our Time* (Cambridge: Harvard University Press, 1956), pp. 274-78, 338-41.

5. The politics of the intra-party struggle are covered in Griffith, *op. cit.*, pp. 17-21.

6. V. Shvetz, "Ukreplenie Ekonomiki Albanii," *Vneshniaia Torgovlia*, Vol. 28, No. 1 (January, 1948), p. 28.

7. *Ibid.*, pp. 24-27.

8. *White Book on Aggressive Activities by the Governments of the USSR, Poland, Czechoslovakia, Hungary, Rumania, Bulgaria and Albania toward Yugoslavia* (Belgrade: Government Printing Office, 1951), pp. 304-5. Hereafter referred to as *White Book*.

9. *Economic Treaties and Agreements of the Soviet Bloc in Eastern Europe 1945-1951* (New York: Mid-European Studies Center, 1952), p. xxiii.

10. V. Shvetz, "Uspekhi Albanskoi Norodnoi Respubliki," *Vneshniaia Torgovlia*, Vol. 31, No. 2 (February, 1951), p. 11.

11. R. Nechaeva, "Ekonomika Albanii na Pod"eme," *Vneshniaia Torgovlia*, Vol. 30, No. 9 (September, 1950), p. 6. Poland gave Albania ships, Hungary gave machinery, etc.

12. V. Shvetz, "Uspekhi Albanskoi Narodnoi Respubliki," p. 11.

13. *Zeri i Popullit,* December 30, 1961 (translated in *Facts,* p. 67). Albanian workers and peasants had received training in the USSR as early as 1949. For an account of Soviet assistance of this type in the 1949-50 period, see E. Lazumkin and D. Stepanov, "Borba Albanskikh Trudiashchikhsia za Demokratii i Sotsializm," *Vneshniaia Torgovlia,* Vol. 30, No. 11 (November, 1950), p. 49.

14. F. Gormunov, "Uspeshnoe Razvitie Albanskoi Narodnoi Respubliki," *Vneshniaia Torgovlia,* Vol. 32, No. 10 (October, 1952), p. 31.

15. K. Danilov, "Razvitie Ekonomiki Albanii," *Voprosy Ekonomiki,* Vol. 10, No. 11 (November, 1956), pp. 101-2.

16. The Albanians have recently published an account of this period: "In May 1955, Khrushchev, without consulting other parties, decided to go to Belgrade at the head of a Soviet party and government delegation. The date for this visit had been set for 26 May whereas on 23 May Khrushchev sent our party a letter requesting the abrogation of the Cominform resolution of November 1949 and the re-examination of the June resolution of 1948. A similar letter was sent to all participants of the Cominform. At the same time Khrushchev requested our approval of the text of a 'decision' on this issue drafted by him and to be published in the name of the Cominform but without its convocation." Sotir Madhi, "The Struggle of the AWP Against Rightest Opposition During 1949-55," *Studime Historike,* No. 3, 1967 (translated in Radio Free Europe Situation Report: Albania, March 15, 1968).

17. Translated in Griffith, *op. cit.,* p. 184.

18. Radio Tirana, April 18, 1957.

19. *Ibid.*

20. *Ibid.*

21. *The New York Times,* August 29, 1957.

22. At this point, Khrushchev was beginning to pay serious attention to the possibilities of economic integration of the nations of East Europe in CMEA. For further information on this point, see Michael Kaser, *Comecon* (London: Oxford University Press, 1967), pp. 69-91.

23. For a detailed history of the events of 1957-60, see Stavro Skendi, "Albania," in *East Central Europe and the World: Developments in the Post-Stalin Era,* ed. Steven D. Kertesz (Notre Dame, Ind.: University of Notre

Dame Press, 1962); and Daniel Tretiak, "The Founding of the Sino-Albanian Entente," *China Quarterly*, No. 10 (April-June, 1962), pp. 123-42.

24. The Soviet and Chinese comments are found in *The Soviet-Yugoslav Controversy, 1948-58: A Documentary Record*, ed. Robert Bass and Elizabeth Marbury (New York: Prospect Books, 1959).

25. *Foreign Trade of the Peoples Republic of China*, No. 11 (June, 1959), p. 20.

26. Albanian Telegraphic Agency (ATA), January 17, 1959 (Tirana Radio Home Service).

27. Radio Moscow, in Albanian to Albania, December 24, 1961 (reprinted in Griffith, *op. cit.*, p. 299).

28. *The New York Times*, May 26, 1959.

29. *The New York Times*, May 27, 1959.

30. *Pravda*, June 7, 1959, cited in Jan S. Prybyla, "The Economic Causes of the Soviet-Albanian Quarrel," *Bulletin—Institute for the Study of the USSR* (Munich), Vol. 10, No. 3 (March, 1963), p. 18. Hoxha stated in a speech, reprinted in *Zeri i Popullit*, of November 4, 1962, "We rejected Tito's nonsensical idea to plant only sunflowers, on the pretext that he would supply us with wheat from the Vojvodina; likewise, we rejected Khrushchev's advice that we should grow only fruit trees and vineyards since he would supply us with wheat grown on his virgin lands; he said the quantity we needed was 'no more than that consumed by our mice,' yet he did not give it to our people when they needed it" (translated in Griffith, *op. cit.*, p. 400).

31. *Peking Review*, Vol. 7, No. 19 (May 8, 1964), p. 12.

32. For a description of the Albanian economy in the pre-war period, see Skendi, *Albania*, pp. 148-58, 173-76; and *Twenty Years of Socialism in Albania* (Tirana: Naim Frasheri State Publishing House, 1964), pp. 47-51.

33. M. Iakovlev, "Razvitie Narodnogo Khoziaistva v Narodnoi Respublike Albanii," *15 Let Narodnoi Albanii*, ed. Nesti Nase (Moscow: Institut Mezhdunarodnykh Otnoshenii, 1959), p. 89.

34. Skendi, *Albania*, p. 144.

35. *Ibid.*, p. 230.

36. *White Book*, p. 307.

37. *Ibid.*, p. 310.

38. K. Dmitrov, "Ekonomicheskie Uspekhi Narodno-Demokraticheskoi Albanii za Desiat Let," *Vneshniaia Torgovlia*, Vol. 34, No. 11 (November, 1954), p. 76.

39. *Albania* (Tirana: Naim Frasheri State Publishing House, 1964), p. 34.

40. *Twenty Years of Socialism in Albania*, p. 54.

41. A discussion of the raw material shortage facing the Soviet bloc in this period is found in Stanley J. Zyzniewski, "Industry and Labor," in *Eastern Europe in the Sixties*, ed. Stephen Fischer-Galati (New York: Frederick A. Praeger, 1963), pp. 90-91.

42. Griffith, *op. cit.*, p. 178.

43. Kocho Teodosi, "Stroitel'stvo Sotsialisticheskoi Ekonomiki v Narodnoi Respublike Albanii," *Voprosy Ekonomiki*, Vol. 12, No. 11 (November, 1959), p. 130.

44. Nesti Nase, "The Albanian People's Fight for Socialism," *International Affairs* (Moscow), Vol. 5, No. 6 (June, 1959), p. 27.

45. Radio Tirana, July 20, 1954.

46. Radio Tirana, July 4, 1959.

47. *Ibid.*

48. *Ibid.* The USSR also had given Albania 716 technical documents by 1960. *Mirovaia Sotsialisticheskaia Sistema Khoziaistva*, Vol. IV (Moscow: Mysl', 1967), p. 37.

49. *U.N. Yearbook of International Trade Statistics, 1963*, p. 43. Hereafter referred to as *U.N. Yearbook*, with appropriate year.

50. *Vneshniaia Torgovlia SSSR za 1960* (Moscow: Vneshtorgizdat, 1961), pp. 61-64.

51. Data from Griffith, *op. cit.*, p. 179.

52. *U.N. Yearbook, 1963*, p. 43.

53. *Vneshniaia Torgovlia SSSR za 1960*, p. 65.

54. *Ibid.*, p. 7.

55. *U.N. Yearbook, 1963,* p. 43.

56. A. Poliakova, "Rol' Vneshnei Torgovli v Ekonomike Albanii," *Vneshniaia Torgovlia,* Vol. 38, No. 10 (October, 1958), p. 13.

57. See Griffith, *op. cit.,* pp. 35-176, for an extensive treatment of the ideological issues.

58. *Zeri i Popullit,* December 30, 1961 (translated in *Facts,* p. 70).

59. *Ibid.*

60. *Ibid.*

61. Cited in Griffith, *op. cit.,* p. 40.

62. In the *Zeri i Popullit* of January 9, 1962, the Albanians stated their feelings about Khrushchev's talk with Venizelos in the following terms: "Should we, perhaps, for the sake of peaceful coexistence make concessions to the Greek Chauvinists in their territorial claims on Southern Albania, as N. Khrushchev did during his talk with Venizelos?" Translated in Griffith, *op. cit.,* p. 308.
    Earlier Hoxha had stated that he had criticized Khrushchev "in a comradely fashion when he raised the hopes of Sophokles Venizelos for the autonomy of Southern Albania." *Zeri i Popullit,* November 8, 1961 (translated in Griffith, *op. cit.,* p. 250).

63. *Zeri i Popullit,* March 25, 1962 (translated in *Facts,* p. 40). The Russians have openly admitted that members of the Albanian party supplied them with information. Letter of Central Committee of CPSU to Central Committee of the CPC, February 22, 1964 (reprinted in *Peking Review,* Vol. 7, No. 19 [May 8, 1964], p. 23).

64. Griffith, *op. cit.,* p. 179.

65. *Zeri i Popullit,* March 25, 1962 (translated in Griffith, *op. cit.,* p. 339), stated that Khrushchev refused to sell grain.

66. Excerpt of Hoxha's speech to the Conference of Eighty-One Parties in Moscow; cited in Griffith, *op. cit.,* p. 55.

67. *Zeri i Popullit,* March 25, 1962 (translated in Griffith, *op. cit.,* p. 339).

68. *Ibid.*

69. Radio Tirana, August 23, 1960.

70. *Zeri i Popullit,* March 25, 1962 (translated in Griffith, *loc. cit.*).

71. See description by Harrison Salisbury in *The New York Times,* October 7, 1960.

72. Radio Free Europe Special Report: Albania, February 2, 1961.

73. Radio Tirana, October 10, 1960.

74. *Zeri i Popullit,* March 25, 1962 (translated in Griffith, *op. cit.,* p. 341).

75. Radio Moscow, November 10, 1960.

76. *Ibid.* The construction work on the Palace, according to the Albanians, was slowed in December, 1960, and the USSR had stopped sending supplies by January, 1961. *Zeri i Popullit,* December 20, 1961 (translated in *Facts,* p. 58).

77. *Zeri i Popullit,* March 25, 1962 (translated in Griffith, *loc. cit.*).

78. New China News Agency, November 23, 1960. Hereafter referred to as NCNA.

79. *Rabotnichesko Delo,* November 30, 1960 (reprinted in Foreign Broadcast Information Service Daily Report, December 6, 1960).

80. Radio Moscow, November 29, 1960.

81. Radio Moscow, November 29, 1960. This is not to say that Khrushchev's only purpose in improving relations with Yugoslavia was to bring pressure on Albania, but this was certainly an effect.

82. *The New York Times,* November 30, 1960.

83. NCNA, November 29, 1960.

84. *Zeri i Popullit,* December 19, 1960 (translated in *Facts,* pp. 48-49).

85. Radio Moscow, February 8, 1962 (reprinted in Griffith, *op. cit.,* p. 319).

86. *Zeri i Popullit,* March 25, 1962 (translated in Griffith, *op. cit.,* p. 341).

87. *Ibid.*

88. There was no mention of the usual "atmosphere of friendship and mutual understanding." *Vneshniaia Torgovlia,* Vol. 41, No. 2 (February, 1961), Supplement, p. 11.

89. *Zeri i Popullit,* December 19, 1961 (translated in *Facts,* p. 51).

90. Albanian Telegraphic Agency (ATA), June 10, 1968 (translated in Radio Free Europe Situation Report: Albania, June 18, 1968).

91. *Foreign Trade of the Peoples Republic of China,* No. 17 (January, 1962), p. 6. The agreement was signed on February 2, 1961.

92. *Pravda,* October 28, 1961 (translated in *Current Digest of the Soviet Press,* Vol. 14, No. 5 [February 28, 1962], p. 20). Mistreatment of Soviet specialists was also given as the reason for their withdrawal from Yugoslavia in 1948 (see Chapter 2).

93. *Zeri i Popullit,* December 6, 1961 (translated in Griffith, *op. cit.,* pp. 277-78).

94. *Review of International Affairs* (Belgrade), Vol. 12, No. 249 (April 20, 1961), p. 16.

95. *Foreign Trade of the Peoples Republic of China,* No. 17 (January, 1962), p. 7.

96. Statement by Canadian Minister of Agriculture Alvin Hamilton, *The New York Times,* August 10, 1961.

97. *Zeri i Popullit,* March 25, 1962 (translated in Griffith, *op. cit.,* p. 342).

98. *Pravda,* April 26, 1961 (cited in Griffith, *op. cit.,* p. 78n).

99. *Zeri i Popullit,* December 19, 1961 (translated in *Facts,* p. 55).

100. There remains some question as to whether the Russian submarines were expelled or whether they were purposely withdrawn. The result—in the form of the removed Soviet military presence—was the same. See Leo Heinman, "Peking's Adriatic Stronghold," *East Europe,* Vol. 13, No. 4 (April, 1964), pp. 15-17.

101. *The New York Times,* June 24, 1961.

102. Cited in *East Europe,* Vol. 10, No. 8 (August, 1961), p. 47. East European tourists had also ceased coming to Albania by mid-June. *The New York Times,* October 22, 1961.

103. NCNA, November 23, 1960.

104. *Zeri i Popullit*, December 30, 1961 (translated in *Facts*, pp. 68-73).

105. Griffith, *op. cit.*, p. 38.

106. *Zeri i Popullit*, November 8, 1961 (translated in Griffith, *op. cit.*, p. 267). Here Khrushchev was suggesting that with a change in Albanian leadership, economic aid from the USSR might once again be available.

107. Contents of verbal communication from N. P. Firyubin, Vice Minister of Foreign Affairs of the USSR, to the Interim Charge d'Affaires of the Peoples Republic of Albania to the USSR, Gac Maxi; reprinted in *Facts*, p. 9. This was not, however, an "unprecedented" act. Earlier in the year, the Cuban government had used a similar tactic to provoke the United States into breaking relations.

108. *50 Let Sovetskoi Vneshnei Torgovli* (Moscow: Mezhdunarodnye Otnosheniia, 1967), p. 140.

109. *Pravda*, December 17, 1961 (translated in *Current Digest of the Soviet Press*, Vol. 13, No. 50, p. 32).

110. *U.N. Yearbook, 1965*, p. 45. Trade agreements were signed with Poland, Hungary, East Germany, Rumania, Bulgaria, and Czechoslovakia for such products as machine tools, electric generators, cables, etc. For a listing of the East European trade agreements with Albania, see *East Europe*, Vol. 11, No. 4 (April, 1962), p. 37.

111. Griffith, *op. cit.*, p. 145.

112. For a discussion of Albania's foreign trade with capitalist countries for the 1962-65 period, see Radio Free Europe Situation Report: Albania, April 4, 1966.

113. *The New York Times*, December 28, 1961.

114. *Zeri i Popullit*, December 10, 1961 (translated in *Facts*, p. 40).

115. *Ibid.*, pp. 40-41.

116. Khrushchev, in his speech to the 22nd CPSU Congress, asserted: "Our great party has more than once been subjected to bitter and filthy attacks from open and covert enemies of Communism. But it must be said outright that we do not recall an instance in which anyone shifted with such dizzying speed from protestations and vows of eternal friendship to unbridled anti-Soviet slander as the Albanian leaders have done.

"Presumably they expect in this way to lay the groundwork for earning handouts from the Imperialists. The Imperialists are always willing to pay thirty pieces of silver to those who cause a split in the ranks of the Communists. But pieces of silver have never brought anyone anything but dishonor and shame." *Pravda,* October 29, 1961 (translated in Griffith, *op. cit.,* p. 233).

117. A 1959 estimate of the Albanian State Planning Commission disclosed that 25 per cent of Albania's gross industrial production came from machinery and equipment supplied by the USSR and another 15 per cent from the other communist countries. In particular, 90 per cent of the equipment for Albania's oil industry, 65 per cent of its agricultural machinery, and 82 per cent of its tractors came from the Soviet bloc. *Zeri i Popullit,* July 18, 1962 (cited in *East Europe,* Vol. 11, No. 11 [November, 1962], p. 30).

118. Cited in Radio Free Europe Situation Report: Albania, September 17, 1962.

119. Translated in Radio Free Europe Situation Report: Albania, September 9, 1962.

120. Translated in Radio Free Europe Situation Report: Albania, August 30, 1966.

121. *Ibid.*

122. *Albanian Statistical Yearbook, 1963* (Tirana, 1964) (translated in Radio Free Europe Research Report: Albania, September 17, 1964).

123. Translated in Radio Free Europe Situation Report: Albania, June 11, 1964.

124. *Ibid.*

125. *Ibid.*

126. *Zeri i Popullit,* November 8, 1961 (translated in Griffith, *op. cit.,* p. 267).

127. Anthony Sylvester, "Revisionists and Stalinists in the Balkans," *East Europe,* Vol. 16, No. 1 (January, 1967), p. 8.

128. *Zeri i Popullit,* July 21, 1962 (translated in *East Europe,* Vol. 11, No. 10 [October, 1962], p. 27). The situation had not markedly changed by 1964. According to an article in *Zeri i Popullit* of October 3, 1964 (translated in Radio Free Europe Situation Report: Albania, November 10, 1964): "Machines often stop because there are workers and specialists who do not

know how to operate them. There are also cases where machines are damaged due to improper handling. This happens precisely because of the low professional level of the workers . . . or because many industrial enterprises employ workers who have a low professional rating for processes which require highly qualified personnel."

129. Radio Moscow, January 9, 1962 (reprinted in Griffith, *op. cit.,* p. 302).

130. Harry Hamm, *Albania: China's Beachhead in Europe* (New York: Frederick A. Praeger, 1963), p. 33. After leaving Soviet bloc countries, many Albanian students went to China to study. Somewhat ironically, they were forced to leave China in 1966 at the outbreak of the cultural revolution.

131. Editorial of party journal *Rruga e Partise,* June, 1963 (translated in Radio Free Europe Situation Report: Albania, August 8, 1963).

132. *Ibid.*

133. Cited in Radio Free Europe Situation Report: Albania, December 5, 1963.

134. Translated in Radio Free Europe Situation Report: Albania, September 2, 1964.

135. *Ibid.*

136. Translated in Radio Free Europe Situation Report: Albania, July 27, 1965.

137. NCNA.

138. Radio Moscow, January 8, 1963; reprinted in Radio Free Europe Situation Report: Albania, January 20, 1963.

139. Radio Moscow, September 12, 1964.

140. Radio Moscow, November 10, 1964.

141. Radio Tirana, November 13, 1964.

142. A *Zeri i Popullit* editorial on November 18, 1964, bitterly protested Yugoslavia's admission which, according to the Albanians, was illegal because Albania had not agreed to it (cited in Radio Free Europe Special Report: Albania, November 18, 1964).

143. *The New York Times,* November 28, 1964.

144. Cited in Radio Free Europe Situation Report: Albania, February 3, 1965.

145. *Ibid.* On this point, see also Anton Logoreci, "Albania and China: Incongruous Alliance," *Current History,* Vol. 52, No. 308 (April, 1967), pp. 227-31.

146. *The New York Times,* February 24, 1966.

147. *Zeri i Popullit,* March 21, 1966 (cited in UPI dispatch from Albania, ATA, September 30, 1967). For an examination of Sino-Albanian relations since the fall of Khrushchev, see Jan S. Prybyla, "Albania's Economic Vassalage," *East Europe,* Vol. 16, No. 1 (January, 1967), pp. 9-14; and Nicholas C. Pano, *The People's Republic of Albania* (Baltimore: Johns Hopkins Press, 1968), Chapter 6.

148. Cited in Radio Free Europe Situation Report: Albania, October 11, l967.

149. Radio Moscow, November 29, 1967.

150. *Pravda*, November 28, 1969 (translated in *Current Digest of the Soviet Press,* Vol. XXI, No. 48 [December 23, 1969], p. 22).

CHAPTER 4

SOVIET USE OF ECONOMIC PRESSURE AGAINST CHINA

"Politics are the concentrated expression of economics. . . . Politics cannot but have precedence over economics. To argue differently means forgetting the ABC of Marxism. . . . Without a proper political approach to the subject, the given class cannot maintain its rule and consequently cannot solve its own production problems." (Lenin criticizing Trotsky and Bukharin)

Peking Review, July 17, 1964

In examining the Soviet Union's use of economic pressure against China, it is necessary to start from the fact that Soviet relations with China in the period preceding the open split in 1960 were substantially different from its relations with either Yugoslavia or Albania in corresponding periods. The Soviet Union had minimal relations with both Yugoslavia and Albania in the inter-war period; Soviet activities of an economic, political, and even military nature in China, however, were widespread and bore a marked resemblance to Russian activities in China during the Czarist era. The question of allegedly insufficient Soviet economic assistance to Albania and Yugoslavia in the post-1945 period played a relatively minor role in the two nations' conflicts with the USSR, but Soviet unwillingness to provide China with as much economic aid as the Chinese leaders felt they needed was a central factor in the deterioration of Sino-Soviet relations.

This case study begins with a brief historical description of Sino-Soviet relations from 1919 until the Chinese Communists came to power in 1949 and then examines the close interrelationship between economic and political factors in Sino-Soviet relations in the period 1949 to 1960. The second section of the chapter analyzes Communist China's vulnerability to the various forms of economic pressure the USSR could exert. The following section contains an analysis of Khrushchev's implementation of economic pressure against China, a far more varied and protracted process than similar Soviet efforts against Yugoslavia or Albania. The fourth section deals with the failure of the attempts of Khrushchev's successors to employ successfully offers of renewed economic cooperation to effect a reconciliation with the Communist Chinese. An evaluation of the role of economic pressure in over-all Soviet policy toward China in the 1960-69 period is presented in the final section.

THE HISTORICAL BACKGROUND

As a result of Czarist expansion at China's expense, by the time of the Russian Revolution Russia dominated both Northern Manchuria and Outer Mongolia and had a significant degree of influence in Sinkiang as well.[1] Despite the Karakhan declaration of 1919, which theoretically renounced the gains made by Czarist Russia at the expense of China,[2] the next two decades were to witness a further increase in Russian influence in China, particularly in Mongolia and Sinkiang. Mongolia, after shifting back and forth between the Chinese, White Russians, and Bolsheviks, became a Soviet satellite in 1921, and Russian troops later fought a series of bloody battles with the Japanese in the 1930's to keep it under Soviet control.

In Sinkiang, Soviet military and economic aid and pressure had turned the Chinese province into a virtual Russian protectorate by 1940.[3] In the early 1930's, Sinkiang was tied to Soviet Central Asia through the Turksib railway at a time when communications and transportation to Eastern China were extremely tenuous. Russian troops were called in to suppress rebellions in 1931 and 1937 and remained in large numbers following the 1937 rebellion. In return for the Russian aid, the ruler of Sinkiang, General Sheng-Shih-Tsai, gave the USSR a series of economic concessions for the extraction of tungsten, oil, and tin. Sheng also joined the CPSU and converted Sinkiang into a Soviet-type state.

In Manchuria, there was a major battle between Russian and Chinese troops in 1929 when the Chinese Nationalists, who had just suppressed the Chinese Communists, attempted unsuccessfully to gain control over the Chinese Eastern Railroad.[4] Soviet domination of Northern Manchuria came to a halt, however, in 1935 when the Russians, in a move to appease Japan, sold it the Chinese Eastern Railroad.

World War II saw the temporary eclipse of Russian power in the Far East. In Sinkiang, General Sheng, sensing a Russian defeat, in 1942 purged his Soviet supporters, secured the withdrawal of Russian troops, and went over to the Chinese Nationalists. Following the war, however, there was a resurgence of Soviet pressure along the entire periphery of China. At the close of the war in 1945, the USSR assisted native revolts against the Chinese Nationalist government in Sinkiang, and Soviet pressure on its one-time protectorate was kept up until 1949 when the Chinese Communists secured control over the province. Alan Whiting in his book *Sinkiang: Pawn or Pivot?* has stated that the Russians, after trying unsuccessfully to obtain mineral concessions in Sinkiang from the Nationalist government, then tried to bribe the new Nationalist ruler of Sinkiang, General Tao Shih Yeath, into declaring Sinkiang independent on the pattern of Outer Mongolia—in return for protection against the Chinese

Communists.[5] Although the offer was refused, the Russians were able to acquire partial economic control over Sinkiang in 1950 when the Chinese Communists grudgingly consented to the establishment there of joint-stock companies in oil and non-ferrous metals.

Soviet policies met with even more success in Mongolia and Manchuria. At Yalta, Stalin obtained international acceptance of the status quo in Mongolia (i.e., its continuation as a Russian satellite) and achieved a powerful position in Manchuria through the lease on Port Arthur, the internationalization of Darien, and the agreement for joint Sino-Soviet operation of the Chinese Eastern and South Manchurian railroads.[6] In the closing days of the war, Soviet troops invaded Manchuria and defeated the weak Japanese forces defending the area.[7] As in Eastern Europe, a great despoilment of the industries of the region under Soviet occupation took place. The Pauley mission estimated the value of Soviet removals of stockpiles, food, machine tools, power generators, and other equipment at $858 million and the total destruction caused by Soviet forces in Manchuria at over $2 billion.[8] In addition, the Russians by threatening not to withdraw their troops from Manchuria tried to force the Nationalist government to agree to joint administration—in the form of joint-stock companies—of the main industrial and mining enterprises in the region.[9] Although the Chinese Nationalists with U.S. support were able to resist these demands, the Soviets managed to time their withdrawal from Manchuria in such a way as to enable certain Chinese Communist forces to gain control over the region's northern section. The Russians then signed trade agreements with the government of the so-called Northeast Liberated Area led by Chinese Communist Central Committee member Kao Kang.[10] There is some evidence that Soviet maneuvers in Manchuria in the 1948-49 period may have been primarily directed toward assisting Kao Kang in seizing power. The preferential treatment given Kao Kang's representatives in Moscow in 1950, his purge in 1954 prior to the visit of Khrushchev to Peking, and Khrushchev's defense of his friendship with the USSR lend substance to the view that Stalin was trying to build a client state in Manchuria under Kao Kang somewhat similar to the one already existing in Mongolia.[11]

In any case, the Russian despoilment of Manchuria was deeply resented not only by the Chinese Nationalists, but by the Chinese Communists as well. Although the Chinese Communist trade union leader Li-Li-San de-emphasized the problem in a 1946 speech in Harbin, he did not absolve the USSR of blame: "I feel that the movement of the machinery is not an important problem at all. Of course the Soviet Union moved some machinery, but not a large amount compared with its war losses."[12] In 1957, during China's "Hundred Flowers" period, more open attacks on Soviet activities in Manchuria were made. Lung Yun, vice-chairman of China's National Defense Council and a former Nationalist governor of Yunan Province, stated publicly: "The Soviet army dismantled and removed a portion of the machinery in our factories when it liberated Northeast China. How much did the Soviet Union pay for it? Will we be compensated for it?"[13] Although Lung Yun was strongly rebuked by the Chinese Communist government for his anti-Russian statement, the official counterstatement contained some anti-Russian innuendoes of its own:

When China with the aid of the Soviet Union liberated the North East
(Manchuria) the Americans dropped KMT troops there by plane. If the
machinery had not been removed (and taken to Siberia) from these
areas, it would have fallen into Chiang Kai-shek's hands. The Rightist
opposition elements among us know very well that the aid given by
the Soviet Union since the liberation outweighs many times over the
value of the machinery removed from the North East and that the
Soviet Union is granting us credit at a low rate of interest.[14]

The rehabilitation of Lung Yun in April, 1959,[15] at a time of deteriorating
Sino-Soviet relations indicates that although the Chinese Communists kept
their bitterness under control in the 1946-58 period when they were in great
need of Soviet support, the Russian despoilment of Manchuria coupled with
the subsequent failure of the Soviet government to reimburse China for its
losses through free grants of similar equipment or a cash gift of equal value still
rankled deeply.

But in 1949 the Chinese Communists had additional grievances against the
Soviet Union. These included the satellite status of Mongolia, which at one
time had been a Chinese province, and the Russian machinations in Sinkiang to
which reference has already been made. In addition, there were conflicts on the
party level. Stalin had made disastrous mistakes in China in the late 1920's. He
first forced the fledgling Communist Party of China into an alliance with the
Nationalists and, when this backfired, then sponsored unsuccessful and
bloodily suppressed uprisings against the Nationalists in China's major cities,
uprisings that almost destroyed the Communist Party.[16] After having increased
their power greatly as a result of World War II, the Chinese Communists could
only have resented Stalin's advice in 1946 (which they rejected) to form
another coalition with Chiang Kai-shek's Nationalists. Nonetheless, having just
conquered China and desperately in need of economic aid to rebuild their
war-torn country, the Chinese Communists "leaned to one side" and went to
Russia for aid.

The negotiations prior to the signing of the Sino-Soviet Treaty of
Friendship, Alliance, and Mutual Assistance and the economic agreements
between the two nations were far different in nature from the mere formalities
preceding the treaties Stalin dictated to his European satellites. There was
apparently considerable bargaining, and Mao Tse-tung, who on January 2,
1950, had predicted a visit of only "several weeks,"[17] remained in Moscow for
almost two months before the main treaty was signed. Indeed, in a TASS
interview on Radio Moscow, Mao frankly remarked that the most important
issues to be discussed during the negotiations were "the existing Treaty of
Friendship and Alliance between China and the USSR; the question of Soviet
credits for the Peoples Republic of China; and the question of trade and a trade
agreement between our countries."[18] Although the treaty and agreements that
were finally signed contained benefits for both sides,[19] the result was a
continued Russian presence in Sinkiang, Mongolia, and Manchuria.

The most important provision of the treaty guaranteed to China
Soviet support in case of an "attack by Japan or any state allied with

Japan" (i.e., the United States), but there were also important economic provisions. The Russians presented the Chinese with a loan of $300 million:

> To be used in payment for deliveries from the USSR of equipment and materials including equipment for electric power stations, metallurgical and engineering plants, mining equipment for the extraction of coal and ores, railway and other transport equipment, rails and other materials for the restoration and development of the economy of China.[20]

In all, the USSR was to help in the construction and rehabilitation of 50 industrial projects, most of which were located in Manchuria, thus demonstrating the continued Soviet interest in the region. This was to be the first installment of a series of Soviet credits which although not free grants (this agreement carried a 1 per cent interest charge) nonetheless provided the basis for China's industrialization. The Soviet loan of $300 million was, however, meager, in comparison not only to American Marshall Plan aid but even to the $450 million loan the USSR had given Poland in 1948. Although the Chinese Communists, who had nowhere else to go for aid, publicly praised the Soviet economic assistance, their later statements attest to their bitterness as to its limited nature:

> In recent years the leaders of the C.P.S.U. have habitually played the benefactor and frequently boasted of their "disinterested assistance." When commemorating the 14th anniversary of the signing of the Sino-Soviet Treaty of Friendship, Alliance and Mutual Assistance in February this year (1964), *Pravda, Izvestia* and other Soviet propaganda media again beat the drum to the same tune. We have not yet made a systematic reply in the press, but we must point out that, so far from being gratis, Soviet aid to China was rendered mainly in the form of trade and that it was certainly not a one-way affair. China has paid and is paying the Soviet Union in goods, gold or convertible foreign exchange for all Soviet-supplied complete sets of equipment and other goods, including those made available on credit plus interest. It is necessary to add that the prices of many of the goods we imported from the Soviet Union were much higher than those on the world market. . . .
>   As for the Soviet loans to China, it must be pointed out that China used them mainly for the purchase of war material from the Soviet Union, the greatest part of which was used up in the war to resist U.S. aggression and aid Korea.[21]

In addition to the loan, Mao secured Stalin's agreement that by the end of 1952 Russia would withdraw from Port Arthur and turn over to China the Soviet share of the two Manchurian railroads (joined into one railroad called the "Chinese Changun Railroad" under joint Sino-Soviet control in 1946). A further Soviet concession was the decision to "transfer without compensation to the government of the People's Republic of China the property acquired in Manchuria from Japanese owners by Soviet government organizations."[22]

Nonetheless, the Chinese Communists had to pay a stiff price for the limited amount of Soviet economic aid and the return of what had originally been Chinese property. First, Mao had to acknowledge the "independent status" of Outer Mongolia. Second, he had to agree to the formation of two joint-stock companies in Sinkiang: "Sovkitmetall," which would prospect for uranium and other non-ferrous metals, and "Sovkitneft," whose task was to drill for oil.[23] (It should be remembered that the USSR had tried unsuccessfully to gain similar concessions from the Chinese Nationalist government.) A third Chinese concession was the promise to "compensate the Soviet Union for expenses it has incurred in restoring and constructing installations (in Port Arthur) since 1945."[24]

Communist China's entry into the Korean War greatly increased her economic dependence on the USSR. By 1951, 48 per cent of the Chinese budget was taken up by military expenditures and the Chinese Communists were heavily dependent on the Soviet Union for shipments of military equipment.[25] But although the Chinese perhaps expected the Russians would display their "fraternal Socialist spirit" by supplying the military material free of charge, such was not to be the case. Stalin sent the material on credit during the war, but he stipulated that the Chinese would have to repay it over a ten-year period once the war was over. Stalin's successors did not change his policy in this regard. The requirement for repayment placed a heavy strain on the Chinese balance of payments.[26]

In 1957, it was again Lung Yun who voiced Chinese displeasure over the repayment requirement in a comparison of American and Russian policies toward their allies:

> It is unreasonable for China to bear all the expenses of the resist-America aid-Korea war. . . . During the Second World War the United States granted loans and leases to her allies. Later some of these allies refused to pay back the loans while the United States excused some from repayment. It will take us more than ten years to repay the loans from the USSR if we ever repay them. Besides, we have to pay interest to the Soviet Union. China fought for Socialism but look at the result.[27]

While Lung was officially rebuked for his "anti-Soviet" attitude, there was no rebuttal of his argument.[28] Indeed, seven years later, the Chinese Communists were openly to deride the Soviet Union for its lack of free economic aid during the Korean War:

> In the war against U.S. aggression the Korean people carried by far the heaviest burden and sustained by far the heaviest losses. The

Chinese people, too, made great sacrifices and incurred vast military expenses. The Chinese Communist Party has always considered that this was the Chinese People's . . . internationalist duty and that it is nothing to boast of. For many years we have been paying the principal and interest on these Soviet loans, which account for a considerable amount of our yearly exports to the Soviet Union. Thus even the war materiel supplied to China in the war to resist U.S. aggression and aid Korea has not been given gratis.[29]

Relations between the two communist nations remained strained throughout the Korean War and until Stalin's death. The Soviet leader, always wary of communists he could not control, exploited China's great dependence on the USSR to keep the Chinese in a subordinate position in the alliance. Trade between the two nations rose sharply (see Table 6), but the Peking regime had to agree to the establishment of two more joint-stock companies in 1951 in shipbuilding ("Sovkitsudostroi") and civil aviation ("Skoda"). (As late as June, 1955, the Chinese publicly maintained that these joint enterprises helped in the development of the Chinese economy.[30]) In 1952, Stalin obtained Chinese consent to the continuation of the Soviet naval base in Port Arthur past the 1952 deadline.* By the end of 1952, the Soviet dictator seemed increasingly reluctant to give the Chinese any further economic aid. Despite the fact that they were waging a costly war in Korea, the Chinese began in 1952 to draft their first five-year plan. In order to successfully complete the plan which had as its goal the doubling of Chinese industrial production, aid from the USSR in the form of both capital equipment and technical assistance was a vital requirement. Yet when Li Fu Chin, Vice Chairman of the Chinese Peoples Republic's Committee on Economics and Finance, went to Moscow to negotiate the necessary agreements, he encountered serious difficulties. He remained in the Soviet capital from August, 1952, until May, 1953, when after Stalin's death an agreement was finally reached.[31]

The agreement called for Soviet delivery of 91 more industrial plants to China** together with the technicians and scientists necessary to put them into operation.[32] The joint-stock companies, however, remained in effect. On September 18, 1953, at the time when the new agreement was first made public, *Pravda* stated, "The Soviet-Chinese companies are working successfully on the basis of full equality and mutual interest."[33] Indeed, even after Stalin's death, the Russians attempted to establish additional joint-stock companies in China, but the Chinese leaders successfully resisted the pressure.[34]

Khrushchev and Bulganin's trip to Peking in October, 1954, seemed to mark a turning point in Sino-Soviet relations. It appeared at the time that Khrushchev, who was in the Chinese capital for the Fifth Anniversary celebrations of the Chinese Peoples Republic (CPR), had made a major effort

---

*The Manchurian railroads, however, were returned on schedule.

**These plants were in addition to the 50 plants the Russians had promised to provide in the 1950 agreement.

TABLE 6

Sino-Soviet Trade, 1949-68
(in millions of new rubles; one ruble = 1.11 U.S. dollars)

Year	Soviet Exports	Chinese Exports	Soviet Balance	Total Trade
1949	179.7	128.9	+ 50.8	308.6
1950	349.4	169.5	+179.9	518.9
1951	430.6	298.2	+132.4	728.8
1952	498.8	372.4	+126.4	871.2
1953	627.8	427.2	+200.6	1,055.0
1954	683.4	520.5	+162.9	1,203.9
1955	673.5	579.2	+ 94.3	1,252.7
1956	659.7	687.8	− 27.9	1,347.5
1957	489.7	664.3	−174.6	1,154.0
1958	570.6	793.1	−222.5	1,363.7
1959	859.1	990.3	−131.2	1,849.4
1960	735.4	763.3	− 27.9	1,498.7
1961	330.6	496.3	−138.7	826.9
1962	210.1	464.7	−254.6	674.8
1963	168.5	371.7	−203.2	540.2
1964	121.8	282.8	−161.0	404.6
1965	172.5	203.0	− 30.5	375.5
1966	157.8	128.8	+ 29.0	286.6
1967	45.2	51.1	− 5.9	96.3
1968	53.4	33.0	+ 20.4	86.4

Sources:

1949-66: *Vneshniaia Torgovlia SSSR 1918-1966* (Moscow: Mezhdunarod-nye Otnosheniia, 1967), pp. 66-67.

1967: *Vneshniaia Torgovlia,* Vol. 48, No. 6 (June, 1968), p. 56.

1968: *Vneshniaia Torgovlia,* Vol. 49, No. 7 (July, 1969), p. 57.

to improve relations between the two communist nations. He extended a long-term loan of $130 million and committed the Soviet Union to sell equipment (and technicians) for another 15 major construction projects.[35] In addition, the Soviet leader agreed to sell to China the Soviet shares of the joint-stock companies and turn the companies over to sole Chinese control by January, 1955. In another Soviet concession, Khrushchev agreed to remove all Soviet troops from Port Arthur and turn over all the installations the Russians had built there to the Chinese free of charge. This was a major concession to the Chinese, because the 1950 treaty had stipulated that they would have to pay for the installations. The Russians would, however, have to be reimbursed for stockpiles of military equipment they left in the port.

The Russians have characterized this trip as a turning point in Sino-Soviet relations. Mikhail Suslov, in his report to the Central Committee of the CPSU on February 14, 1964, stated:

> Soviet-Chinese cooperation achieved its greatest development after 1953 when, on the initiative of the CPSU and Comrade N. S. Khrushchev personally, the elements of inequality in the relations between our two countries that had been a phenomenon of the Stalin cult were eliminated.[36]

The CPSU letter to China of March 7, 1964, went into detail on these "elements of inequality":

> On its own initiative the CC of the CPSU corrected Stalin's errors and restored the Leninist principle of equality in its relations with fraternal parties and countries. We withdrew our troops from countries where they had previously been stationed *including our troops from Port Arthur. We liquidated the economic joint companies in China and in other countries* [emphasis added].[37]

Despite the loan and the Soviet concessions, all was not complete harmony during Khrushchev's visit to Peking. Information has recently come to light that reveals that Mao tried to reach an agreement with the Russians on the reincorporation of Mongolia into Communist China. In the words of the Chinese leader, however, "They (the Soviet leaders) refused to talk to us" about it.[38] The Soviet unwillingness to grant China any more capital loans after 1954 may well have been related to the Chinese challenge to the entire Soviet position in Asia.

Perhaps related to this was the Soviet requirement for the Chinese to pay for the Russian shares in the joint-stock companies and for the military stockpiles left in Port Arthur. Although the USSR gave China a $160 million transfer credit in 1955 to cover the cost of Soviet equipment invested in these companies, coupled with the continuing requirement for repayment of the Korean War debt, this was to place a major strain on China's balance of payments. Indeed, the Chinese were unable to pay off their debts to the Russians (through a surplus of exports over imports) until 1964 (see Table 6).

It is interesting to note that although the USSR canceled repayment requirements for the Soviet shares in the Eastern European joint-stock companies following the Hungarian Revolution, similar action was not taken to relieve the Chinese of this burden.

The Soviet unwillingness to assist the Chinese to any significant extent became still more evident in 1955 as Soviet exports to China began to drop (see Table 6). In 1956, Chinese exports to the USSR for the first time exceeded Chinese imports from it. In addition, in the same year the Russians suggested to the Chinese that the Russian technical advisors who were assisting the Chinese economy in many areas be withdrawn.[39] Although the Russians acceded to a Chinese request to allow the advisors to remain,[40] by 1956 the Chinese must have realized that they could not count on the Soviet Union to provide long-term credits for their economy. Indeed, the only major economic agreement signed between the two nations that year provided for the USSR to *sell* machinery, equipment, and technical assistance for 55 additional plants.[41] Lest there be any doubt, the Soviet Foreign Trade Journal *Vneshniaia Torgovlia*, beginning in 1957, strongly hinted to the Chinese that they had best rely on their own resources. Thus an article in the July, 1957, issue stated:

> Thanks to the utilization of the experience of the USSR and the production initiative of Chinese workers, technicians and engineers, *it has been possible to discover and exploit large reserves* in many branches of industry of the Chinese Peoples Republic [emphasis added].[42]

In an article in the same journal in October, 1957, M. Sladkovskii stated:

> The successful fulfillment of the economic plan in 1956 and in the first half of 1957 gives the Chinese the possibility before the appointed time of raising the percentage of domestically produced equipment in equipping enterprises which are being constructed. *In connection with this, in 1957 there has been a contraction in machinery imports from the Soviet Union* [emphasis added—see Table 7].[43]

An article in the October, 1957, issue of *Voprosy Ekonomiki* similarly implied the need for China to depend on its own resources:

> Of the states of the Socialist Camp, apart from the Soviet Union, *only a land so rich in immense human and natural resources as the Chinese Peoples Republic can assume the comparable task of creating a completely developed economy which will fully satisfy all the needs of the country* [emphasis added].[44]

TABLE 7

Soviet Machinery and Equipment Exports to China, 1949-68
(in millions of new rubles; one ruble = 1.11 U.S. dollars)

Year	Amount
1949	17.373
1950	37.208
1951	98.833
1952	140.896
1953	145.217
1954	178.964
1955	206.615
1956	274.274
1957	244.401
1958	286.165
1959	537.768
1960	453.527
1961	97.281
1962	24.594
1963	37.969
1964	51.944
1965	69.296
1966	77.596
1967	22.178
1968	13.409

Sources: *Vneshniaia Torgovlia SSSR 1918-1966* (Moscow: Mezhdunarodnye Otnosheniia, 1967), pp. 208-9; *Vneshniaia Torgovlia SSSR za 1968* (Moscow: Mezhdunarodnye Otnosheniia, 1969), p. 231.

The reluctance of the Soviet Union to grant China capital aid during this period—a reluctance that antedated the Hungarian Revolution*—was seen by the Chinese leaders as a pernicious consequence of Khrushchev's advocacy of such doctrines as "peaceful coexistence," "peaceful transition to Communism," and "peaceful competition with the West." Indeed, by November, 1957, Chinese dissatisfaction with Khrushchev's doctrines had given rise to sharp polemics between the two nations. This debate has been discussed in considerable detail elsewhere, but it is nonetheless necessary to review it here in order to set the background for an examination of Sino-Soviet economic relations in the 1957-59 period.[45]

Khrushchev had introduced the concept of a peaceful transition to socialism in his February, 1956, address to the 20th Congress of the CPSU. This concept had a number of negative implications as far as the Chinese were concerned. First, the emphasis on peaceful coexistence lessened China's importance to the USSR as a potential wartime ally against the "Imperialists" and consequently reduced the Soviet Union's need to give China assistance in its industrialization (on which Chinese military power would ultimately be based). Indeed, if there was to be "peaceful coexistence," and economic competition was to be the main area of conflict between capitalism and communism, then priority in the allocation of Soviet resources would have to be given to the Soviet economy in order to defeat the United States in the productivity competition. The fact that as a concomitant to Khrushchev's policy the Soviet Union began a vigorous policy of economic assistance to certain "neutral" underdeveloped nations at this time in order to "win them over to Socialism,"[46] must also have been a bitter pill for the Chinese leaders to swallow, since they had not received any Soviet capital aid since the 1954 agreement.

By the time of the November, 1957, meeting of ruling communist parties, Chinese dissatisfaction with Soviet policy had, according to a later Chinese report, reached the level of "sharp debate" with the Soviet delegation:

> At the time of the meeting of the representatives of the Communist and Workers parties in 1957, the delegation of the CCP engaged in a sharp debate with the delegation of the CPSU on the question of the transition from capitalism to socialism.[47]

The Chinese delegation then agreed to sign the final conference document (which predominantly echoed the Soviet view of the debated issues) according to the *Peking Review* report only "to make allowances for the internal needs"

---

*Some observers have argued that the huge outlays the Soviet Union had to make to Eastern Europe following the Hungarian Revolution was the reason for both decreased shipments of goods to China and the Soviet unwillingness to grant China aid.

The Soviet unwillingness actually predates the Hungarian Revolution, and Soviet aid to certain non-communist countries such as India (see note 46 at end of chapter) indicates that rubles were available for causes Khrushchev deemed worthwhile. A higher priority was also assigned to the improvement of the living standard of the Russian people.

of the CPSU and "for the common struggle against the enemy."[48] A more likely explanation for the Chinese willingness to sign the document, however, lies in the fact that on October 15, 1957, the two nations signed an agreement on "new technology for national defense."[49] The Chinese later claimed that this agreement committed the Russians to supply them with a sample atomic bomb and technical information relating to its manufacture. In agreeing to give the Chinese a sample atomic bomb, the Russians made a major contribution to the Chinese economy by enabling the Chinese to avoid a lengthy and costly research and development process that would have consumed large amounts of scarce Chinese resources.

Despite the nuclear weapons agreement, however, the Russians persisted in their refusal to grant China capital aid. An editorial appearing in the March, 1958, issue of *Vneshniaia Torgovlia*, after citing a speech by Khrushchev that emphasized that the main goal of the Soviet people was to overtake the United States in production,[50] then went on to describe economic cooperation between the Soviet Union and China in these terms:

> *The most important form* of economic cooperation between the Soviet Union and the People's Republic of China is foreign trade, for the development of which there are broad possibilities. . . . In the trade relations of the USSR with China are found the clear expression of equality, mutual profit and fraternal cooperation [emphasis added].[51]

This was the first explicit listing of Soviet priorities in its economic relations with China; previous articles dealing with Sino-Soviet economic cooperation in the same journal had stated only that foreign trade was "*an* important form of economic cooperation" and that "allocation of credits" was also "*an* important form of economic cooperation."[52] Although in August, 1958, the USSR agreed to *sell* China another 47 plants and the necessary technical assistance to put them into operation, this was still not the economic assistance the Chinese economy needed; and although Soviet exports to China rose sharply in 1958, Chinese exports to the Soviet Union rose even more sharply as the Chinese continued to pay back previous Soviet aid.[53]

By the spring of 1958, this lack of Soviet aid has posed severe problems for the Chinese leadership. Although the industrial sector of their economy had made significant gains by the close of the first five-year plan, agricultural production had not shown a corresponding increase. Indeed, the rise in agricultural production had barely exceeded the increase in population over the period. Whereas 35 per cent of China's exports to the Soviet Union in 1957 consisted of agricultural products, and the unwillingness of the Russians to supply long-term credits forced the Chinese to increase their exports in order to pay for imports of Soviet machinery, the Chinese leaders faced the dilemma of not only feeding their own population but of securing sufficient agricultural products for export as well.[54] The "Great Leap Forward" and the "Commune" movement, which was the latest of a series of agricultural reorganizations aimed at increasing production, were the Chinese responses to this dilemma.*

The Chinese development of Communes—institutions the Russians had tried and rejected—had a major impact on Sino-Soviet relations. In proclaiming their "short-cut to Communism," the Chinese appeared to challenge the Soviet "model" of "Socialist construction"—and Soviet leadership of the communist movement—at least in the underdeveloped areas of Asia, Africa, and Latin America.[55] Leonid Ilychev, in a June, 1964, article in *Kommunist* in which he accused the Chinese of "petty-bourgeois impatience" and "great power aspirations" stated in retrospect:

> Having proclaimed in 1958 the "Big Leap" and "Peoples Communes" slogans, the Chinese leaders declared at that time that the Soviet Union had gotten stuck at the stage of Socialism and was marking time, while China was advancing to Communism with seven-league strides.[56]

A temporary compromise was worked out between China and the USSR at the time of the 21st CPSU Congress. In his speech to the Congress, Chou En-lai dropped the claim that the Chinese were building communism and stated instead that China was building "Socialism." Khrushchev responded with the equivocal statement that all socialist countries would enter communism "more or less simultaneously," thus implying that the USSR would aid the more backward. The Soviet leader appeared to make a step in this direction several days later when the USSR agreed to sell China 78 more plants in the period 1959-67. The cost of the Soviet equipment and technical assistance was to come to $1,250 million.[57] Nonetheless, although a long-term commitment of Soviet resources, it was still a regular trade agreement with no credits involved, and although Soviet exports were to increase by more than 50 per cent in 1959 over 1958, Chinese exports increased almost as sharply; and the end result was that China had an "export surplus" with the USSR of $145 million for that year. The real Soviet attitude toward assisting the underdeveloped nations of the Camp was clearly expressed several years later in an article in *Kommunist*:

> A few years ago . . . it was asserted that the obligation of Socialist countries that had moved forward in their economic development allegedly consisted in "waiting for" the lagging ones, and giving them everything that had been created by the forward moving countries, as distinct from the lagging ones. *This parasitical understanding of the*

---

*The Chinese leaders could, of course, have adopted other alternatives such as increasing investment in agriculture so as to concentrate on raising agricultural production (investment in fertilizer factories, tractors, etc.). Alternatively, they could have turned to the West for industrial credits; the special "Chincom" embargo had been eased the previous year. Nonetheless, although these very alternatives were to be adopted after 1961, in 1958 the Chinese leaders preferred a rapid increase in both industrial and agricultural production in the context of increased trade with the USSR, which at that time appeared to be a dependable supplier. The August, 1958, agreement, mentioned above, appeared to substantiate this belief.

*principles of proletarian internationalism with regard to the relations
between Socialist countries was in radical contradiction to Leninism*
[emphasis added] .[58]

The tone of Soviet descriptions of Sino-Soviet economic relations, as reflected in the economic press, hardened further in 1959. In the February issue of
Vneshniaia Torgovlia, I. Andreev, after listing some of China's industrial accom-
plishments since 1950, bluntly stated: "The grand successes achieved by the
Chinese people in Socialist construction are *inseparable* from the all-around,
prolonged and disinterested aid of the Soviet Union" (emphasis added).[59]

This article began a running debate in *Vneshniaia Torgovlia* between
Chinese and Soviet economists as to the importance of Soviet aid in Chinese
industrial growth. In the June, 1959, issue, Chan Wa-doon, trade councillor of
the Chinese Embassy in the USSR, wrote that foreign trade was only "an
important form" of economic cooperation between the USSR and China and
stressed in his article the earlier credits granted by the USSR in 1950 and
1954.[60] The article concluded with a sharp attack on Khrushchev's new
rapprochement policy with Yugoslavia:

> All of these agreements will . . . deliver a serious blow to the intrigues
> of the imperialists and modern revisionists who are dedicated to the
> undermining of close cooperation and fraternal friendship between
> the Chinese Peoples Republic and the USSR.[61]

The debate became even more pointed in the October, 1959, issue where
Yeh Chi-chang, China's Minister of Foreign Trade, stated:

> In the area of foreign trade it is necessary to pursue a course
> decisively. The development of our state by our own resources—this
> is the main thing. Receipt of foreign aid—this is secondary. This
> course is the main direction of Socialist construction in China.[62]

After discussing the Western embargo against China, which had been
considerably relaxed two years earlier, Yeh Chi-chang went on to say:

> Some *consider* that we could not manage without trade with Western
> states and therefore try to fish in troubled waters, cherishing unre-
> alizable hopes to make use of trade with our state in their mercenary
> motives. However, this is a flagrant error [emphasis added] .[63]

Given the fact that China had managed comparatively well without Western trade
during the embargo period, it seems strange that the Chinese Foreign Trade
Minister should use the present tense in making his allegation. It could be, however, that he was making oblique reference to Soviet leaders who may well have
reasoned that China could not get along without Soviet trade. Indeed, hints to
that effect had already been dropped by Soviet leaders as early as June, 1959.

In a radio broadcast to Hungary on June 2, 1959, which was very similar to the now famous article in *Sovetskaia Latvia* fourteen months later, Anatoly Kurov stated:

> The Socialist world system unites highly industrialized countries like the USSR, Czechoslovakia and the DDR and countries like the Chinese Peoples Republic, Albania and the Democratic Republic of Vietnam which have only just begun to develop their industries and are at various stages of economic development.
>
> The fraternal cooperation between the socialist countries plays an important role in bringing the different levels of development to a common one. *How, for instance, would the development of the Chinese Peoples Republic have looked, a country which is now advancing toward becoming one of the world's great industrial powers if she had had to build socialism on her own as the Soviet Union once had to do?* The pace of development would naturally have been high, since this is the common law of socialism, but the Chinese people would have had to overcome many other difficulties in creating their own industry and training experts.
>
> All of these problems can be solved much more quickly in the CPR because of the vast aid given by the Soviet Union and the Peoples Democracies. About 300 enterprises have been built in China with Soviet help. The problem of training cadres is also being quickly solved thanks to the assistance of the Soviet Union and other Socialist countries. These countries have either sent their experts to China or have trained Chinese in their own universities. . . . It is obvious that such fraternal assistance has made it possible for China to develop at an exceptionally fast rate and to approach more quickly the level of the leading socialist countries [emphasis added].[64]

By June, 1959, however, the issue of Soviet economic aid was not the only one marring Sino-Soviet relations. The Chinese were also dissatisfied with the lack of Soviet support during their offshore islands confrontation with the United States in the fall of 1958. For their part, the Russians were alarmed at the prospect of being pulled into a war over an area of only tertiary interest to the Soviet Union.[65] It was probably following the end of this crisis that the Russians, according to a later Chinese statement, put forth "unreasonable demands designed to bring China under military control."[66] These Soviet demands were related to the nuclear weapons agreement of October, 1957, and probably involved Soviet control over any nuclear weapons given to China. The Chinese rejection of these demands was followed on June 20, 1959, by a Soviet cancellation of the weapons agreement itself.[67] This Soviet action, coming at a time when the Chinese leaders had come to the realization that the "Great Leap Forward" had been a failure, helped to precipitate a major crisis in the Chinese Communist Party.

By refusing to grant China a sample nuclear weapon, Khrushchev was forcing the Chinese to go through the long and expensive research and development program they had apparently been spared by the 1957 agreement. In addition, coming at a time when the question of allocating China's limited resources had again become a matter of sharp debate because of the failure of the "Great Leap" and the Communes to solve China's problem of capital formation, the cancell-ation was a severe blow to the Chinese economy. All these factors helped precipi-tate a split in the Chinese Communist Party.

There were elements in the Chinese party that had opposed the "Great Leap," the Commune movement, and the resultant deterioration of relations with the USSR. These elements were apparently led by P'eng Teh-huai, China's De-fense Minister, and operated with at least the cognizance if not the full support of Khrushchev himself.[68] P'eng had met Khrushchev in Tirana on May 26, 1959, interrupting his Eastern European tour to fly to the Albanian capital. In June, P'eng had gone to Moscow and apparently told Khrushchev of his dissatisfaction with the Communes and the "Great Leap" at that time. In late July, P'eng openly attacked Mao at the Lushan Plenum of the Chinese Communist Party but failed in his attempt to change the policies of the party; he was purged and demoted to the post of superintendent of the "Sino-Soviet Friendship" state farm in Heilung-kang. Khrushchev's later support for P'eng was bitterly resented by the Chinese leaders and became a matter of public conflict at the Bucharest Conference in June, 1960.

Following the demotion of P'eng Teh-huai, relations between the USSR and China deteriorated even more sharply. Khrushchev's visit to the United States clearly did not meet with Chinese approval, but an even more serious irritant for the Chinese was the USSR's neutral stand on a Sino-Indian border clash that took place just before Khrushchev left for the United States.* In retrospect, the Chinese, who may have staged the border incident to embarrass Khrushchev, stated:

> The tearing up of the agreement on new technology for national defense by the leadership of the CPSU and its issuance of the statement of the Sino-Indian border clash on the eve of Khrushchev's visit to the United States were ceremonial gifts to Eisenhower so as to curry favor with U.S. Imperialists and create the so-called "Spirit of Camp David."[69]

---

*The Chinese date this incident as the first serious conflict between China and the Soviet Union. In an editorial in the *Peking Review* of March 1, 1963, the Chinese stated:

"The truth is that the internal differences among the fraternal parties were first brought into the open, not in the summer of 1960, but on the eve of the Camp David talks, on September 9, 1959 to be exact. On that day a socialist country, turning a deaf ear to China's repeated explanations of the true situation and China's advice, hastily issued a statement on a Sino-Indian border incident through its official news agency. Making no distinction between right and wrong, the statement expressed 'regret' over the border clash and in reality condemned China's correct stand. They even said it was tragic and deplorable. Here is the first instance in history in which a socialist country, instead of condemning the armed provocations of the reactionaries of a capitalist country, condemned another fraternal socialist country when it was confronted with such armed provocations."

The Soviet offer of a $375 million loan to India three days after the TASS announcement on the border clash was also deeply resented by the Chinese.[70]

Relations between the two communist nations continued to deteriorate in early 1960, and the Soviet Union began to drop even stronger hints of the possibility of a cutoff in Soviet "aid." In the February, 1960, issue of *Vneshniaia Torgovlia*, F. Kleimonov in an article entitled "Fruitful Cooperation" reminded the Chinese that "in its movement forward China depends upon the continual and thorough aid of the USSR and other Socialist states."[71] Kleimonov concentrated on the importance of Soviet technical assistance in his article and summed up its importance to the Chinese economy in these words:

> The utilization of Soviet technical documents and Soviet experience to a significant degree facilitated Chinese mastery of the production of the means of production and the means of transportation—all of which had a decisive significance for the successful solution of the tasks of rapid development of the Chinese economy.[72]

Kleimonov concluded his article by stating:

> Cooperation (between the USSR and China) makes possible an extremely rapid development of science and technology in both states. It helps the Chinese people more quickly possess many branches of science and the newest technology necessary for the construction of modern industry and modern agriculture and to solve successfully the tasks laid down by the Chinese Communist Party—"in the course of 12 years to achieve or bring near a modern level of world science and technology in most areas."[73]

Less than five months later, the Soviet technicians assisting the Chinese in "modern technological development" were withdrawn from China on Khrushchev's orders. But before this and other acts of Soviet economic pressure against China are examined in detail, it is necessary to examine Chinese vulnerability to such pressure.

CHINA'S ECONOMIC VULNERABILITY

China was considerably less vulnerable to Soviet economic pressure than either Yugoslavia or Albania despite the large share of the USSR in its total trade in 1959 (47.4 per cent of its imports and 49.5 per cent of its exports).[74] Not only were the Chinese not dependent on Soviet loans—which were not available anyway—but Chinese exports to the Soviet Union were of much greater value to the USSR than Yugoslavia's or Albania's had been. Nonetheless, because of China's severe shortage of trained technicians and its inability to acquire large amounts of machinery elsewhere, the Chinese economy was vulnerable to Soviet economic pressure.

As stated above, the early development of Chinese industry was heavily dependent on supplies of Soviet machinery and technical assistance. Although

China had to pay for much of this assistance in the form of exports, the existence of the Western economic embargo precluded China from acquiring large amounts of modern equipment elsewhere.[75] Thus without the Soviet supplies, it is doubtful whether China could have achieved the industrial production levels it reached in 1957. According to Soviet statistics, by 1957, the USSR had exported $1,483,639,288 worth of machinery and equipment to China, of which $785,797,000 worth was in the form of complete plants.[76] The willingness of the USSR to supply China with complete factories together with the technicians who knew how to set them up was unquestionably the major factor in the success of China's first five-year plan (1953-57). By 1957, approximately 57 per cent of Communist China's steel production and 50 per cent of her coal production came from enterprises constructed or rebuilt with Soviet help.[77] Thanks in large part to Russian assistance, Chinese steel production tripled and coal production doubled over the five-year period.[78]

Beginning in 1956, however, China's relative dependence on Soviet machinery imports began to drop. Although approximately 94 per cent of Chinese imports of this commodity came from Soviet bloc nations in 1955, this figure declined to 88 per cent in 1956 and to 80 per cent in 1957.[79] The decrease was due in part to a drop in Soviet exports (see Table 6) but also to a sharp rise in imports from Western European countries and Japan as a result of the lifting of most of the embargo restrictions against China in 1957. In addition, by 1957 China had acquired the ability to produce about 60 per cent of the machinery it needed domestically.[80] This tendency toward a decreasing dependence on Soviet bloc machinery imports was reversed, however, in 1958. The Chinese decision, embodied in the August, 1958, and February, 1959, trade agreements, to rapidly increase trade with the USSR heavily committed Chinese export capabilities to the Soviet market rather than to Western Europe or Japan.[81] China's agricultural crises in the 1960-61 period then precluded the possibility of a turn to the West for machinery and equipment when the Soviet Union curtailed exports of these commodities, because the agricultural goods the Chinese had earlier planned to exchange for the machinery were not available.[82] Indeed, the Chinese had to sell silver in the West to both pay off their earlier debts and purchase much-needed grain.[83] Given the unwillingness of the Western nations to supply China with industrial credits during this period, the Soviet decision to sharply reduce machinery exports found the Chinese economy in a particularly vulnerable condition.

The Chinese economy was also vulnerable to the cessation of Soviet technical assistance that accompanied the curtailment of exports in 1960. Soviet provision of technical assistance to the Chinese had been of major importance in her industrialization up to 1960. In a country with so few engineers and technicians of its own at the time of the communist take-over, such technical aid was as important if not more important than capital equipment deliveries. In 1952, the Russians began to help build a Chinese technical intelligentsia by agreeing to grant Chinese students half-scholarships for study and training in the USSR.[84] According to the Russians, by 1962 "more than 11,000 students and higher degree candidates graduated from Soviet higher educational institutions." In addition, "some 10,000 Chinese engineers, technicians and skilled workers and about 1,000 scientists underwent instruction, scientific training and practice in the USSR."[85] In 1954, China and Russia set up a joint commission for scientific and technical collaboration, and in 1956 Communist China joined CMEA as an "observer." It was also in 1956 that Chinese scientists entered the Soviet bloc institute for nuclear research at Dubna.[86]

Soviet technicians working in China also played a major role in training the Chinese, and the Chinese Communists themselves stated in 1964, four years after Khrushchev had abruptly pulled the technicians out of China, that: "The overwhelming majority of them (the specialists) were hard-working and helpful to China's socialist construction. We have always highly appreciated their conscientious work and still miss them to this day."[87] Between 1950 and 1960, the Soviet Union supplied China with some 10,000 technicians.[88] In addition, the Russians supplied during this period 1,250 kinds of blueprints for factories, shops, and enterprises and 4,000 working drawings for machinery.[89] Although a number of Chinese had been trained by 1959, the role of the Soviet technicians in assisting the development of the Chinese economy was still very important. A description of the scope of the activity of the Russian technical assistance was given in a June, 1959, *Vneshniaia Torgovlia* article by Chang Wa-doon, the trade representative of the Chinese Embassy in the USSR:

> In the process of building enterprises, the Soviet Union gives us many-sided technical aid including: collection of initial data, research work, selection of construction sites, construction, supply of equipment, installation and adjustment of equipment, training of cadres, supply of technical drafts and materials, and mastering production of the final product.[90]

In the area of commodity vulnerability, China was, as stated above, most vulnerable to curtailment of Soviet machinery and equipment exports, as these composed approximately 50 per cent of its imports from the USSR in 1958 and 1959.[91] Next in importance were Soviet petroleum exports which accounted for 12 per cent of Soviet exports to China in 1958 and 9 per cent in 1959.[92] Soviet deliveries of petroleum products comprised 85 per cent of Chinese imports of these commodities in 1958 and almost 100 per cent in 1959.[93] Soviet awareness of this Chinese vulnerability was shown in the article on Sino-Soviet economic cooperation in the May, 1958, issue of *Vneshniaia Torgovlia* by N. Shiriaev:

> In connection with the fact that in old China there were no geological surveys or searches, and the extraction of oil was in embryo, the oil industry of Communist China has made significant progress, although it is not yet able to completely satisfy the growing demand of the economy for petroleum products. However, *under present conditions,* this is not an obstacle to the rapid development and growth of the industrial and agricultural production of the state

because China completely fills this shortage with imports of petroleum products [emphasis added].[94]

Chinese Minister of Foreign Trade Yeh Chi-chang summed up China's economic dependence on the USSR in an article in the September, 1959, issue of the Chinese foreign trade magazine *Foreign Trade of the People's Republic of China*:

> Through the channel of trade we have obtained large amounts of economic aid from the fraternal socialist countries, particularly the USSR. The goods imported from these countries are all essential to the economic construction of China, or to her peoples living with the overwhelmingly greater part consisting of machinery and equipment so very useful to the development of her industrial and agricultural production, scientific and technological research and transportation. Of these, complete sets of plant equipment supplied us for some of our large industrial projects by the Soviet Union and the socialist countries of Eastern Europe are the important items.[95]

Although Soviet exports to China played a major role in Chinese economic development, the benefits accruing to the Soviet economy from large-scale trade with China should also not be underestimated. China sent the USSR a number of valuable mineral products such as lithium concentrates, beryllium concentrates, wolfram concentrates, piezoelectric quartz, mercury, molybdenum concentrates, and tin.[96] Although these minerals averaged only approximately 10 per cent of China's annual exports to the USSR in 1958 and 8 per cent in 1959, they were nonetheless quite important.[97] Tungsten and molybdenum, for example, were embargoed by the West, and Russia obtained all of its tin imports from China.[98]

Of greather weight in Chinese exports to the USSR were food and consumer goods, particularly textiles, and building materials. Some Western specialists have argued that in agreeing to accept these goods, which were not of major importance to the Soviet economy, the Russians may have actually subsidized the Chinese.[99] This, however, does not appear to be the case. A large part of Chinese trade with the USSR in these commodities went to the Soviet provinces bordering China to the north and east. These provinces have traditionally had difficulty feeding themselves, and although certain mining and large-scale machine-building enterprises are located in these regions, light industry is far less developed than it is in Western Russia. Although no data is available on the exact amounts of Chinese trade with the bordering Russian provinces in such commodities as food, consumer goods, and building materials, the Soviet press has repeatedly stated that these were the commodities in which the best future lay for an expansion of Sino-Soviet trade. Sladkovskii, in his February, 1957, article in *Vneshniaia Torgovlia* wrote:

> It is a significant interest of the USSR to be assured of many types of agricultural raw materials and several types of finished industrial

goods for our Far East, Sakhalin, Kamchatka, and Northern Littoral.[100]

An editorial in the March, 1958, *Vneshniaia Torgovlia* stated:

The coal, cement, and pig iron supplied the USSR by China assures the needs of the Far Eastern sections of our country. For the satisfaction of the needs of our population, particularly in the Far East, the USSR purchases from China in large quantities citrus fruits, apples and a number of foodstuffs.[101]

Considerable transportation costs were saved by importing these goods from China instead of shipping them thousands of miles from the more agriculturally and industrially developed areas of European Russia.

For these reasons, Soviet trade with China was of considerably greater importance to the Soviet economy than trade with Albania or Yugoslavia had been, both in volume and in commodities imported. This may have been one of the reasons for the more gradual enactment of Soviet economic pressure against China than against the other two countries, a development to be studied in the following section.

SOVIET ECONOMIC PRESSURE AGAINST CHINA DURING THE KHRUSHCHEV PERIOD

Soviet economic pressure against China during the Khrushchev era was not restricted to the withdrawal of specialists and the gradual curtailment of trade. Other Soviet policies have included a sharp increase in trade and economic assistance to India—China's main Asian enemy—and a curtailment of economic assistance and military aid to North Korea, which was China's main Asian ally in the Sino-Soviet conflict. Each of these policies will be discussed in this section along with an examination of the Chinese response to the various forms of Soviet economic pressure.

As late as March, 1960, the USSR was apparently still willing to increase trade with China. On March 29, a trade protocol was signed calling for a 10 per cent increase in trade between the two nations for 1960.[102] One month later, however, an event occurred that according to the Russians marked the turning point in Sino-Soviet relations. This was the major polemical attack launched by the Chinese against the USSR in a series of articles issued in commemoration of Lenin's birthday. In these articles, the Chinese strongly condemned the Russian position on peaceful coexistence and clearly implied that the Russians had strayed from the true path of Leninism. The Chinese continued their attacks during the World Federation of Trade Unions meeting in early June in Peking, but Khrushchev had his revenge several weeks later at the Bucharest Conference where, in the words of the Chinese, he launched a "dastardly attack on the CPC." Following the conference, Khrushchev began to exert economic pressure to augment his ideological position. The Chinese have described the situation in these terms:

> Immediately after the Bucharest Conference (where Khrushchev launched a dastardly attack on the CPC) the Russians brought more pressure to bear on China by taking a series of steps to extend the ideological differences between the Chinese and Soviet Parties to the sphere of state relations. . . .
>
> Moscow withdrew 1,390 experts, tore up 343 contracts and supplementary provisions concerning experts and annulled 257 items of scientific and technical cooperation. After that they heavily slashed the supplying of whole sets of equipment and crucial parts of installations. This caused heavy losses to China's work of construction and dislocated its original plan for the development of the national economy, greatly aggravating our difficulties. . . .
>
> Apparently the leaders of the CPSU imagined that once they waved their baton, gathered a group of hatchet men to make a converging assault and applied immense political and economic pressure they could force the Chinese Communist Party to abandon its Marxist-Leninist and proletarian stand and submit to their revisionist and great power behests.[103]

Khrushchev's move, coming at a time of severe economic crisis in China, was a naked use of Soviet economic power to coerce the dissident Camp member into obedience. With the Soviet technicians withdrawn, the Chinese were hard put to cover their own factories and plants; yet at the same time they were challenged to take the place of Russian specialists who had begun to leave Albania as well.

Almost four years after the specialists were withdrawn, the Chinese Communists revealed the vital role they played in the industrialization of China. In an open letter to the CPSU in which Soviet economic pressure was bitterly attacked, the Chinese gave the following information:

> You were well aware that the Soviet experts were posted in over 250 enterprises and establishments in the economic field and the fields of national defense, culture, education and scientific research, and that they were undertaking important tasks involving technical design, the construction of projects, the installation of equipment, trial production and scientific research. As a result of your peremptory orders to the Soviet experts to discontinue their work and return to the Soviet Union, many of our country's important scientific research projects had to stop halfway, some of the construction projects in progress had to be suspended, and some of the factories and mines which were conducting trial production could not go into production according to schedule. *Your perfidious action disrupted China's original national economic plan and inflicted enormous losses upon China's socialist construction.*

You were going completely against Communist ethics when you took advantage of China's serious natural disasters to adopt these grave measures.

Your action fully demonstrates that you violate the principle of mutual assistance between socialist countries and *use the sending of experts as an instrument for exerting political pressure on fraternal countries, butting into their internal affairs* and impeding and sabotaging their socialist construction [emphasis added].[104]

The Russians gave a somewhat less credible reason for withdrawing their specialists. Not only had the specialists' advice gone unheeded, claimed the Russians, but beginning in 1960 the Chinese had even attempted to subvert them:

Beginning in the spring of 1960 the Chinese authorities began to "work on" the Soviet specialists trying to turn them against the CPSU Central Committee and the USSR government; this evoked the legitimate indignation of our people.

The USSR government repeatedly called the attention of the Chinese authorities to all these disturbing instances and insistently requested that they create normal conditions for the work of the Soviet specialists. But in answer the Chinese authorities only adopted an even more hostile and insulting attitude toward our workers, looking down on them as "conservatives" and began to defame Soviet experience and technology in every way. Surveillance of Soviet people increased, and searches of their personal belongings and so on became more frequent. Under such conditions, the recall of our specialists was the only solution.[105]

Soon after the withdrawal of the specialists, the Russians openly warned China of further retribution if she persisted in her ideological attacks against the USSR.

In an article in *Sovetskii Flot* on August 9, S. Titarenko, a candidate of the Historical Sciences, stated:

Under present conditions it is impossible to imagine the victory of socialism in a country without close ties with the mighty Soviet Union and all the Socialist states, and without the brotherly help of these states. In 1956 counter-revolutionary revolt in Hungary revealed with particular poignancy how dangerous the situation of the socialist countries would be but for the fact that the attempts of imperialist reaction encounter the common rebuff of the USSR and the entire Socialist camp.[106]

One week later, he mentioned the Chinese by name in a similar warning in the now famous article in *Sovetskaia Latvia*:

Could one imagine the successful construction of socialism going on in present day conditions even in so great a country as, let us say China, if that country were in a state of isolation and could not rely on the collaboration and aid of all the other socialist countries? While being subjected to an economic blockade by the capitalist countries such a country would be subjected simultaneously to military blows from the outside. It would experience the greatest difficulties even if it succeeded in withstanding the furious attacks of the enemy.[107]

The Russians apparently did not wait too long to carry out their threat. The official Soviet trade statistics reveal a drop in Sino-Soviet trade for 1960 (see Table 8), particularly in locomotives although the Russians actually increased deliveries of such important commodities as steel plate and bulldozers. The precipitous drop in trade was not to occur until 1961 when, after the Conference of the Eighty-One Communist Parties, the Russians severely slashed their exports to China. At that Conference, both China and Russia openly lobbied for support among the numerous communist parties, and the Chinese delegation, whose main spokesman was Teng Hsiao-p'ing, delivered a series of biting attacks against the Russians. Included among the Soviet policies Teng denounced were the low level of Russia's aid to China and CMEA's proposal for a division of labor among the communist states.[108]

Mid-way through the Conference, Chen Yi in an interview with Japanese journalists both denigrated Russian aid and stated that China was not afraid to stand alone:

I take exception to the view that without Soviet aid China would not have developed to the present stage. Our rehabilitation and construction depend on our own efforts. Of course we received aid from the USSR, East Europe, Vietnam and Korea. Soviet aid was especially great. Aid is not a cure-all, however. When a man is alive, a drug may prove effective, but once he is dead, no doctor can do anything for him. Soviet aid thus extended to China is roughly equivalent to China's aid extended to Southeast Asian nations.[109]

Nonetheless, despite the bitter debate at the Conference, China eventually signed the Moscow Declaration which, although it was later to be subject to different interpretations, primarily backed the Soviet ideological position. Edward Crankshaw has contended that the Chinese agreed to sign the Declaration in return for a Russian promise to send their technicians back to China.[110] A related explanation for China's action may stem from the fact that the Chinese economy was in such a state of chaos in late 1960 due both to the "Great Leap" and poor weather conditions that the Chinese requested some respite in repaying the Soviet credits that had become due. In any case, in February, 1961, a Russian economic mission went to Peking; and on April 7, 1961, a number of economic agreements were finally worked out. The primary

TABLE 8

Soviet Commodity Exports to China, 1959-68
(selected commodities in millions of new rubles; one ruble = 1.11 U.S. dollars)

	1959	1960	1961	1962	1963	1964	1965	1966	1967	1968
Machinery and Equipment	537.768	453.527	97.281	24.594	37.969	51.944	69.296	77.596	22.178	13.409
Complete Plants	359.785	336.459	71.018	7.960	13.113	11.186	3.513	.230	1.500	.277
Oil Products (thousand met. tons)										
crude oil	2,412	2,395	2,928	1,856	1,408	504	38	40	6.9	7.6[a]
benzine (gasoline)	635	567	0	0	0	0	0	0	0	---
kerosine	1,256	1,055	1,325	764	455	269	32	28	3.9	---
diesel fuel	380	386	512	488	476	139	2	4	0.4	---
	556	709	841	378	333	79	4	7	1.9	---
Rolled Steel Products	26.450	33.427	16.645	15.031	15.036	12.984	22.086	8.142	5.127	5.037
steel plate	8.025	10.840	4.704	3.150	3.110	4.771	6.837	1.770	.630	.025
stainless steel plate	2.209	4.780	1.870	1.025	1.650	2.263	3.383	1.643	.023	—[b]
Pipes	12.961	12.260	7.728	6.213	6.501	3.641	5.909	3.484	1.759	2.591
oil pipes	9.523	8.042	4.625	3.016	3.330	1.334	1.496	.969	.092	.776
Excavators and Road-Building Equipment	3.616	5.064	.419	.002	.298	.494	6.110	6.509	.295	.108
excavators (number)	49	150	15	0	9	5	30	68	5	0
bulldozers (number)	82	107	7	0	9	11	222	194	2	0

	1959	1960	1961	1962	1963	1964	1965	1966	1967	1968
Pump-Compressor Equipment	4.228	4.395	1.042	.111	.032	.127	1.327	.573	.021	.143
pumps (number)	718	602	159	29	0	5	23	118	3	7
compressors (number)	191	204	13	10	0	0	238	95	0	0
Tractors (number)	941	1,579	33	62	979	688	993	1,192	0	0
Rolling Stock	67.861	4.889	.317	0	.042	.041	.012	.008	.003	—b
locomotives (number)	950	50	0	0	0	0	0	0	0	—
Heavy Trucks (number)	8,046	13,666	710	1,619	1,487	788	2,406	3,910	54	108
Electrical Equipment	5.687	6.316	1.869	.471	.438	.300	1.357	.998	.404	.159
Total Soviet Exports	859.100	735.400	330.600	210.100	168.500	121.800	172.500	157.800	45.300	53.400

aThis category not broken into its component parts in data issued for 1968.

bThis category not listed in statistics for 1968.

Sources:

1959, 1960: *Vneshniaia Torgovlia SSSR za 1960* (Moscow: Vneshtorgizdat, 1961), pp. 162-67.
1961: *Vneshniaia Torgovlia SSSR za 1961* (Moscow: Vneshtorgizdat, 1962), pp. 179-85.
1962, 1963: *Vneshniaia Torgovlia SSSR za 1963* (Moscow: Vneshtorgizdat, 1964), pp. 205-9.
1964, 1965: *Vneshniaia Torgovlia SSSR za 1965* (Moscow: Mezhdunarodnye Otnosheniia, 1966), pp. 252-57.
1966, 1967: *Vneshniaia Torgovlia SSSR za 1967* (Moscow: Mezhdunarodnye Otnosheniia, 1968), pp. 243-48.
1968: *Vneshniaia Torgovlia SSSR za 1968* (Moscow: Mezhdunarodnye Otnosheniia, 1969), pp. 231-34.

Russian concession was their agreement to a five-year moratorium on the $320 million the Chinese owed the USSR. The debt was to be repaid in four installments: $9 million in 1962, $55 million in 1963, $128 million in 1964, and $128 million in 1965.[111]

The Russians published this agreement with some glee in the May, 1961, issue of *Vneshniaia Torgovlia* which repeatedly told its readers that the USSR had given China the debt moratorium because the Chinese were unable to pay their debts.[112] In a two-page article describing the agreements, V. Kuplenski reiterated this fact no less than three times. In one place, he bluntly stated:

> As a result of temporary agricultural difficulties which arose, as already stated above, because of natural calamities, the *Chinese foreign trade organizations were not able to assure the fulfillment of their obligations in supplying the Soviet Union in 1960 with agricultural and certain other goods.* This led to the formation of a debt on the part of the Chinese to the USSR in trade operations in 1960 for the sum of 288 million rubles [emphasis added].[113]

One reason for the rather large spread given to the Chinese moratorium announcement might have been a Russian attempt to dissuade Western nations from entering into close economic relations with Peking, whom the Russians hoped to portray as a poor credit risk. If this was indeed the Soviet intention, it proved to be unsuccessful, and, as will be shown later, Chinese trade with the West and Japan began to rise as her trade with Russia and the East European communist states declined.

In addition to signing the debt repayment agreement, the two nations also signed a trade agreement for 1961. The Chinese leaders had now shifted their priorities to concentrate on agricultural production and for that reason were probably not interested in purchasing as much industrial equipment as before, but available evidence indicates that the USSR was unwilling to supply China with even the kinds of goods the Chinese leaders wanted.* In describing the trade negotiations, Kuplenski stated:

> In the course of these (trade) negotiations, the Soviet and Chinese trade delegations basically agreed on the list of Chinese goods and *exchanged opinions on the list of Soviet goods* planned to be sent in 1961 [emphasis added].[114]

Trade statistics for the year 1961 indicate the severe cut in Soviet exports (see Table 8). Total Soviet exports dropped from $817 million in 1960 to $367 million in 1961—a decline of no less than 55 per cent. Soviet machine and

---

*It is difficult to measure with any degree of exactitude the effect of the withdrawal of Soviet technicians or the subsequent Soviet curtailment of trade on China's economy. The dislocations caused by the failure of the "Great Leap Forward" as well as the poor weather of 1959 and 1960 also played a role in the Chinese decision to emphasize agricultural development, particularly the manufacture of fertilizer.

equipment exports were cut by 79 per cent, complete plant equipment by 79 per cent, and steel plate by 56 per cent. In addition, exports of Soviet tractors were reduced from 1,579 in 1960 to only 33 in 1961—a figure not destined to significantly help Chinese agricultural production. Other major reductions included trucks (13,666 in 1960 to only 710 in 1961) and bulldozers (107 in 1960 to only 7 in 1961).

Interestingly enough, however, the Soviets did not capitalize on China's vulnerability in refined oil.[115] Although the Soviet Union sent no more crude oil in 1961, it actually increased deliveries of gasoline and diesel fuel. In addition, the USSR, which had been a net importer of grain from China before 1961, shipped the Chinese 100,000 tons each of wheat and rye[116] in that year. Soviet willingness to provide these goods indicates an attempt to maintain some trade links with China. Nonetheless, as the Russians were able to export some 7.1 million tons of grain in 1961 (wheat, oats, rye, and barley),[117] the limited amount provided to China that year must have seemed a mere pittance to the Chinese; they had to spend many millions of dollars in scarce foreign exchange in 1961 to acquire grain from capitalist countries. The fact that China also turned to England rather than the USSR to purchase aircraft in 1961 may well indicate a reluctance on the part of the USSR to supply China with this type of good.[118]

As relations between China and the USSR continued to deteriorate during 1962, so too did trade relations. Despite the recovery of the Chinese economy, there was another sharp drop (75 per cent) in Soviet supplies of machinery and equipment, and Soviet deliveries of complete plant equipment fell to 11 per cent of the 1961 figure. Soviet exports of electrical equipment, which had fallen 66 per cent in 1961, fell an additional 75 per cent in 1962. Gasoline exports now also began to drop (1,325,000 tons in 1961 to 764,000 in 1962) as did diesel fuel (841,000 tons in 1961 to 378,000 in 1962). In addition, deliveries of railroad rolling stock and road-building equipment came to a complete halt. The Chinese have characterized the Soviet unwillingness to sell them the goods they needed in these terms:

In pursuance of your policy of further imposing restrictions on and discriminating against China in the economic and commercial fields, since 1960 you have deliberately placed obstacles in the way of economic and trade relations between our two countries and held up or refused supplies of important goods which China needs. You have insisted on providing large amounts of goods which we do not really need or which we do not need at all, while holding back or supplying very few of the goods which we need badly. *For several years you have used the trade between our countries as an instrument for bringing political pressure to bear on China.* How could this avoid cutting down the volume of Sino-Soviet trade? [emphasis added].[119]

In apparent retaliation for the cut in Soviet deliveries, the Chinese ordered the closing of the Soviet consulates in Shanghai, Darien, Harbin, Urumchi, and Inim in September, 1962.

Trade continued to decline in 1963 as a result of the rapid deterioration of Sino-Soviet relations following the Cuban missile crisis and the Chinese invasion of India. Despite a meeting between Chinese and Soviet representatives in July where, according to a Soviet report, the Russians offered to return some technicians to China, Soviet exports dropped to $180 million.[120] Gasoline exports continued their decline to 455,000 tons and diesel fuel to 333,000 tons.

On September 7, 1963, there was a serious incident at the Naushki border railway station in which Chinese students on their way to the Soviet Union vociferously protested the removal of anti-Soviet propaganda by Russian border guards.[121] Several weeks later, the Soviet government issued a statement attacking the Chinese leaders for their stand on the partial nuclear test ban treaty, for their invasion of India, and for such "dangerous experiments" as the Communes and the "Great Leap Forward." The Soviet statement went on to attribute the "serious economic difficulties" plaguing China to the mistakes of the Chinese leadership and then pointedly remarked:

> It is not our fault that the leaders of the Peoples Republic of China have curtailed economic cooperation with the Soviet Union and thereby deprived the Chinese people of a chance to benefit from the Soviet Union's unselfish help.[122]

The Russians also threatened China with loss of the Soviet shield:

> The Chinese leaders now say cynically in their statement of September 1: "Well, Soviet leaders, protect us with your nuclear weapons, but we shall still criticize you."
>   In this connection, one cannot but recall the old Russian proverb: "Don't foul the well; you may need the water."[123]

In the middle of October, however, there was an apparent change in Soviet policy toward China. Khrushchev, perhaps realizing that he would not be able to secure a sufficiently strong majority at a proposed international communist conference either to force the Chinese to capitulate or else to excommunicate them from the international communist movement, decided to take a more conciliatory position. William Griffith contends that it was probably for this reason that Khrushchev called for a cessation of Sino-Soviet polemics on October 25, 1963.[124] An indication of the Soviet desire to improve relations had come twelve days earlier when a Sino-Soviet railway agreement was signed which was probably aimed at avoiding a repetition of railway border incidents such as the one that occurred at the Naushki station.[125]

Khrushchev followed up the railway agreement in late November, 1963, in a letter to Mao Tse-tung and the Chinese Communist Central Committee in which he proposed a major improvement in Sino-Soviet relations. After once again calling for a cessation of polemics, the Soviet leader offered an economic incentive to the Chinese:

Now that the CPSU and the CCP, as well as other fraternal Parties, have stated their views on the questions in dispute, it would be correct not to concentrate attention on the problems on which there are differences between us but to let them wait until the heat of passion has cooled, to let time do its work. We are certain that life will demonstrate the correctness of the Marxist-Leninist line. At the same time, we could develop our cooperation in those spheres where favourable possibilities exist. Such cooperation is in the interest not only of the Soviet Union and China but also of all the peoples of the socialist community. . . .

Particularly great possibilities exist for the strengthening of ties between the People's Republic of China and the USSR in the economic field and in the fields of scientific-technical co-operation and culture. In this letter, we would like to make a series of practical proposals, the realization of which could serve the cause of strengthening friendship between our countries. . . .

Specifically, it would be possible to start in the immediate future to draw up jointly agreed preliminary plans for the exchange of goods between the CPR and the Soviet Union. In the course of the next few years the USSR could increase its export to China of goods in which you are interested, and the import of goods from China into the USSR, which would be in the interest both of our economy and of yours.

As is known, the Protocol of May 13, 1962 concluded by the governments of our two countries provides for the renewal next year of negotiations concerning the delivery to the People's Republic of China of whole sets of equipment the manufacture of which was postponed for two years at the request of the Chinese side. If your side shows interest, it would be possible in our view to come to an understanding on the broadening of technical aid to the CPR in the building of industrial enterprises and specifically to discuss the possibility of aid in the development of the petroleum industry and the building of enterprises in the mining and other industries on terms beneficial to both our countries.

Once again we affirm our readiness to send Soviet specialists to the People's Republic of China should you consider it necessary. . . .

We understand, of course, that each nation builds socialism and communism by relying mainly on its own forces because no one except the people of a given country will build socialism there. But it is also evident that co-operation among socialist countries facilitates and accelerates the construction of socialism by each nation. The restoration and strengthening of the economic co-operation between our countries will help not only to accelerate the growth of the national economies of the USSR and China and the economy of the entire socialist system, but also to create favourable conditions for normalizing relations in other fields [emphasis added].[126]

Part of the Soviet offer may have been tied to a quid pro quo whereby the Chinese would end their polemics over the border areas acquired by the Czars from China. Khrushchev followed up his offer of renewed economic assistance with these words:

> Experience shows that the development of trading, economic and other ties improves the atmosphere in mutual relations and helps to straighten out other problems on which the relations between our countries depend. And such problems unfortunately do exist and demand solution.
>
> You will probably agree that the situation which has arisen in recent years along different sections of the Soviet-Chinese border cannot be regarded as normal. The Soviet government has already proposed that friendly consultations take place to define accurately the boundary in different sections, considering that this will result in the removal of the causes of the present misunderstanding. . . .
>
> Statements have recently been made in China concerning the aggressive policy of the Czarist government and the unjust treaties imposed upon China. Naturally, we will not defend the Russian Czars who permitted arbitrariness in laying down the state boundaries with neighboring countries. We are convinced that you, too, do not intend to defend the Chinese emperors who by force of arms seized not a few territories belonging to others.[127]

There may, however, have been another reason for this striking change in Khrushchev's policy. By August, 1963, the Chinese economy had recovered sufficiently for the Chinese to place a number of orders for complete plants in the West. In addition, China's trade with the West had risen rapidly as its trade with the USSR and Soviet bloc countries had declined. (In 1963, China's trade with non-communist countries was more than 50 per cent of her total trade whereas in 1959 it had been only 30 per cent.[128]) Although Chinese purchases of industrial equipment from the West (including Japan) by 1963 did not match the level of its purchases from the USSR in the late 1950's,[129] the potential for a rapid increase appeared to be present, particularly with Japan.[130]

China's rapid increase in trade with the West is yet another example of the limitation inherent in the Soviet Union's policy of curtailing trade as a means of economic pressure—the target nation can usually turn somewhere else for the necessary supplies. Perhaps the Russians felt that because of the virulent nature of Chinese propaganda against "Imperialism" and the abortive Chinese attempt at economic warfare against Japan in the 1958-60 period, the industrialized capitalist nations would hesitate to do business with China. But Western businessmen (and their governments—with the notable exception of the United States) were swayed neither by ideological polemics nor by the Russian attempt of 1961 to portray China as a poor credit risk. Just as in 1949 China "leaned to one side" not only in her political but also in her economic relations, she now began to swing back the other way because of the increasingly bitter Sino-Soviet conflict. In 1964, an article in the *Peking Review* attempted to give ideological justification for China's increase in trade with such capitalist nations as Canada, France, and Australia:

> The U.S. imperialist attempt to seize the intermediate zone is bound to run up against the opposition of all the peoples and countries in that region. This vast intermediate zone is composed of two parts. One part consists of the independent countries and those striving for independence in Asia, Africa, and Latin America; it may be called the first intermediate zone.
>
> The second part consists of the whole of Western Europe, Oceania, Canada and the other capitalist countries; it may be called the second intermediate zone. Countries in this second intermediate zone have a dual character. While their rulers are exploiters and oppressors, these countries themselves are subjected to U.S. control, interference and bullying. They therefore try their best to free themselves from U.S. control. In this regard, they have *something in common with the socialist countries and the peoples of various countries.* By making itself anatagonistic to the whole world, U.S. imperialism inevitably finds itself tightly encircled [emphasis added].[131]

Given Peking's economic turn to the West (and its potential political turn as well), Khrushchev may have decided to make his offer of renewed technical aid and increased trade to arrest this development. The Chinese answer to Khrushchev's offer, however, was contemptuous in tone:

> Now you (the Soviets) have again suggested sending experts to China. To be frank, the Chinese people cannot trust you. They have just healed the wounds caused by your withdrawal of experts. . . .
>
> We would like to say in passing that, basing ourselves on the internationalist principle of mutual assistance among countries in the socialist camp, we are very much concerned about the present economic situation in the Soviet Union. If you should feel the need for the help of Chinese experts in certain fields, we would be glad to send them.[132]

Nonetheless, despite the negative Chinese response, Khrushchev pushed ahead with this policy. Although total Soviet exports declined in 1964, particularly in gasoline and diesel fuel, Soviet shipments of machinery and equipment increased, as did shipments of steel plate and stainless steel plate. Soviet propaganda put forth the thesis that the USSR had given large amounts of aid to China in the past and could be expected to do so in the future if the Chinese would change their policies. A Soviet broadcast in Mandarin to China on October 2, 1964 (two weeks before Khrushchev was toppled), echoes this theme:

> Since the founding of the CPR, the economic and cultural relations between China and the Soviet Union and other fraternal countries

have developed extensively. Cooperation between China and the Soviet Union and Soviet aid to China have been an important factor in building socialism in China. The Soviet Union has sent 8,500 experts to China during 1950 to 1960 rendering assistance in designing, building, installing, and adjusting equipment as well as technical assistance in industrial production. About 1,500 experts have been sent from the Soviet Union to assist China in developing science, higher education, health protection, and culture. Nearly 10,000 Chinese engineers, technicians, and skilled workers and 1,000 scientists have studied, received academic training, or practiced in the Soviet Union between 1951 and 1962. During this period, 11,000 Chinese college students and postgraduates have graduated from Soviet institutions of higher learning.

Through supplying equipment and offering technical assistance, the Soviet Union has taken part in constructing all of the large enterprises in China. More than 200 enterprises have been built and commissioned with Soviet assistance. . . .

With the assistance of the GDR, Poland, Czechoslovakia, Rumania, and Bulgaria nearly 100 industrial projects have been built in China. Meanwhile, these countries have obtained from China many goods necessary for their national economy, such as mineral ores, minerals, and agricultural products. The overall aid from the Soviet Union and other fraternal countries has intensified the Chinese people's efforts to carry out social reform, eliminate economic and technical backwardness, and pushed their own country to march forward along a path of building socialism. *Such friendly support is an expression of loyalty to proletarian internationalism by the Soviet Union and other fraternal countries* [emphasis added] .[133]

The increased trade between China and Russia's Eastern European allies (East Germany, Poland, Czechoslovakia, Bulgaria, and Hungary) in 1964 seems to have been a reflection of Khrushchev's changed policy (see Table 9). Although it was actually Rumania that took the lead in increasing trade with China in 1963, the other nations followed suit in 1964. The Rumanian leaders utilized the increased leverage given them by the Sino-Soviet conflict to improve their own position and sabotage Khrushchev's plan for a supra-national planning body in CMEA which was to control the economies of the Eastern European countries. China, for her own reasons, strongly supported the Rumanians in their opposition to the planning body.[134]

In December, 1962, when Sino-Soviet relations had hit a new low following the Cuban missile crisis and the Chinese invasion of India, a Chinese trade delegation went to Bucharest. After lengthy discussions, the two nations announced a 10 per cent increase in trade for 1963. As the Rumanians shifted away from the Russian position in the Sino-Soviet conflict toward a more neutral stance, the Chinese increased their open support for Rumania in her struggle with CMEA—a conflict from which the Rumanians ultimately emerged victorious. But the increase in Sino-Rumanian trade was of more than just

TABLE 9

China's Trade with Eastern Europe, 1962-65
(in millions of U.S. dollars)

	Chinese Exports				Chinese Imports			
	1962	1963	1964	1965	1962	1963	1964	1965
Rumania	10.5	14.1	18.0	22	2.2	13.8	15.9	27
Albania	42.1	41.7	61.7	70	11.7	23.4	23.9	25
Bulgaria	3.2	2.3	1.1	1	3.3	1.3	1.5	1
Czechoslovakia	25.6	29.0	20.6	13	11.9	9.3	9.3	19
East Germany	32.0	24.7	19.5	25	21.9	10.4	15.6	26
Hungary	11.0	20.0	14.9	11	11.9	3.3	4.3	15
Poland	22.7	24.8	25.0	25	15.1	11.2	15.0	19
Total	147.1	156.6	160.8	167	78.0	72.7	85.5	132

Source: Robert L. Price, "International Trade of Communist China 1950-65," *An Economic Profile of Mainland China*, Vol. II (Washington, D.C.: U.S. Government Printing Office, 1967), p. 596.

symbolic value. Rumania began to ship to China some of the very goods the Russians had begun to embargo. Included among the Rumanian exports were refined oil (including gasoline, aviation fuel, and diesel oil), oil-drilling rigs, and petroleum-processing installations.[135]

The emulation of the Rumanian policy by Khrushchev's Eastern European allies appears to have been part of his new policy to maintain some contacts with the Chinese lest they become completely dependent on the West. This policy was similar to that employed toward Albania, where trade contacts were maintained by the Soviet Union's allies. In the case of China, it seems that Khrushchev, having finally realized that his policy of economic pressure had not forced that nation to renounce its "anti-Soviet" position, wished to prevent relations between China and Soviet bloc countries from being completely destroyed. It may well be that Khrushchev also hoped for a change in Chinese leadership that would lead to improved relations with the USSR. By maintaining contacts on the economic level, Khrushchev hoped to facilitate this process when such change occurred. Although it has been suggested that the increase in Eastern European trade with China was an initiative taken by the East Europeans themselves,[136] it is extremely doubtful whether such nations as East Germany and Czechoslovakia (in 1964) would have taken such an independent step without at least the tacit approval of Moscow.

Nonetheless, Russia's East European allies did have a strong economic interest in increasing trade with China. Almost all had been hurt by the curtailment of trade with China in the early 1960's. Although the Soviet Union was far less dependent on trade with China than China was on trade with the Soviet Union, the opposite was the case in respect to Chinese trade with Eastern Europe. Czechoslovakia and East Germany were particularly hard hit by the 1960 trade curtailment. Until 1960, approximately 15 per cent of Czechoslovakia's engineering exports were sold to China, and the Czechs had planned a large increase in their sales during the 1961-65 period.[137] The drop in sales to China was a severe blow to the Czechoslovak engineering industry, which found it very difficult to sell the equipment built for Chinese specifications on the world market.[138] In addition, the corresponding reduction in China's agricultural exports to Czechoslovakia was a damaging blow to her food supply.[139] The East Germans faced similar problems. Due to the rapid decline in Sino-German trade, they were deprived of their major source of soybeans for margerine.[140]

The resurgence of trade between China and Eastern Europe in 1964 included the sale of complete plants to the Chinese who now began to get them from communist as well as non-communist sources. By the end of 1966, Hungary had sold China two complete stainless steel tube plants, Poland a complete mining plant, and Bulgaria, perhaps Russia's closest ally, no less than 28 hydroelectric power stations.[141] Thus although Soviet trade with China diminished, Soviet bloc trade gradually increased and, despite increasingly poor political relations, economic relations were maintained, and the Chinese did not become entirely dependent on trade with the West.

In addition to the withdrawal of technicians and the reduction of trade with China, Khrushchev pursued two other policies of economic pressure against the Chinese. The first involved a sharp increase both in trade and in economic assistance to India, China's main competitor and enemy in Asia. The other policy involved a cessation of economic and military assistance to North Korea, China's closest Asian ally. Both policies will be examined in order to complete the description of Soviet economic pressure against China during the Khrushchev era.*

Mention has already been made of the effect of cordial Soviet-Indian relations on Sino-Soviet relations. The rapid rise in Soviet aid to India could only have angered the Chinese who had received less than half the non-military loans given to India by 1961. Of particular irritation to the Chinese was the Soviet loan of $375 million to India on September 12, 1959, for the construction and expansion of a number of industrial establishments. Not only was the loan larger than any the Chinese had received (the Chinese had also obtained *no* developmental loans since 1954), but it came at the same time as the USSR's "neutral" stand on the Sino-Indian border incident. An article in *Red Flag* summed up China's view on Soviet aid to India:

> As for their aid to India, here Soviet ulterior motives are especially clear. India tops the list of newly independent countries to which the Soviet Union gives economic aid. This aid is obviously intended to encourage the Nehru government in its policies directed against Communism, against the people and against the Socialist countries (particularly China). Even the American Imperialists have stated that such Soviet aid is "very much to our (U.S.) interests."[142]

The very nature of Soviet aid to India, as well as its magnitude, indicates that the Soviet Union under Khrushchev was trying to build up Indian military power to help balance the Chinese in Asia. As early as November, 1960, the Soviets agreed to supply India with 12 heavy transport planes which the Indians could pay for in rupees. In 1961, the Indians secured a number of helicopters from Russia, but most important of all, in August, 1962, the Russians agreed to construct in India a jet engine factory with the capacity of producing Soviet MIG-21 jet engines, an installation the Chinese had never obtained. The Russians also agreed to supply India with MIG-21 aircraft, which have a clear superiority over the MIG-17 which were the most modern aircraft the Chinese had obtained from the USSR.[143]

The Chinese reaction to the Soviet decision to equip India with a jet engine factory and send MIG-21 aircraft was delivered by the Albanians who acted as spokesmen for the Chinese in the early stages of Sino-Soviet polemics. In a *Zeri i Popullit* article of September 19, 1962, the Albanians stated:

> The N. S. Khrushchev group, while seeking to weaken the defensive might of the socialist countries—as, for example, in the case of the

---

*For a different viewpoint toward Khrushchev's strategy of economic pressure against China, see Peter J. Wiles, *Communist International Economics* (New York: Frederick A. Praeger, 1969), pp. 509-14.

People's Republic of Albania—has even gone so far as to sell Indian reactionary circles arms and airplanes which are in fact used to oppress the Communists and progressives and for armed provocations against the socialist countries.[144]

An examination of the Soviet-Indian trade statistics indicates a direct relationship between the drop in Sino-Soviet trade beginning in 1960 and the rise of Soviet-Indian trade, particularly in the area of machinery and equipment. Table 10 compares Soviet exports of machinery and equipment and complete plants to China and India from 1960 to 1964. In each of these years, Soviet machinery and equipment exports accounted for well over half of total Soviet exports to India. Soviet exports of diesel fuel were also of major significance to India, rising from 11,500 tons in 1960 to 350,400 tons in 1964.[145] Although Soviet exports were of considerable value to the Indians, it appears that Indian exports to the USSR were of less value to the Russians than previous Chinese exports had been. India's main exports to the Soviet Union over the 1960-64 period were tea (20 per cent), leather products (25 per cent), and tobacco (12 per cent).[146]

TABLE 10

Comparison of Soviet Machinery and
Complete Plant Exports to India and China, 1960-64
(in thousands of rubles)

Year	Soviet Machinery Exports		Soviet Complete Plant Exports	
	China	India	China	India
1960	453,527	22,742	336,459	16,343
1961	97,281	48,524	71,018	35,648
1962	24,594	69,925	7,960	58,262
1963	37,969	107,886	13,113	73,230
1964	51,944	163,697	11,186	119,403

Source: Vneshniaia Torgovlia SSSR 1918-1966 (Moscow: Mezhdunarodnye Otnosheniia, 1967), p. 209.

The statistics on total trade between India and the USSR from 1955 to 1964 (see Table 11) indicate the nature of Soviet subsidization of the trade relationship. The total Soviet trade subsidy for the 1955-64 period amounted to 298.5 million rubles ($331.3 million).

TABLE 11

Soviet-Indian Trade, 1955-64
(in millions of rubles)

Year	Soviet Exports	Indian Exports	Soviet Balance
1955	6.6	4.0	2.6
1956	36.4	16.5	19.9
1957	76.2	37.8	38.4
1958	117.0	45.8	71.2
1959	61.2	54.5	6.7
1960	42.4	61.6	−19.2
1961	85.9	60.2	25.7
1962	112.3	64.5	47.8
1963	119.7	85.3	34.4
1964	211.3	140.3	71.0

Source: Vneshiaia Torgovlia SSSR 1918-1966 (Moscow: Mezhdunarodnye Otnoshcniia, 1967), pp. 208-9.

In addition to increasing both trade and aid to India, Khrushchev followed a similar policy of improving economic relations with the other major Asian non-communist states. As can be seen from Table 12, Soviet exports to Indonesia tripled between 1960 and 1964. Even more important was Soviet bloc economic and military aid to Indonesia which totaled nearly $1 billion by 1965.[147] Soviet trade with Japan also increased sharply, rising from 123.9 million rubles in 1960 to 322 million rubles in 1964.[148] By increasing trade with all three major Asian non-communist states and by offering sizable amounts of aid to both India and Indonesia, Khrushchev was making a major effort to strengthen the Soviet position in Asia in order to outflank the Chinese. The Russian subsidization of the Mongolian economy (see Table 12), in return for which the Mongolian leaders dutifully echoed the Soviet line on all important issues including the Sino-Soviet conflict, was part of this policy, which the Chinese Communists have called "the revisionist attempt to encircle China."[149]

Soviet economic relations with Communist North Korea during the Khrushchev era were of a considerably different nature from its relations with either Communist Mongolia or neutral India. The Soviet-North Korean trade statistics (see Table 13) show a marked absence of Soviet developmental aid after 1959.[150] Indeed, in the 1955-64 period it was actually North Korea that shows a favorable balance of trade (1.5 million rubles over the ten-year period).

The reason for the Soviet unwillingness to grant North Korea developmental loans after 1959 stems from the North Korean position in the Sino-Soviet conflict.

TABLE 12

Soviet Trade with Selected Asian Nations, 1955-68
(in millions of rubles; one ruble = 1.11 U.S. dollars)

Country	1955	1960	1961	1962	1963	1964	1965	1966	1967	1968
MONGOLIA										
Total trade	157.9	125.3	135.6	167.9	149.1	178.5	169.8	198.3	223.8	222.3
Soviet exports	109.5	74.6	83.2	113.6	102.6	126.8	114.1	142.2	167.9	174.5
Soviet imports	48.4	50.7	52.4	54.3	46.5	51.7	55.7	56.1	55.9	47.8
NORTH KOREA										
Total trade	76.4	102.7	140.5	152.0	153.2	147.2	160.3	160.1	196.5	263.8
Soviet exports	39.7	35.5	69.3	72.6	73.9	74.6	80.8	77.0	99.3	155.0
Soviet imports	36.7	67.2	71.2	79.4	79.3	72.6	79.5	83.1	97.2	108.8
NORTH VIETNAM										
Total trade	0.3	42.8	60.3	76.4	82.8	74.2	94.9	84.2	151.7	159.4
Soviet exports	0.3	22.0	37.2	49.2	51.0	42.9	67.4	61.4	132.9	143.3
Soviet imports	0	20.8	23.1	27.2	31.8	31.3	27.5	22.8	18.8	16.1
JAPAN										
Total trade	3.6	123.9	161.6	232.9	260.3	322.1	326.0	417.0	466.8	518.6
Soviet exports	2.0	68.5	101.7	101.7	111.5	148.2	166.4	215.0	317.7	352.1
Soviet imports	1.6	55.4	59.9	131.2	148.8	173.9	159.6	202.0	149.1	166.5

Country	1955	1960	1961	1962	1963	1964	1965	1966	1967	1968
INDIA										
Total trade	10.6	104.0	146.1	176.8	285.0	351.6	362.9	346.0	308.8	329.6
Soviet exports	6.6	42.4	85.9	112.3	199.7	211.3	193.5	174.0	146.1	165.0
Soviet imports	4.0	61.6	60.2	64.5	85.3	140.3	169.4	172.0	162.7	164.6
INDONESIA										
Total trade	3.4	42.9	58.7	87.5	71.7	65.6	77.8	32.0	26.6	21.9
Soviet exports	0.1	14.6	28.2	52.7	44.9	42.4	49.0	4.3	4.7	4.7
Soviet imports	3.3	28.3	30.5	34.8	26.8	23.2	28.8	27.7	21.9	17.2

Sources:

1955-1966: *Vnesbniaia Torgovlia SSSR 1918-1966* (Moscow: Mezhdunarodnye Otnosheniia, 1967), pp. 66-68.

1967: *Vnesbniaia Torgovlia*, Vol. 48, No. 6 (June, 1968), p. 56.

1968: *Vnesbniaia Torgovlia*, Vol. 49, No. 7 (July, 1969), p. 57.

TABLE 13

Soviet-North Korean Trade, 1955-64
(in millions of rubles)

Year	Soviet Exports	North Korean Exports	Soviet Balance
1955	39.7	36.7	3.0
1956	48.4	46.1	2.3
1957	54.0	56.3	−2.3
1958	52.2	42.4	9.8
1959	73.6	46.4	27.2
1960	35.5	67.2	−31.7
1961	69.3	71.2	−1.9
1962	72.6	79.4	−6.8
1963	73.9	79.3	−5.4
1964	74.6	72.6	2.0

Source: *Vneshniaia Torgovlia SSSR 1918-1966* (Moscow: Mezhdunarodnye Otnosheniia, 1967), pp. 66-67.

The North Korean leaders, along with leaders of other communist states, made no secret of their desire to industrialize rapidly. In a discussion of North Korea's first five-year plan (1957-61), Radio Pyongyang stated:

Industrial output will increase more than 2.6 times during the five year plan period, and this includes output of the means of production to be increased more than 2.9 times and the output of consumer goods more than 2.2 times. . . . Industrialization of construction will be promoted in every possible way . . . and large capital construction in particular.[151]

Foreign trade was to be a major factor in the five-year plan, not only because North Korea needed machinery, but also because of its relatively limited resource base, particularly in coking coal, petroleum products, and synthetic rubber. North Korea also depended on foreign suppliers for the bulk of its cotton, wool, and sugar.[152] On this point, Radio Pyongyang stated:

Economic relations and technical cooperation with the Soviet Union and other socialist countries will be further strengthened and the international division of labor with these countries will be developed, and foreign trade with them will be further promoted.[153]

The Soviet Union had extended economic assistance to North Korea well before the start of the five-year plan. In 1953, at the end of the Korean War, the Soviet Union gave Korea a loan of $244.75 million for reconstruction. This aid included machinery, railroad equipment, fishing vessels, tractors, agricultural equipment, fertilizer, and consumer goods. The USSR also extended technical assistance in the form of trained cadres and technical documents.[154]

In August, 1956, the Russians gave North Korea another loan, this time of $74.93 million, for its five-year plan. By this agreement, the Soviet Union was to send machinery, equipment, rolled ferrous metals, cables, trucks, tractors, lumber, sugar, grain, and cotton thread.[155] The trade statistics for the years 1958 and 1959 indicate that the Soviet Union was indeed extending aid to North Korea, particularly in the area of machinery and equipment. It should be noted that at this time the North Koreans had nowhere else to turn for sophisticated machinery other than the USSR, Poland, East Germany, Hungary, or Czechoslovakia—all countries closely tied to the USSR. Whereas China has a Hong Kong to generate foreign exchange, not only does North Korea lack such an outlet, but its relations at that time with the nations of the West were so bad that it was unable to acquire any loans or long-term credits from them.[156]

North Korea's economic and political relations with the USSR began to deteriorate with the development of the Sino-Soviet conflict. Its flirtation with a Commune-like movement, together with its neutral position during 1960 and 1961 in the Sino-Soviet dispute, brought Soviet retaliation in the form of severely curtailed shipments of machinery and equipment (see Table 14). Soviet shipments of petroleum products continued, however, and grain shipments were also not reduced. In this instance, Soviet economic pressure was of a limited character. In addition, competition from China in granting aid probably spurred the USSR into an announcement on November 1, 1960 (just before the opening of the Conference of Eighty-One Parties), that it had canceled $172 million in North Korean debts and eased repayment terms for another $35 million.[157] Nonetheless, although these debts were canceled, no new loans were forthcoming. This stood in contrast to a $105 million loan from China on October 13, 1960 (coming after the Soviet advisors were withdrawn), which followed an earlier grant of $219.4 million on November 23, 1953, and loans totaling $52.5 million on September 17, 1958.[158]

Relations between North Korea and the USSR appeared to improve somewhat following the *coup d'état* in South Korea in May, 1961. The two nations signed a defensive pact in August of that year, at which time, significantly enough, Kim Il-sung heartily thanked Khrushchev for Soviet economic aid.[159] Soviet exports of machinery and equipment to North Korea more than doubled the next year. Nonetheless, the improvement in relations was to be brief. As a result of the Cuban missile crisis and the Chinese invasion of India, the North Koreans veered sharply toward Peking. Beginning in late 1962, the North Koreans began to attack the USSR—although not by name—for its rapprochement with "revisionist" Yugoslavia and for its cowardly stand in the Cuban missile crisis. The North Koreans also joined in Chinese propaganda attacks against the Indian "reactionaries." These policies caused the North Korean delegations increasing difficulty at the East European party congresses in the winter of

TABLE 14

Soviet Commodity Exports to North Korea, 1959-68
(in millions of new rubles; one ruble = 1.11 U.S. dollars)

Item	1959	1960	1961	1962	1963	1964	1965	1966	1967	1968
Machinery and Equipment	26.577	9.010	8.105	18.228	20.987	25.258	26.242	26.535	17.972	42.496
electrical	2.647	.416	.638	.860	.636	.692	.536	.425	.868	1.158
light industry	2.683	.701	.166	.464	.095	.240	.237	.025	.336	.974
Complete Plants	2.047	.808	1.112	8.824	12.373	16.839	11.847	15.760	2.829	15.148
Tractors (number)	756	250	4	0	0	0	0	0	0	0
Trucks (number)	1,960	10	0	0	0	0	0	102	140	410
Gasoline (thous. met. tons)	124	119	135	180	238	209	172	181	186	714 (petroleum and petroleum products)a
Diesel Fuel (thous. met. tons)	78	63	123	192	162	169	175	143	178	
Rolled Ferrous Metal Products	1.488	.369	1.085	1.536	1.169	.970	.970	.717	1.289	1.229

Item	1959	1960	1961	1962	1963	1964	1965	1966	1967	1968
Cardboard and Paper Products	4.062	.077	.051	.048	.040	.058	.043	.023	.077	.077
Wheat (thous. tons)	40	60	240	50	50	0	100 (maize)	118	251	105
Cotton (thous. tons)	0	2.0	10.0	10.3	9.4	8.3	10.2	9.7	10.1	13.2
Tires (thousand)	33	5	53	73	84	78	65	70	85	92
Ballbearings	1.038	1.258	1.300	1.845	2.044	.997	1.129	1.328	1.216	1.166
Total Soviet Exports	73.600	35.500	69.300	72.600	79.300	72.600	79.500	83.100	99.300	155.000

aThis category not broken down into its component parts in statistics issued for 1968. There can be no doubt that the figures indicate a sharp increase in Soviet shipments of petroleum products, however, as the corresponding figure for 1967 is only 447,600 tons.

Sources:

1959,1960: *Vneshniaia Torgovlia SSSR za 1960* (Moscow: Vneshtorgizdat, 1961), pp. 172-75.
1961:   *Vneshniaia Torgovlia SSSR za 1961* (Moscow: Vneshtorgizdat, 1962), pp. 189-92.
1962,1963: *Vneshniaia Torgovlia SSSR za 1963* (Moscow: Vneshtorgizdat, 1964), pp. 212-16.
1964,1965: *Vneshniaia Torgovlia SSSR za 1965* (Moscow: Mezhdunarodnye Otnosheniia, 1966), pp. 259-63.
1966,1967: *Vneshniaia Torgovlia SSSR za 1967* (Moscow: Mezhdunarodnye Otnosheniia, 1968), pp. 249-53.
1968:   *Vneshniaia Torgovlia SSSR za 1968* (Moscow: Mezhdunarodnye Otnosheniia, 1969), pp. 235-38.

1962-63, and the Korean delegate was even prohibited from speaking at the East German Congress.[160]

The outbreak of polemics in 1963 between the Chinese and Russians was joined by the North Koreans who took the occasion to air some of their own grievances against the Soviet Union. In a *Nodong Sinmun* editorial of April 23, 1963, the North Koreans castigated the Soviet Union for using economic aid as an instrument of pressure against socialist countries.

> It is precisely the policy of imperialism to use aid as a bait in enslaving other countries and thereby encroach upon their independence and sovereignty in order to achieve aggressive designs. . . . Among socialist countries aid cannot be used as a means of interfering in the internal affairs of other countries.[161]

Six months later, a *Nodong Sinmun* editorial criticized the USSR for attempting to interfere in the direction of the Korean economy:

> [During the past few years] some countries failed to show due understanding or support of our party's policy for socialist construction. Without a clear notion of our actual conditions they took issue with us saying: "The five year plan is an illusion"; "You need not build a machine-building industry"; "The speed of your agricultural collectivization is too fast"; "How can you collectivize the rural economy without agricultural machinery?" and so on. Of course we did not suffer great losses on account of these counsels because we acted independently as we had determined. It is not difficult to imagine that we would have suffered certain damages if we had acted otherwise.[162]

When the Soviet Union in a radio broadcast reminded the North Koreans of the aid the USSR had given to the North Korean economy, the Koreans responded with the claim that the Russians had cheated them in their mutual trade following the war:

> In rendering aid after World War II you furnished us with equipment, stainless steel plate and other materials at prices much higher than world market prices and took away from us scores of tons of gold, quantities of valuable nonferrous metals and raw materials at prices much lower than world market prices.[163]

The Soviet response to the North Korean ideological alignment with Peking was a sharp cut in military assistance.[164] It is probably for this reason that Premier Kim Il-sung stated at the Fifth Plenum of the Fourth Party Congress (December 10-14, 1962) that Korean economic development might have to suffer because of the need for increased expenditures on defense.[165] Indeed, the North Koreans were forced to shift resources from economic development to defense industries with the end result that in 1966 it was acknowledged that the target date for achieving the planned goals of the seven-year plan would have to be postponed from 1967 to 1970.[166]

The USSR cut off military assistance, but it did not terminate trade. Nor did Khrushchev markedly reduce Soviet exports to the Koreans. Soviet supplies of machinery and equipment remained approximately at 1962 levels for 1963 and 1964 (see Table 14). In addition, there was no significant reduction in either gasoline or diesel fuel shipments, commodities the North Koreans needed and the Chinese would have been hard put to supply. Soviet exports of cotton also continued at only slightly reduced levels, and the drop in tractor and truck deliveries can perhaps be explained by the Korean claim of self-sufficiency in the production of these goods in 1963.[167]

North Korean exports to the Soviet Union, although valuable, were not essential to the Soviet economy during the 1960-64 period, so it is doubtful whether mere considerations of economic need played a major role in the decision to keep trading with Korea. The main exports of North Korea to the USSR were rolled steel—an item the Russians themselves produced in ample quantity—and also zinc and lead.[168] The latter two commodities were sent in large quantities to the USSR, but the Russians themselves exported considerably more lead and zinc than they imported at this time.[169] Indeed, one might hazard a guess that Soviet exports of lead and zinc may have included re-exports from North Korea.

Thus the use of Soviet economic pressure against North Korea can be seen as a deliberate—though still limited—attempt to discipline a former Soviet satellite that had opted for the Chinese side. Unlike the case of Albania, trade was not cut off; nor was it sharply reduced after 1962 as in the case of China. The Soviet-North Korean conflict was also limited by the fact that the exchange of polemics never reached the stage of name-calling or personal insults characterizing both the Albanian and Chinese cases. The Soviet Union simply made it clear to North Korea that it could not expect either military or economic assistance so long as it maintained its alignment with Communist China. On the other hand, channels of trade were kept open with Pyongyang, and the North Koreans were neither forced into the arms of China (as Albania had been) nor forced to turn to a Western nation, such as Japan, for assistance.

Thus, in summation, Soviet economic pressure against China in the period between July, 1960, and October, 1964, when Khrushchev was deposed, consisted of a gradual decrease in trade, following the withdrawal of Soviet technicians, coupled with periodic offers of improved economic relations. While increasing economic pressure, the Russians held out the possibility of improved relations. The Chinese, however, responded negatively to these offers, and acquired instead alternate suppliers in the West.

As an added form of pressure on China, Khrushchev embarked on a policy of rapidly increasing both trade with and aid to India—including substantial amounts of military assistance—in an effort to help develop India as an alternate power in Asia. In addition, there was a sharp increase in Soviet trade with the other major Asian non-communist nations—Indonesia and Japan—as Khrushchev sought to outflank China. At the same time, by cutting military assistance to North Korea and refusing to give that nation developmental economic aid, Khrushchev was penalizing the North Koreans for their alignment with Peking and serving notice on other communist states of the penalties such an alignment might bring.

As the next section will indicate, the fall of Khrushchev brought only a temporary improvement in relations between Moscow and Peking. Soviet relations with North Korea, however, showed a marked improvement, and Khrushchev's successors succeeded in removing the North Koreans from their ideological alignment with Peking.

ECONOMIC ASPECTS OF THE BREZHNEV-KOSYGIN RAPPROCHEMENT ATTEMPT

Following the fall of Khrushchev, there was temporary improvement in Sino-Soviet economic and political relations. Although the major policy editorial in *Pravda* on October 17, 1964, had little to say about the "Socialist Commonwealth," the one paragraph dealing with Soviet relations with other communist nations stated:

> The world socialist system, a commonwealth of equal and sovereign peoples advancing along the path of Socialism and Communism is a very great achievement of the International Revolutionary movement. The CPSU and the entire Soviet people regard as their duty the development of fraternal relations with the Socialist countries, *wide cooperation in all spheres of economic, sociopolitical and cultural life* [emphasis added].[170]

This offer of "wide cooperation" bore fruit on April 29, 1965, when, after long negotiations, a trade protocol was signed between Russia and China. In addition to calling for an increase in trade, the protocol added helicopters to the list of goods the USSR was to ship China.[171] It is interesting to note that the protocol was signed despite the fact that one month earlier Chinese students had clashed with Soviet police and army troops in an attack on the U.S. Embassy in Moscow—an event that evoked bitter protests from the Chinese.

On June 12, 1965, a further step in economic cooperation was taken when a protocol was signed in Moscow providing for a resumption in the exchange of technicians and engineers "to study scientific and technical experience in various branches of the economy."[172] Despite an increasing number of Chinese polemical attacks against the new Soviet leadership and Chinese efforts to prevent the USSR from participating in the "Second Bandung Conference" in Algeria, Sino-Soviet trade rose in 1965 with Soviet exports increasing from 122 million rubles in 1964 to 173 million rubles in 1965. Soviet shipments of machinery and equipment, rolled steel, and pipes increased sharply as did Soviet exports of bulldozers, compressors, tractors, and heavy trucks. It appears that by increasing its exports in this way the USSR was striving to improve state relations despite negative developments in intra-party relations.

The Soviet decision to supply China with helicopters and greatly to increase deliveries of heavy trucks suitable for military use may also have been related to an attempt to appeal to a military faction in the Chinese Communist leadership. Khrushchev's successors may have reasoned that this group might prove amenable to an improvement in Sino-Soviet relations following the U.S. bombing of North Vietnam and the landing of American soldiers in South Vietnam. Indeed, an article in the August 5, 1966, issue of *Peking Review* branded the military faction as the one most sympathetic to the Russians.[173] It may well be that just as Khrushchev attempted to utilize P'eng Teh-huai to split the Chinese party in August, 1959, Khrushchev's successors have attempted to use leading military figures in the party hierarchy to factionalize for improved Sino-Soviet relations. The purge of Chinese chief of staff Lo Jui-ch'ing and Party Secretary Teng Hsiao-p'ing, who appears to have advocated improved relations with Moscow for the sake of modernizing the Chinese economy, indicates, however, that although the Soviet leaders may have struck some responsive chords in the Chinese party by their overtures, these elements did not have the power to control the party.[174] Indeed, the Mao Tse-tung/Lin P'iao group proved willing to sacrifice both military and economic assistance from the USSR to maintain its own version of ideological purity. The quotation at the beginning of this chapter sums up the attitude of the dominant faction of the Chinese party toward this question.

Following the outbreak of the Cultural Revolution and the purge of those members of the Chinese leadership favorably inclined toward a limited rapprochement with the USSR, Sino-Soviet trade relations again began to suffer. Soviet exports in 1966 dropped to 157.8 million rubles, but the full effect of the Cultural Revolution and such incidents as the humiliating departure of Soviet diplomats and their wives from Peking was not felt in Sino-Soviet trade until 1967 when Soviet exports plummeted to only 45.2 million rubles—the lowest amount since the Chinese Communists came to power.[175]

Economic and political relations continued to deteriorate in 1968, and in 1969 open warfare broke out along the Sino-Soviet border. Although it is not possible at the time of this writing (January, 1970) to determine who was responsible for initiating the hostilities, one interesting facet of the subsequent Soviet offer to begin negotiations on the border problems was the fact that the Russian leaders attempted to tie offers of increased trade to the start of negotiations.[176] Thus an entire section of the official Soviet note of March 29, 1969, was devoted to a history of previous Soviet economic aid to China. The section concluded with the following statement:

> During that (1949-59) period Soviet-Chinese trade was developing on a very broad scale: by 1959 its annual volume had reached almost 2,000,000,000 rubles. This was equitable and mutually advantageous

cooperation. Had it not been for the Chinese side's position, trade, economic and scientific-technical cooperation between our countries could undoubtedly have developed further. *This still holds true today* [emphasis added].[177]

The Chinese answer to this offer came in the official CPR statement of May 24, 1969:

Harboring ulterior motives, the Soviet government, moreover, talked glibly about Soviet assistance to China in its statement. It is true that under the leadership of the great Lenin and Stalin the Soviet people rendered assistance to the Chinese people which the Chinese people will never forget. In turn the Chinese people, led by their great leader, Chairman Mao, also rendered assistance to the Soviet people, which the Soviet people will never forget either. . . . However, it must be pointed out that in the past decade the Soviet government has completely betrayed the internationalist foreign policy of Lenin and Stalin, done all evils against China and committed towering crimes against the Chinese people.
It is not qualified at all to talk about assistance rendered to the Chinese people at the time of Lenin and Stalin. At present, the Soviet government is everywhere perpetrating acts of aggression and plunder against the peoples of other countries under the signboard of "assistance." Such practice of the Soviet government is exactly the same as that of U.S. imperialism.[178]

Despite this rebuff, the Russian leaders pressed ahead with their attempts to tie offers of improved economic relations to a solution of the border conflict. Although the official Soviet note of June 12, 1969, made no mention of Sino-Soviet economic relations, the Chinese revealed on October 7, 1969, that during his surprise trip to Peking the previous month, Soviet Premier Aleksei Kosygin had discussed increased trade (together with a number of other issues) with Chou En-lai.[179] Indeed, according to "authoritative Soviet sources" cited by *New York Times* reporter Bernard Gwertzman on December 20, 1969, the Soviet strategy in its border talks with China that had begun two months earlier was to try to reach agreement on such "easy" issues as trade relations first in order to create a positive atmosphere for solution of the far more difficult border question.[180] If this report is accurate, it will not have been the first time Soviet leaders have pursued the strategy of offering economic inducements to improve political relations. Whether they will be able to successfully implement this strategy, however, is at the time of this writing a very moot point.[181]

Khrushchev's successors had considerably more success in improving relations with North Korea than they did with China—although this development was due, at least in part, to events in Vietnam. The American escalation of the war in Vietnam turned out to have a negative effect on Sino-Soviet relations, but it had a positive effect on Russian relations with North Korea. The North Korean leadership, unable to manufacture domestically or to acquire from China the sophisticated anti-aircraft weapons needed to counter a potential American bombing of their homeland, turned to the Soviet Union for assistance. Indeed, the day after the United States launched a major air strike against North Vietnam in retaliation for an attack against an American base in South Vietnam, a large number of Russian military leaders appeared at a reception given by the North Korean military attache in Moscow.[182] In May, 1965, a high-level North Korean army mission arrived in the USSR for talks and on May 31 Radio Moscow reported that an agreement had been signed between the USSR and North Korea which "provided assistance for the further strengthening of the defensive potential of the Democratic People's Republic of Korea."[183]

The gradual improvement of Soviet-North Korean relations, which resulted in an estrangement of North Korea from Peking, was highlighted by the North Korean decision to attend the 23rd CPSU Congress in March, 1966—an event the Chinese Communists conspicuously boycotted. The North Koreans were rewarded for their move away from China on June 21, 1966, when the Russians agreed to assist North Korea in enlarging an iron and steel mill, and in building a thermal power station, an oil refinery, and other industrial installations. This Soviet decision must have been especially welcome to the North Korean leaders in that it implicitly ratified their decision to build an independent economy with their own steel mill and oil refineries. It was also announced on June 21 that Soviet-North Korean trade would be "considerably increased" for the 1967-70 period.[184] In fact, the trade statistics for 1968 already indicate a doubling of Soviet exports in comparison to 1966, with a sharp increase in Soviet supplies of machinery and equipment (see Table 14).

By September, 1966, the North Koreans had moved so far from the Chinese position that they attacked their former ideological ally for interference in their internal affairs. Then on March 5, 1967, Radio Pyongyang reported another defense agreement had been signed with the Soviet Union.[185]

Thus in the post-Khrushchev period, the Soviet leadership made a deliberate attempt to improve relations not only with China but with its Asian ally, North Korea, as well. Soviet exports to China were increased, and offers of renewed cooperation were made following the U.S. escalation of the Vietnamese War. Although certain members of the Chinese leadership, especially the professional military, may have wished for an improvement in relations, the purge of Lo Jui-ch'ing and Teng Hsiao-p'ing at the start of the Cultural Revolution was followed by a sharp deterioration in Sino-Soviet relations in both the political and economic spheres—a trend that had not been reversed by early 1970.

Soviet relations with North Korea, however, did improve. The North Koreans were in need of sophisticated Soviet weaponry which the post-Khrushchev leadership proved willing to supply. Then, as a result of Soviet military and later economic assistance, North Korea shifted to a neutral position in the Sino-Soviet conflict.

SUMMARY

The implementation of Soviet economic pressure against China in the post-1960 period has been in some ways similar to the examples of Soviet economic warfare examined in the first two case studies, but has been in other ways quite different. As in the cases of Yugoslavia and Albania, major aspects of Soviet economic pressure involved the withdrawal of technical assistance and the curtailment of trade relations. But the USSR canceled long-term capital aid agreements with both Yugoslavia and Albania, whereas similar action was not taken against China because the Chinese had not received any capital loans from the USSR since 1954. Indeed, the failure of the Soviet Union to grant China developmental capital loans after 1954 had been one of the factors causing the Chinese leaders to undertake the "Great Leap Forward" and establish Communes. The ideological challenge inherent in these experiments, together with Chinese dissatisfaction at the lack of Soviet aid and other Soviet policies, brought the Chinese into conflict with the USSR.

Khrushchev's application of economic pressure against China was considerably more gradual than his implementation of economic pressure against Albania or Stalin's employment of such pressure against Yugoslavia. Despite the cancellation of the nuclear weapons agreement in June, 1959, Khrushchev was willing as late as March, 1960, to increase trade with the Chinese. Nonetheless, the launching of a major ideological attack by the Chinese in April, 1960, and the open clash between the two major communist nations at the Bucharest Conference in June led Khrushchev to recall Soviet technicians from China in July. Unlike the cases of Yugoslavia and Albania, however, the withdrawal of technicians was not followed by a trade embargo. Instead, there was a gradual decrease in trade extending from 1960 until Khrushchev was deposed in October, 1964.

There are several explanations that might be put forth for the failure of the USSR to enact an embargo against China. The first is an economic one; namely, that trade was too valuable to the Russians to permit a complete interruption. Although there is certainly some validity to this argument, it would appear that political factors played a more important role in the decision. In the course of the 1960-64 period, Khrushchev made several offers to return Soviet technicians to China, and in November, 1963, he also offered the Chinese a substantial increase in trade. Up until November, 1963, Khrushchev seems to have hoped that with each increase in economic pressure the Chinese leadership (which was also plagued by a series of natural disasters) would either reach the limits of its endurance and give in to Soviet demands or else split and relinquish power to a more pro-Russian faction. By October, 1963, however, the recovery of the Chinese economy and the Chinese turn to the West (and Japan) not only for machinery and equipment but also for complete plants seems to have prompted Khrushchev to make offers of increased trade, lest China, which was already "leaning to the other side" economically, soon do so politically as well, as Yugoslavia had done in the

1950-53 period. Despite the Chinese rejection of Khrushchev's offers, the USSR's Eastern European allies increased their trade with China in 1964, thus preserving at least some links between China and the Soviet bloc.

Additional forms of economic pressure against China during the Khrushchev period were the major increases in Soviet economic and military assistance to India, which was China's main competitor and enemy in Asia, and a cancellation of such assistance to North Korea, which was China's main Asian ally in the Sino-Soviet conflict. By increasing economic aid to India, the USSR assisted in that nation's development; and by providing important military equipment, the Russians forced the Chinese to divert resources to their military production to match the Indians. Khrushchev's cancellation of military and economic aid to North Korea, on the other hand, forced the Chinese to extend their limited economic and military resources to assist that nation.

Khrushchev's successors began their reign with a relatively conciliatory approach to China, and despite certain Chinese provocations Sino-Soviet trade increased in 1965. There is some evidence that, especially after the American escalation of the war in Vietnam, the Soviet leaders may have entertained the hope that certain military elements in the Chinese leadership might prove amenable to an improvement in Sino-Soviet relations. Indeed, the Soviet decision to resume sales of helicopters to China in 1965 may well have been made to increase pro-Soviet feeling among this group. Nonetheless, the onset of the "Cultural Revolution" and the purge of the Chinese officials who appeared favorable even to a limited rapprochement with the USSR ended Soviet hopes in this regard. Consequently, trade again began to fall in 1966 and dropped precipitously in 1967 following the humiliation of the Soviet diplomats and their wives at the Peking airport. Sino-Soviet relations had indeed deteriorated so badly by 1969 that a border conflict broke out between the two nations. On the other hand, relations between the USSR and North Korea improved markedly following the fall of Khrushchev, thanks in large measure to the resumption of Soviet military supplies to the Koreans following the escalation of U.S. involvement in Vietnam in 1965.

NOTES

1. The two best books dealing with Sino-Russian relations both before and after the communists rose to power in each country are Klaus Mehnert, *Peking and Moscow* (New York: G. P. Putman's Sons, 1963); and Harry Schwartz, *Tsars, Mandarins and Commissars* (Philadelphia: J. P. Lippincott, 1964). Both books give excellent accounts of the clashes of national interest between China and Russia irrespective of the nature of the ruling governments.

2. Schwartz, *op. cit.*, p. 94.

3. For a good discussion of Russia's relations with Sinkiang in both the Czarist and communist periods, see Alan S. Whiting, *Sinkiang: Pawn or Pivot?* (East Lansing: Michigan State University Press, 1958).

4. Schwartz, *op. cit.*, p. 110.

5. Whiting, *op. cit.*, p. 117.

6. Schwartz, *op. cit.*, p. 132.

7. A description of the military engagements between Japan and the Soviet Union (and the initial Soviet occupation of Manchuria) is found in Raymond L. Garthoff, "The Soviet Intervention in Manchuria," in *Sino-Soviet Military Relations,* ed. Raymond L. Garthoff (New York: Frederick A. Praeger, 1966), Chapter 4.

8. Schwartz, *op. cit.*, p. 139.

9. Max Beloff, *Soviet Policy in the Far East 1944-1951* (New York: Oxford University Press, 1953), pp. 36-39.

10. Schwartz, *op. cit.*, p. 142.

11. For further information on this point, see Beloff, *op. cit.*, p. 76; and S. Y. Teng, "Comments (to Chalmers Johnson's article)," *China in Crisis,* Vol. 1, Book 1, ed. Ping-ti Ho and Tang Tsou (Chicago: University of Chicago Press, 1968), p. 443n.

12. Cited in David J. Dallin, *Soviet Russia and the Far East* (New Haven, Conn.: Yale University Press, 1948), p. 245.

13. New China News Agency, June 18, 1957 (cited in Mehnert, *op. cit.*, p. 250). This news agency is hereafter referred to as NCNA.

14. NCNA, July 15, 1957 (cited in Mehnert, *op. cit.*, p. 250).

15. Raymond L. Garthoff, "Sino-Soviet Military Relations 1945-66," in *Sino-Soviet Military Relations,* p. 94.

16. For a discussion of Stalin's policies in China during this period, see Robert C. North, *Moscow and the Chinese Communists* (Stanford, Calif.: Stanford University Press, 1963).

17. *The New York Times,* January 2, 1950.

18. *Ibid.*

19. The text of the treaty is translated in Henry Wei, *China and Soviet Russia* (Princeton: D. Van Nostrand, 1956), pp. 343-47.

20. *Ibid.*, p. 347.

21. *Peking Review,* Vol. 7, No. 19 (May 8, 1964), pp. 13-14.

22. Communique on signing of treaty; translated in Wei, *op. cit.,* p. 344.

23. Schwartz, *op. cit.,* p. 147.

24. Agreement on Chinese Changun Railroad *et al.;* translated in Wei, *op. cit.,* p. 345.

25. Robert Rigg, "Red Army in Retreat," *Current History,* January, 1957, p. 3 (cited in Garthoff, "Sino-Soviet Military Relations 1945-66," *op. cit.,* p. 85).

26. Alexander Eckstein, *Communist China's Economic Growth and Foreign Trade* (New York: McGraw-Hill, 1966), p. 142.

27. Cited in Schwartz, *op. cit.,* p. 148.

28. *Ibid.,* p. 149.

29. *Peking Review,* Vol. 7, No. 19 (May 8, 1964), p. 14.

30. Yeh Tsi Wan, "Vneshniaia Torgovlia Kitaia," *Vneshniaia Torgovlia,* Vol. 35, No. 6 (June, 1955), p. 2.

31. Eckstein, *op. cit.,* p. 142.

32. M. Sladkovskii, "Uspekhi Sovetsko-Kitaiskoi Torgovli," *Vneshniaia Torgovlia,* Vol. 37, No. 10 (October, 1957), p. 3.

33. Cited in David J. Dallin, *Soviet Foreign Policy After Stalin* (Philadelphia: J. B. Lippincott, 1961), p. 424.

34. Seweryn Bialer, "Polish Grievances Before the Twentieth Congress," in *The Development of the Communist Bloc,* ed. Roger Pethybridge (Boston: D. C. Heath and Company, 1965), p. 154. Bialer had access to the notes of a CPSU Central Committee meeting that discussed this affair.

35. Sladkovskii, *op. cit.,* p. 4.

36. *Pravda,* April 3, 1964 (translated in *Current Digest of the Soviet Press* [hereafter *Current Digest*], Vol. 16, No. 14 [April 29, 1964], p. 3). Suslov's speech, as translated, will hereafter be referred to as the *Suslov Report.*

37. *Peking Review,* Vol. 7, No. 19 (May 8, 1964), p. 26.

38. Dennis J. Doolin, *Territorial Claims in the Sino-Soviet Conflict* (Stanford: Hoover Institution, 1965), p. 43.

39. *Suslov Report,* p. 5.

40. *Ibid.*

41. Sladkovskii, *op. cit.,* p. 5.

42. A. Golubkov, "Sovetsko-Kitaiskoe Nauchno-Teknicheskoe Sotrudnichestvo," *Vneshniaia Torgovlia,* Vol. 37, No. 7 (July, 1957), p. 3. Whenever the Soviet economic press talks about "discovering and exploiting reserves," this almost always means that less aid is coming from the center.

43. Sladkovskii, *op. cit.,* p. 5.

44. V. Kraigl, "Bratskoe Sotrudnichestvo i Mezhdunarodnoe Razdelenie Truda v Mirnom Sotsialisticheskom Lagere," *Voprosy Ekonomiki,* Vol. 10, No. 10 (October, 1957), p. 37.

45. The best account of the debate is found in Donald Zagoria, *The Sino-Soviet Conflict 1956-61* (Princeton: Princeton University Press, 1962), pp. 39-199.

46. In 1955, the USSR gave India a $137.5 million loan. In 1956, Afghanistan and Indonesia each obtained $100 million loans, and Egypt was promised substantial aid for the Aswan Dam. In 1957, Syria received an $87.5 million loan, and India obtained a loan of $125 million. Kurt Muller, *The Foreign Aid Programs of the Soviet Bloc and Communist China: An Analysis* (New York: Walker and Company, 1967), pp. 219-25.

47. *Peking Review,* Vol. 7, No. 14 (April 3, 1964), p. 8.

48. *Ibid.,* pp. 8-9.

49. *Peking Review,* Vol. 6, No. 37 (September 13, 1963), p. 12.

50. "Krepnet Sovetsko-Kitaiskoe Sotrudnichestvo," *Vneshniaia Torgovlia,* Vol. 38, No. 3 (March, 1958), p. 3.

51. *Ibid.,* p. 5.

52. Cf. "Velikie Uspekhi Kitaiskogo Naroda v Stroitel'stve Sotsialisma," *Vneshniaia Torgovlia,* Vol. 36, No. 2 (February, 1956), p. 4; and Iu. Pekshev, "Ekonomicheskoe Sotrudnichestvo Sovetskogo Soiuza i Kitaiskoi Narodnoi Respubliki," *Vneshniaia Torgovlia,* Vol. 35, No. 2 (February, 1955), p. 2.

53. M. Sladkovskii, "Razvitie Torgovli Sovetskogo Soiuza s Kitaiskoi Narodnoi Respublikoi," *Vneshniaia Torgovlia,* Vol. 39, No. 10 (October, 1959), p. 9.

54. *Vneshniaia Torgovlia SSSR za 1957* (Moscow: Vneshtorgizdat, 1958), pp. 127-31.

55. The ideological impact of the Commune movement is discussed in detail in Zagoria, *op. cit.,* Chapter III.

56. Leonid Ilyichev, "Revolutionary Science and Our Age: Against the Anti-Leninist Course of the Chinese Leaders," *Kommunist,* No. 11, 1964 (translated in William E. Griffith, *Sino-Soviet Relations, 1964-65* [Cambridge: MIT Press, 1966], p. 362).

57. M. Sladkovskii, "Razvitie Torgovli Sovetskogo Soiuza s Kitaiskoi Narodnoi Respublikoi," p. 9.

58. "Marxism-Leninism Is the Basis for the Unity of the Communist Movement," *Kommunist,* No. 15 (October 18, 1963) (translated in *Current Digest,* Vol. 15, No. 43 [November 20, 1963], p. 3).

59. I. Andreev, "Druzhba i Sotrudnichestvo Sovetskogo i Kitaiskogo Narodov," *Vneshniaia Torgovlia,* Vol. 39, No. 2 (February, 1959), p. 7.

60. Chan Wa-doon, "Krepnet Sovetsko-Kitaiskaia Druzhba," *Vneshniaia Torgovlia,* Vol. 39, No. 6 (June, 1959), p. 8.

61. *Ibid.,* pp. 9-10.

62. Yeh Chi-chang, "Vneshniaia Torgovlia Nashei Strany za Desiat Let," *Vneshniaia Torgovlia,* Vol. 39, No. 10 (October, 1959), p. 15.

63. *Ibid.,* p. 16.

64. Radio Moscow, June 2, 1959.

65. For a discussion of this crisis and the role played by the Soviet Union, see Zagoria, *op. cit.,* Chapter VII.

66. *Peking Review,* Vol. 6, No. 37 (September 13, 1963), p. 12.

67. *Ibid.*

68. This account of the P'eng Teh-huai affair is based on David A. Charles, "The Dismissal of Marshal P'eng Teh-huai," *China Quarterly,* No. 8 (October-December, 1961), pp. 63-76.

69. *Peking Review,* Vol. 6, No. 37 (September 13, 1963), p. 12.

70. Muller, *op. cit.,* p. 223. The large loan was given for the development of various industrial plants during India's third five-year plan (1961-65). Granting this loan to the Indians so soon after the border incident was a definite sign of support for them and a clear slap in the face for the Chinese.

71. F. Kleimonov, "Plodotvornoe Sotrudnichestvo," *Vneshniaia Torgovlia,* Vol. 40, No. 2 (February, 1960), p. 15.

72. *Ibid.,* p. 17.

73. *Ibid.,* p. 20.

74. Percentage figures for this section, except where otherwise noted, are taken from the tables in Eckstein, *op. cit.,* pp. 98, 106-7, 114-15, 146, 150-51, 190-91.

75. There is some evidence that both China and the USSR acquired certain goods from Western Europe during the period when the embargo was most rigidly enforced. On this point, see Gunnar Adler-Karlsson, *Western Economic Warfare 1947-67* (Stockholm: Almqvist and Wiksell, 1968), Chapters 5 and 6.

76. *Vneshniaia Torgovlia SSSR 1918-1966* (Moscow: Mezhdunarodnye Otnosheniia, 1967), pp. 206-9. Hereafter referred to as *VT SSSR 1918-66.*

77. Estimate by Sidney Klein in "Sino-Soviet Economic Relations 1949-1962," *Current Scene,* June 15, 1963, pp. 7-11.

78. Estimate by A. Doak Barnett, *Communist China and Asia* (New York: Council on Foreign Relations, 1960), p. 50. There is, however, some question as to the quality of the coal produced.

79. Eckstein, *op. cit.,* p. 106; *VT SSSR 1918-66,* p. 208.

80. M. Sladkovskii, "Uspekhi Sovetsko-Kitaiskoi Torgovli," p. 5.

81. Trade with Japan fell off in the 1959-60 period because the Chinese tried to extract political concessions from the Japanese in return for trade. For further information on this subject, see Barnett, *op. cit.,* pp. 274-77.

82. Eckstein, *op. cit.,* pp. 191, 218.

83. *Ibid.,* p. 219.

84. *Ibid.,* p. 324n.

85. *Suslov Report*, p. 3.

86. M. Sladkovskii, "Nerushimaia Sovetsko-Kitaiskaia Druzhba," *Vnesh-niaia Torgovlia*, Vol. 37, No. 2 (February, 1957), p. 4.

87. *Peking Review*, Vol. 7, No. 19 (May 8, 1964), p. 14.

88. Radio Moscow, October 2, 1964.

89. Kleimonov, *op. cit.*, p. 17.

90. Wa-doon, *op. cit.*, p. 1.

91. *VT SSSR 1918-66*, p. 208.

92. *Vneshniaia Torgovlia SSSR za 1959* (Moscow: Vneshtorgizdat, 1960), pp. 144-48. Hereafter this statistical yearbook will be referred to as *VT*, with the appropriate year.

93. *Ibid.*; Eckstein, *op. cit.*, p. 107.

94. N. Shiriaev, "K Itogam Sovetsko-Kitaiskikh Torgovykh Perego-vorov," *Vneshniaia Torgovlia*, Vol. 38, No. 5 (May, 1958), p. 3.

95. Yeh Chi-chang, "China's Foreign Trade in the Past Ten Years," *Foreign Trade of the People's Republic of China*, No. 9 (September, 1959), p. 3.

96. *VT, 1959*, pp. 144-48.

97. *Ibid.*

98. *VT SSSR 1918-66*, p. 105; *VT, 1959*, pp. 144-48.

99. Eckstein, *op. cit.*, pp. 170-71.

100. Sladkovskii, "Nerushimaia Sovetsko-Kitaiskaia Druzhba," p.3.

101. "Krepnet Sovetsko-Kitaiskoe Sotrudnichestvo," p. 3. The Russians, however, have recently changed their evaluation of Chinese exports to the USSR and now imply that they did the Chinese a favor by accepting them. See Yu. Vladimirov, "The Question of Soviet-Chinese Economic Relations in 1950-1966," *Voprosy Istorii*, No. 6, 1969 (translated in *Current Digest*, Vol. 21, No. 33 [September 10, 1969], p. 11).

102. *Vneshniaia Torgovlia*, Vol. 40, No. 4 (April, 1960), p. 33; *Foreign Trade of the People's Republic of China*, No. 11 (June, 1960), p. 2.

103. This statement has been pieced together from two editorials in the *Peking Review,* one on September 13, 1963 (p. 14), and the other dated February 7, 1964 (p. 9).

104. *Peking Review,* Vol. 7, No. 19 (May 8, 1964), p. 14.

105. *Suslov Report,* p. 5. For a first-hand account of the experiences of a Soviet specialist working in China, see M. A. Klochko, *Soviet Scientist in China* (New York: Frederick A. Praeger, 1964).

106. Translated in *Foreign Broadcast Information Service Daily Report,* August 26, 1960.

107. Translated in David Floyd, *Mao Against Khrushchev* (New York: Frederick A. Praeger, 1964), p. 285.

108. William E. Griffith, "The November 1960 Moscow Meeting: A Preliminary Reconstruction," in *Polycentrism,* ed. Walter Laqueur and Leopold Labedz (New York: Frederick A. Praeger, 1962), pp. 112, 114. A detailed account of Teng Hsiao-p'ing's speech is found in Edward Crankshaw, *The New Cold War: Moscow vs. Peking* (Baltimore: Penguin Books, 1963), Chapter 12.

109. Translated in Schwartz, *op. cit.,* p. 182.

110. Crankshaw, *op. cit.,* p. 137. According to Suslov, Mikoyan allegedly told the Chinese at the November, 1960, Conference "that if the Soviet specialists were really needed in China and if normal working conditions were created for them we were ready to send them back to the CPR." *Suslov Report,* p. 5.

111. *Vneshniaia Torgovlia,* Vol. 41, No. 5 (May, 1961), p. 13.

112. V. Kuplenski, "K Itogam Sovetsko-Kitaiskikh Torgovykh Perego-vorov," *Vneshniaia Torgovlia,* Vol. 41, No. 5 (May, 1961), pp. 17-18.

113. *Ibid.,* p. 18.

114. *Ibid.*

115. According to the Chinese, however, the Russians began to threaten termination of their petroleum exports to China in 1960. *Peking Review,* Vol. 12, No. 24 (June 13, 1969), p. 12.

116. *VT, 1961,* p. 185.

117. *Ibid.,* p. 27.

118. *The Financial Times,* December 5, 1961 (cited in Radio Free Europe Background Report: USSR, December 7, 1961). The planes in question were six Vikers Viscount 800 passenger aircraft. This incident may also indicate, however, that the Chinese were now reluctant to become dependent on the USSR for the supply of the aircraft and needed spare parts.

119. *Peking Review,* Vol. 7, No. 19 (May 8, 1964), pp. 14-15.

120. *Suslov Report, loc. cit.*

121. Griffith, *op. cit.,* pp. 174-76, has a detailed description of the incident.

122. Reprinted in William Griffith, *The Sino-Soviet Rift* (Cambridge: MIT Press, 1964), p. 436.

123. *Ibid.,* p. 440.

124. William Griffith, *Sino-Soviet Relations, 1964-65,* p. 13.

125. The Peking Radio report (October 14, 1963) that discussed the agreement stated that discussions had been held "on questions concerning through railway transport" and that "finally an agreement had been reached." Cited in *The New York Times,* October 15, 1963.

126. *Peking Review,* Vol. 7, No. 19 (May 8, 1964), pp. 19-20.

127. *Ibid.,* pp. 20-21.

128. Data from Eckstein, *op. cit.,* pp. 94-95.

129. *Ibid.,* p. 107.

130. On November 9, 1962, Japan and China signed a long-term (five-year) trade agreement. Japan's exports to China increased from only $17 million in 1961 to $40 million in 1962, to $66 million in 1963, and to $160 million in 1964. Robert L. Price, "International Trade of Communist China 1950-65," *An Economic Profile of Mainland China* (Washington, D.C.: U.S. Government Printing Office, 1967), p. 600. For a detailed examination of the development of Sino-Japanese trade in the period 1949-68, see George P. Jan, "Japan's Trade With Communist China," *Asian Survey,* Vol. 9, No. 12 (December, 1969), pp. 900-918.

131. *Peking Review,* Vol. 7, No. 4 (January 24, 1964), p. 7.

132. *Peking Review,* Vol. 7, No. 19 (May 8, 1964), p. 14. The Chinese were referring to the sharp drop in Soviet production in 1964, particularly of agricultural products.

133. Radio Moscow, October 2, 1964.

134. For a detailed account of the Rumanian events, see David Floyd, *Rumania* (New York: Frederick A. Praeger, 1965).

135. Jan S. Prybyla, "The China Trade," *East Europe,* Vol. 16, No. 3 (March, 1967), pp. 17-18.

136. *Ibid.,* p. 19.

137. Eckstein, *op. cit.,* p. 254.

138. Price, *op. cit.,* p. 595.

139. Eckstein, *loc. cit.*

140. Prybyla, *loc. cit.*

141. *Ibid.*

142. *Red Flag,* October 21, 1963 (cited in Marshall I. Goldman, *Soviet Foreign Aid* [New York: Frederick A. Praeger, 1967] , p. 101).

143. *London Times,* August 18, 1962 (cited in Radio Free Europe Background Report: USSR, August 20, 1962); Goldman, *op. cit.,* p. 104.

144. *Zeri i Popullit,* September 19, 1962 (translated in William Griffith, *Albania and the Sino-Soviet Rift* [Cambridge: MIT Press, 1963] , p. 372).

145. *VT SSSR 1918-66,* p. 209.

146. *Ibid.*

147. Goldman, *op. cit.,* p. 131.

148. *VT SSSR 1918-66,* p. 221. The lead article in the March, 1961, issue of *Vneshniaia Torgovlia* was an open appeal for increased trade with Japan. E. Ivanov, "Shirokie Vozmozhnosti Razvitiia Sovetsko-Iaponskoi Torgovli," *Vneshniaia Torgovlia,* Vol. 41, No. 3 (March, 1961), pp. 3-6.

149. For a discussion of Soviet-Mongolian relations, see Robert A. Rupen, "The Mongolian People's Republic and Sino-Soviet Competition," in *Communist Strategies in Asia,* ed. A. Doak Barnett (New York: Frederick A.

Praeger, 1963), pp. 262-92. It is interesting to note that the same day that Radio Moscow announced Mongolia's support of the Soviet plan for a new international communist meeting, it also announced a new aid agreement for Mongolia (December 11, 1967).

150. *VT SSR 1918-66*, pp. 66-67. For a detailed discussion of Soviet political relations with North Korea, see Joungwon A. Kim, "Soviet Policy in North Korea," *World Politics*, Vol. 22, No. 2 (January, 1970), pp. 237-55.

151. Radio Pyongyang, June 12, 1958.

152. *Mirovaia Sotsialisticheskaia Sistema Khoziaistva*, Vol. IV (Moscow: Mysl', 1967), pp. 174-75.

153. Radio Pyongyang, June 12, 1958.

154. S. D. Sergeev, *Ekonomicheskoe Sotrudnichestvo i Vzaimopomoshch' Sotsialisticheskikh Stran* (Moscow: Vneshtorgizdat, 1964), p. 187.

155. *Ibid.*

156. A description of North Korea's problems at this time is found in M. T. Haggard, "North Korea's International Position," *Asian Survey*, Vol. 5, No. 8 (August, 1965), pp. 375-88.

157. Radio Free Europe Background Information: North Korea, September 14, 1961.

158. Muller, *op. cit.*, p. 235.

159. Radio Free Europe Background Information: North Korea, September 14, 1961.

160. A detailed account of these events is found in Radio Free Europe Background Information: North Korea, April 8, 1964.

161. Translated in *ibid*.

162. Translated in Ernst Kux and Joseph C. Kun, *Die Satelliten Pekings* (Stuttgart: Kohlhammer Verlag, 1964), pp. 247-48.

163. *The New York Times*, September 11, 1964.

164. Joseph Kun, "North Korea: Between Moscow and Peking," *China Quarterly*, No. 31 (July-September, 1967), p. 49.

165. Joungwon A. Kim, "The 'Peak of Socialism' in North Korea: The Five and Seven Year Plans," *Asian Survey,* Vol. 5, No. 5 (May, 1965), p. 267.

166. *Mirovaia   Sotsialisticheskaia   Sistema   Khoziaistva,* Vol. IV p. 172.

167. The Korean Central News Agency on January 17, 1964, claimed that in 1963 North Korea had produced 3,033 tractors and 4,022 trucks (cited in Glenn D. Paige, *The Korean People's Democratic Republic* [Stanford: Hoover Institution, 1966], p. 43).

168. *VT SSSR 1918-66*, pp. 212-15.

169. *Ibid.*, p. 87. In 1961, for example, the USSR exported 116,200 tons of zinc and 102,000 tons of lead while it imported 23,600 tons of zinc and 24,200 tons of lead from North Korea. In 1964, the USSR exported 149,800 tons of zinc and 96,100 tons of lead while importing 24,700 tons of zinc and 17,600 tons of lead from North Korea. *Vneshniaia Torgovlia* has also used the term "traditional exports" to describe North Korean exports to the USSR. This term is somewhat derogatory in nature and usually refers to items for which the USSR has no particular need. (Cf. M. Botsin, "Sovetsko-Koreiskoe Ekonomicheskoe Sotrudnichestvo," *Vneshniaia Torgovlia,* Vol. 46, No. 8 [August, 1966], p. 23.)

170. Translated in *Current Digest,* Vol. 16, No. 40 (October 28, 1964), p. 6.

171. Radio Moscow, April 30, 1965.

172. Radio Peking, June 12, 1965.

173. *Peking Review,* Vol. 9, No. 32 (August 5, 1966), p. 9.

174. A detailed description of the individuals and factions who desired an improvement in relations with the USSR in the post-Khrushchev era is found in Donald Zagoria, "The Strategic Debate in Peking," in *China in Crisis,* Vol. II, ed. Tang Tsou (Chicago: University of Chicago Press, 1968), pp. 237-68; and Uri Ra'anan, "Peking's Foreign Policy 'Debate' 1965-66," pp. 23-71 in the same volume.

175. In his detailed description of Sino-Soviet economic relations in the period 1950-66, the Soviet economist Vladimirov dates the 11th plenary session of the CPC Central Committee (August, 1966—the start of the "Cultural Revolution") as the meeting that "brought Soviet-Chinese relations as a whole to the brink of complete rupture." See Vladimirov, *op. cit.,* p. 8.

176. Note the similarity to Khrushchev's offer of November, 1963. A collection of documents pertaining to the border conflict in the period March

to October, 1969, has been published in *Studies in Comparative Communism,* Vol. 2, Nos. 3 and 4 (July/October, 1969), pp. 150-382.

177. *Pravda,* March 30, 1969 (translated in *Current Digest,* Vol. 21, No. 13 [April 16, 1969], p. 2).

178. Radio Peking, May 24, 1969.

179. Official Government Statement of the CPR, published in *The New York Times*, October 8, 1969.

180. *The New York Times,* December 21, 1969.

181. The Soviet economist Abram Frumkin in his book *Modern Theories of International Economics* (Moscow: Progress Publishers, 1969), p. 478, has clearly defined the reasoning behind this facet of Soviet policy: "The interaction of economics and politics, foreign trade and foreign policy . . . is of a dual nature. It is not only a question of politics determining trade, *for foreign trade is itself capable of substantially influencing the global environment. The Soviet Union, for one, has always regarded international trade as an important factor in easing international tension and promoting peace* [emphasis added].

182. Radio Free Europe Situation Report: North Korea, February 11, 1965.

183. Radio Moscow, May 21, 1965.

184. Botsin, *op. cit.,* p. 23.

185. Cited in *The New York Times,* March 6, 1967.

CHAPTER 5

CONCLUSIONS

In the history of international relations, there have been very few instances where foreign economic pressure has succeeded in forcing a government to alter its policies.[1] The period since World War II has not been an exception to this pattern. In addition to the examples of Yugoslavia, Albania, and China on the Russian side, one can also point to similar American experiences with the USSR, China, and Cuba.[2] Indeed, the American experience with Cuba is in many ways analogous to the Soviet experiences with Yugoslavaia and Albania. After issuing several threats in response to what he deemed to be "anti-American" acts of the Castro regime, President Eisenhower slashed the Cuban sugar quota in July, 1960, and ordered a total American embargo on all sales to the Caribbean island three months later. Both the Russians and Chinese then stepped in with large loans and offers to purchase enough sugar to make up for Cuba's lost market in the United States.[3] The end result of the process was that Cuba went over to the Communist Camp. This American experience, together with the case studies of Soviet economic pressure described in this study, illustrate the general proposition that economic warfare is not likely to be an effective policy in an international system where a target state can turn elsewhere for trade and economic assistance.* It has taken the Soviet leadership a considerable amount of time, however, to learn this basic principle of international relations.

In order to understand the reasons for the initially overoptimistic Soviet view of the efficacy of economic pressure, it is first necessary to examine the pattern of its employment by the Soviet leaders. There have been a number of similarities in the Russian and American uses of economic pressure in the post-war period, but there are several areas in which Soviet economic warfare

---

*An important corollary to this proposition is that a major power must maintain a flexible foreign economic policy in order to capitalize on the mistakes of its opponent. It should be noted in this regard, however, that the present American policy of restricting trade with the nations of the Soviet bloc is counterproductive. Indeed, the United States should drop all trade restrictions against these nations (except for *truly* strategic goods) so as to facilitate their obtaining markets and credits if the Soviet Union began to exert economic pressure against them.

within the Communist Camp is distinguishable from its American counterpart within the larger international system. First, because of the nature of economic relations within the Communist Camp the Soviet Union has a much broader spectrum of economic pressures with which it can deal with deviant communist states. This spectrum, which extends all the way from a delay in inter-governmental trade negotiations to the cessation of all trade and economic assistance, has enabled the Soviet leadership to orchestrate more sharply the pressures it has deemed necessary to bring a recalcitrant state into line.

Another distinguishable characteristic of Soviet economic warfare has been its pattern of "gradual escalation." In order for an economic embargo to have its maximum effect, it must be enacted as rapidly as possible so as to give the target regime the minimum possible time to acquire alternate suppliers. Nonetheless, the Soviet leaders did not institute their embargoes against Yugoslavia and Albania until more than eighteen months had passed after the first economic pressure was employed, and in the case of China no embargo has yet been imposed although trade has been significantly cut. (By contrast, there was only a five-month period between the first American warning that economic pressure might be used against Cuba and the imposition of the final embargo.[4]) In each of the case studies examined, the Soviet leaders used minor forms of economic pressure as the first signals of their displeasure with the target regime. When the early signals were not heeded, the economic pressure was stepped up, notch by notch. This pattern of "gradual escalation" would seem to indicate that both Stalin and Khrushchev believed at each turn of the economic screw that the leadership of the target regime would either agree to Soviet demands or else disintegrate under the pressure with the result that a pro-Russian faction would take control. When neither event occurred, the economic pressure was increased another notch until finally, in the cases of Yugoslavia and Albania, a total embargo was enacted.[5]

The reasons for the gradual nature of this escalation lay in the tendency of the Soviet leaders to underestimate the will and cohesiveness of the target regimes. This was due in part to the fact that each of the victims of Soviet economic pressure was in the process of "building socialism" (i.e., indus-trialization) and up to the point of its conflict with the USSR each target state was highly dependent on the Soviet Union for its economic development. In each case, the desire of the leaders of the underdeveloped communist nation for rapid industrialization was reinforced by what might be called the "industrialization ethic" of their Marxist-Leninist ideology. Trade with the USSR and the other members of the Soviet bloc was a major ingredient in their industrialization efforts, along with Soviet technical assistance and, to a lesser degree, Soviet capital aid. In each case, the fact that Russian technicians were assisting in the development of the target state gave the Russian leaders first-hand information on the potential effects of the various forms of Soviet economic pressure. Both Stalin and Khrushchev appear to have concluded that, because of the desire of the target regimes to "build socialism," they would not forgo economic cooperation with the Soviet Union for the sake of doctrinal or national independence. For this reason, both Soviet leaders seem to have felt that minor forms of economic pressure would suffice to bring the target regimes back into line and, when these pressures failed, that more severe pressure would accomplish the purpose. What the two Russian leaders failed to realize, however, was that national independence was a goal of higher priority for the target regimes than economic development. Even though as a consequence of the Soviet economic pressure the somewhat grandiose industrialization plans of the target regimes were revised downward, the target nations were willing to pay this price to continue their independent policies.[6]

The greater importance attributed by the target regimes to political independence over economic development is also evident in the various reconciliation attempts undertaken by the successors of the Soviet leaders initiating economic pressure against the target states. Khrushchev was successful in his rapprochement efforts with Yugoslavia in 1955, but only after he had made substantial political concessions. In the case of Yugoslavia, however, Soviet offers of renewed trade began the reconciliation process. Khrushchev's successors also used offers of renewed or increased trade in similar efforts to improve state relations. It would appear that underlying the Soviet leadership's view that improved economic relations would lead to improved political relations was the belief, fostered by their Marxist-Leninist ideology, that it is impossible to separate economic and political relations. The results of their reconciliation attempts, however, were mixed. In the case of China, the offers of increased trade were only partially successful in securing an improvement in Sino-Soviet relations; and when political relations again began to deteriorate, Sino-Soviet economic relations similarly suffered. Nonetheless, the Russian leaders persevered in this policy, and after border fighting broke out in 1969, the Soviet Union once again made offers of increased trade as an inducement for improved relations between the two communist states. In the case of Albania, the Brezhnev-Kosygin offer of renewed economic cooperation met with even less success as the Hoxha regime insisted on prior Soviet political concessions (unacceptable to the Russians) before it would agree to any improvement in state relations. Only in the case of North Korea was a rapprochement successfully effected, but even here it was the Kim Il-sung regime's desire for military assistance rather than economic development which seems to have been the decisive factor in the reconciliation.

The willingness of the target regimes to forgo rapid economic development, however, was accompanied by ideological pronouncements that justified the correct Marxist-Leninist nature of their policies vis-a-vis the USSR. Indeed, the Chinese citation of Lenin's statement that "politics cannot but have precedence over economics" is an example of just such a justification. Once the conflict between the Soviet Union and the target state had begun in earnest, each side used the same ideological terms to denounce the other. Thus the Soviet leaders, in an attempt to discredit the target regime, maintained that the leaders of the regime had "impeded the construction of Socialism" in their country and had also committed the unpardonable sin of "cooperating with the imperialists." The target regime's leaders counterattacked with the claim that it was the Russians who had become "imperialists" and that the Soviet leaders were the ones responsible for "impeding the construction of Socialism" in the target nation. Here, as in many other areas of intra-Camp relations, the common ideology instead of being a unifying force in times of stress served only as a transmission belt of mutual invective as both sides used it to justify their positions.

A second fallacy in the thinking of the Soviet leaders lay in their view of the cohesiveness (or lack thereof) of the target regimes. Stalin, in a well-known statement, remarked: "I will shake my little finger and there will be no more Tito. He will fall."[7] Although Khrushchev is not known to have made such a statement about Hoxha, the abject international weakness of Albania and its almost total economic dependence on the Soviet bloc probably aroused similar thoughts in Khrushchev's mind. In addition, China's economic condition following the failure of the "Great Leap Forward" probably indicated to Khrushchev that Mao Tse-tung's position as leader of the Chinese Communist Party had been seriously weakened. In both Yugoslavia and Albania, there were members of the party leadership who directed their primary loyalties to the CPSU rather than to their own parties, and both Stalin and Khrushchev evidently hoped to use these individuals in their plans to overthrow the opposing leadership after it had been "softened up" by the initial acts of Soviet economic pressure. Although there was no such "pro-Russian" faction in the Chinese party, there were a number of Chinese leaders, even after the purge of P'eng Teh-huai, who opposed Mao's policy of worsening relations with the USSR.[8] The Soviet use of economic pressure, however, served only to harden the resolve of the target regimes' top leaders and in fact helped them rally the majority of their parties with the call to national independence. Thus, instead of enabling a pro-Russian faction to gain control of the target nation, the Soviet pressure resulted in the elimination of the faction from the target regime's leadership. Hence the utilization of economic pressure had the reverse effect of weakening Soviet influence over the target nation.

Perhaps the major conclusion to be drawn from this study is that the Soviet leadership has gradually become more sophisticated in its use of economic pressure since 1948, and, in fact, seems to have learned from its earlier mistakes. The Soviet leadership in its initial experiences in the exercise of economic pressure seems to have had overly optimistic expectations regarding its efficacy as a means of "deviation control," but subsequent Soviet exercises in economic pressure indicate that the leaders of the CPSU have become considerably more circumspect both in their actions and expectations. Stalin, in enforcing a Soviet bloc embargo against Yugoslavia, succeeded only in eventually forcing Tito over to the side of the West, but later Soviet leaders have tried carefully to avoid a similar realignment on the part of the victims of their economic pressure. Here again, the Soviet leaders seem to have felt that a major economic realignment could lead to a political realignment (as indeed had happened in the case of Yugoslavia). Thus, although Khrushchev enacted a Soviet embargo against Albania, he did not prohibit the other members of the Soviet bloc from trading with the tiny Balkan nation. This may have been due, in part, to Khrushchev's weaker position within the Communist Camp and the greater freedom of action the East European nations possessed as a result of the Sino-Soviet conflict. In addition, some of these nations such as Poland probably tried to moderate Khrushchev's actions as insurance against a time when they might similarly be isolated. Given the available evidence, however, it would seem that the main reason for the continued trade lay in Khrushchev's desire to maintain some Soviet bloc contact with the Albanians. Having failed in his efforts to topple the Hoxha regime, Khrushchev could still prevent an Albanian turn to the West (in the manner of Yugoslavia) or its total dependence on China by continuing to permit trade between the nations of East Europe and Albania. In this way, he could also facilitate Albanian re-entry into the bloc at a future date.

Khrushchev's use of economic pressure against China was considerably more limited than it was against Albania. In the case of China, the Russian levers of economic pressure were weaker, and China's exports to the USSR were more valuable than the Albanian or Yugoslav had been. Furthermore, it is doubtful whether Khrushchev initially felt that his employment of economic pressure would lead to such a serious deterioration in Sino-Soviet relations. Nonetheless, pressed by the need to overcome the Chinese challenge to Soviet leadership in the international communist movement and by China's attempts to form a sub-alliance (including recruits from East Europe) within the Communist Camp, Khrushchev resorted to economic pressure in the form of a cancellation of economic aid and a gradual reduction of trade. Although the Soviet leader may not have entertained much hope of splitting the Mao Tse-tung regime, it appears that he felt that China's serious economic crisis would force the Chinese into political concessions. When the Chinese refused to give in, Khrushchev further reduced Soviet exports and increased the pressure on the Chinese by making a determined effort to build up India and by improving the USSR's relations with the other major non-communist states of Asia. The Soviet Union's terminaion of military and economic assistance to the North Koreans in 1962 increased the pressure on the Chinese still further.

When the Chinese economy began to recover in 1963 and China then turned to the West for capital goods, Khrushchev himself made several offers of increased trade to the Chinese. Although his offers were not accepted, the other members of the Soviet bloc did increase their trade with China. It should also be noted that the USSR never totally severed its trade with China as it had done with Yugoslavia and Albania. Once again, Khrushchev's reasoning seems to have been that the maintenance of Soviet bloc trade relations with China would both facilitate a future reconciliation and prevent a complete Chinese economic turn to the West, which might then lead to a political realignment.

Khrushchev's growing sophistication in the use of economic pressure can be seen most clearly in his treatment of North Korea. The North Koreans, who opted for the Chinese side of the Sino-Soviet conflict in late 1962, were treated far more gently than were the Albanians, who had chosen the same alignment two years earlier. By late 1962, Khrushchev had become aware of the dangers of using too much economic pressure against a target regime, and he limited the Soviet reaction to a cessation of military and economic assistance while trade continued at earlier levels. By limiting economic pressure in this way, Khrushchev did not completely alienate the North Koreans (as he had the Albanians) and thus made it considerably easier for his successors to effect a reconciliation with the Kim Il-sung regime.

The team of Brezhnev and Kosygin has been even more circumspect in its use of economic pressure than was Khrushchev. They have employed only minor forms of economic pressure against Rumania (the curtailment of coke and iron ore deliveries) and Cuba (the limitation of oil exports) despite the relatively serious challenges the policies of these nations have posed for the USSR. The very limited amount of economic pressure employed indicates that the intention of the Soviet leadership was neither to topple the target regime nor even to force it into major political concessions. In addition, it is doubtful whether the pressure was intended to deter other nations from following the examples of Cuba and Rumania, particularly as these two nations had not been deterred by the far more serious economic pressures employed by the USSR against Yugoslavia, Albania, and China. It is possible that the action was taken as a signal to the two regimes that the Soviet leadership had reached the limit of its patience and that further independent steps would bring more serious Soviet action. It seems more likely, however, that the Soviet leaders felt they had to take *some* action to show their displeasure with the target nations. In the absence of a decision to employ military force, economic retaliation was the only pressure the Soviet leadership could take which would make the nature of its displeasure painfully evident. It thus appears that the economic pressure used was employed as much to assuage the pride of the Soviet Union as to hurt the target nation.* By keeping the pressure very limited, however, the Soviet leaders kept open the possibility of rapid reconciliation with the target regimes.

The very limited economic pressure employed against Rumania and Cuba indicates that the Brezhnev-Kosygin leadership has learned from the experience of the past that economic pressure if pushed too far may force the target regime into the camp of one of Russia's enemies. This, however, illustrates a serious dilemma for the Soviet leadership, which possesses few other instruments of "deviation control" within the Communist Camp. In an era when both the Communist Camp and the larger international system are bipolar, when national communist leaders have succeeded in purging Russian agents from their parties, and when the Soviet Union has lost its unquestioned ideological preeminence, there are few meaningful pressures short of an outright military invasion which the Soviet leaders can exert to force a deviant communist nation into line without running the risk of the target nation turning to the Chinese or even to the West for aid. Economic pressure is one of the instruments the Soviet Union can employ to punish deviant regimes, but it is an instument that must be exercised delicately lest the target state change its alignment either within the Communist Camp or within the larger international system. For this reason, the economic pressures used against Rumania** and

---

*The prolongation of the U.S. embargoes against China and Cuba seems to be governed by very similar considerations.

**It should be noted, however, that Rumania has made a major effort to decrease the Soviet bloc percentage of its total trade to reduce its vulnerability to Soviet economic pressure of this type.

Cuba were quite limited in nature. Future Soviet exercises in economic pressure against communist states not occupied by the Russian Army will probably also be limited in nature for this reason.

The reader will have observed that the only communist nations dealt with in this study have been the underdeveloped ones that are net capital importers from the USSR. It may be asked whether the Soviet Union has employed its instruments of economic pressure against the more developed nations of the Communist Camp such as Poland, Hungary, East Germany, and Czechoslovakia, all of whom, in 1966, were net capital exporters to the USSR.[9] There is no question but that Soviet trade with these nations is of far greater value to the USSR than Soviet trade with the less-developed communist states, and for this reason it is likely that the Soviet leaders would be more hesitant about utilizing economic pressure against them. Unfortunately, sufficient data is not available to make a conclusive case study on any of these nations although it should be noted that all four are currently (1970) occupied by the Russian Army, and the very presence of Soviet troops gives the Soviet leaders far more leverage than any form of economic pressure.*

Nonetheless, it would be useful to briefly examine Soviet-Czechoslovak relations during the period of 1968 pior to the Soviet invasion for any indications of Soviet economic pressure in order to test our hypothesis that the Russian leaders have become very careful in the use of that instrument of foreign policy. It is interesting to note that, aside from a Western report that the Russians had delayed wheat shipments to Czechoslovakia (the report was subsequently denied by both Czech and Soviet officials) and a *Pravda* article on July 29, 1968, that pointedly described the advantages the Czechs derived from trade with the USSR, the only significant indication of Soviet economic pressure was the hesitancy of the Russian leaders to respond to a Czech request for a large hard-currency loan. Indeed, the possibility that the Czechs might turn to the West for economic assistance (negotiations were already under-way with West Germany) may well have been one more signal to the Russians that the Czechs had begun to pull away from the Soviet bloc. Were the Soviet leaders to exercise their major levers of economic pressure against Czechoslovakia, as they had earlier done against Yugoslavia and Albania, the result would have been an even more rapid departure. The Soviet invasion, however, precluded just such an eventuality.

In sum, Soviet leaders have been using economic pressure as an instrument of their policy toward communist nations since the Communist Camp came into existence following World War II. The case studies dealt with in this study clearly belie the Soviet claim that among socialist states "international relations of a new type" have come into being. Instead, the Soviet Union has acted as a typical hegemonal power attempting to discipline weaker nations within its sphere of influence. And, just like the United States, the USSR has found that

---

*The reinstatement of pro-Russian conservatives into high posts in the Czechoslovak Communist Party following the Soviet invasion of August 21, 1968, is evidence of this. Furthermore, it is doubtful whether Rumania could have taken so many foreign policy initiatives if Soviet troops had remained on Rumanian soil after 1958.

it cannot convert the economic dependence of another nation into political obedience. At first overoptimistic regarding the efficacy of this instrument of their foreign policy, the Soviet leaders have gradually come to realize that economic pressure is not an effective means of deviation control within the Communist Camp.

Probably the most important lesson political scientists and policy-makers may draw from the Soviet experience in the employment of economic pressure is a greater appreciation for its limitations as a policy instrument. Indeed, as this study has shown, economic pressure may prove to be counterproductive from a policy standpoint. Thus, instead of forcing target nations to change their policies, on several occasions Soviet economic pressure drove them into the camp of Moscow's enemies. Given the dangers inherent in its employment, therefore, it would appear that if statesmen decide to exert economic pressure they would be best advised to do so only in a very limited way. By keeping economic pressure at a low level, the practitioner can demonstrate his displeasure with a target nation's policies but still not force the target nation's leadership to opt for the other side out of economic necessity. Furthermore, there is always the possibility (albeit a slight one) that the *threat* of increased economic pressure inherent in its initial employment may have the desired effect. Most important of all, however, keeping economic pressure at a low level facilitates a future rapprochement, as was shown in the cases of Yugoslavia in 1962 and North Korea in 1965.

All in all, although economic pressure may appear to be a potent weapon in the hands of an economically powerful nation, in reality its usefulness as an instrument of policy is very limited indeed.

NOTES

1. For a view of economic warfare in historical perspective, see Wu Yuan-li, *Economic Warfare* (New York: Prentice-Hall, 1952). The possible use of economic pressure against South Africa to force the government of that nation to alter its apartheid policies is dealt with in *Sanctions Against South Africa,* ed. Ronald Segal (Baltimore: Penguin Books, 1964). For a theoretical study of the use of economic pressure as a means of enforcing arms control, see Morris Bornstein, "Economic Sanctions and Rewards in Support of Arms Control Agreements," *American Economic Review,* Vol. 58, No. 2 (May, 1968), pp. 417-27.

2. The United States experience in waging economic warfare is discussed in Gunnar Adler-Karlsson, *Western Economic Warfare 1947-67* (Stockholm: Almqvist and Wiksell, 1968).

3. *Ibid.*, pp. 208-10.

4. *Ibid.*

5. The initial Soviet-target state relationship in each of these cases in some ways resembled the non-zero-sum games described by Thomas Schelling in *The Strategy of Conflict* (New York: Oxford University Press, 1963). In each instance, the target state would have been better off had it continued to receive economic assistance from the USSR and the USSR would have been better off had it obtained a modicum of political obedience from the target state. Nonetheless, as a result of the Soviet Union's actions, the relationship was rapidly transformed into one of a zero-sum game. This indicates that the Soviet leaders are considerably less adept at settling disputes through the process of intra-alliance bargaining than are their American counterparts. On this point, see Fred Charles Iklé, *How Nations Negotiate* (New York: Harper and Row, 1964), pp. 236-37.

6. It seems that the great powers have a penchant for overestimating the amount of political obedience they can obtain through economic pressure. As recently as June, 1969, U.S. Senator Everett M. Dirksen wrote: "It is time for the United States to tie its trade to global politics, to insist on getting from the Communists something in return—a quid pro quo—for the scientific and technological genius *they need so desperately from us*" (emphasis added). Everett M. Dirksen, "Needed: A Realistic East-West Trade Policy," *Readers Digest,* Vol. 94, No. 566 (June, 1969), p. 133.

7. Nikita S. Khrushchev, "Crimes of the Stalin Era: A Special Report to the 20th Congress of the Communist Party of the Soviet Union" (translated and reprinted in pamphlet form by the *New Leader* [New York: 1962], p. S48).

8. See O. Borisov and B. Koloskov, "The Anti-Soviet Course of the Mao Tse-tung Group," *Kommunist,* No. 7, 1969 (translated in *Current Digest,* Vol. 21, No. 32 [June 18, 1969], p. 5).

9. *Vneshniaia Torgovlia SSSR 1918-1966* (Moscow: Vneshtorgizdat, 1967), pp. 173, 175, 181, 197.

BIBLIOGRAPHY

BIBLIOGRAPHY

Documentary Collections and Statistical Studies

Bass, Robert, and Marbury, Elizabeth (eds.). *The Soviet-Yugoslav Controversy, 1948-58: A Documentary Record.* New York: Prospect Books, 1959.

Dallin, Alexander (ed.). *Diversity in International Communism: A Documentary Record 1961-1963.* New York: Columbia University Press, 1963.

Direction of (Foreign) Trade. New York: United Nations, 1948-68.

Economic Bulletin for Asia and the Far East. New York: United Nations, 1953-68.

Economic Treaties and Agreements of the Soviet Bloc in Eastern Europe 1945-1951. New York: Mid-European Studies Center, 1952.

Ekonomika Stran Sotsializma 1966. Moscow: Ekonomike, 1967.

The Facts about Soviet-Albanian Relations. Tirana: Naim Frashcri State Publishing House, 1964.

50 Let Sovetskoi Vneshnei Torgovli. Moscow: Mezhdunarodnye Otnosheniia, 1967.

Mirovaia Sotsialisticheskaia Sistema Khoziaistva, Volumes III, IV. Moscow: Mysl', 1967.

Monthly Bulletin of Statistics. New York: United Nations, 1959-January, 1967.

Narodnoe Khoziaistvo Sotsialisticheskikh Stran v 1966 Godu. Moscow: Statistika, 1967.

Statistical Yearbook. New York: United Nations, 1959-66.

Statistics of the Foreign Trade of Yugoslavia 1946-49. Belgrade: Federal Statistical Office, 1953.

Vneshniaia Torgovlia SSSR 1918-1966. Moscow: Mezhdunarodnye Otnosheniia, 1967.

Vneshniaia Torgovlia SSSR za 1955-1968 (yearly). Moscow: Vneshtorgizdat (1955-65); Mezhdunarodnye Otnosheniia (1966-68).

White Book on Aggressive Activities by the Governments of the USSR, Poland, Czechoslovakia, Hungary, Rumania, Bulgaria and Albania toward Yugoslavia. Belgrade: Government Printing Office, 1951.

Yearbook of International Trade Statistics. New York: United Nations, 1958-65.

Books

Acheson, Dean. *Present at the Creation.* New York: W. W. Norton, 1969.

Adler-Karlsson, Gunnar. *Western Economic Warfare 1947-67.* Stockholm: Almqvist and Wiksell, 1968.

Allen, Robert Loring. *Soviet Economic Warfare.* Charlottesville: University of Virginia Press, 1960.

Barnett, A. Doak. *Communist China and Asia.* New York: Council on Foreign Relations, 1960.

————. *Communist Economic Strategy: The Rise of Mainland China.* Washington, D.C.: National Planning Association, 1959.

———— (ed.). *Communist Strategies in Asia: A Comparative Analysis of Governments and Parties.* New York: Frederick A. Praeger, 1963.

Beloff, Max. *Soviet Policy in the Far East 1944-1951.* New York: Oxford University Press, 1953.

Bergson, Abram, and Kuznets, Simon (eds.). *Economic Trends in the Soviet Union.* Cambridge: Harvard University Press, 1963.

Bogosavljevic, Miliutin. *The Economy of Yugoslavia.* Belgrade: Prosveta, 1961.

Bromke, Adam, and Uren, Philip E. (eds.). *The Communist States and the West.* New York: Frederick A. Praeger, 1967.

Brown, J. F. *The New Eastern Europe.* New York: Frederick A. Praeger, 1966.

Brzezinski, Zbigniew K. *The Soviet Bloc.* 2nd ed. rev. Cambridge: Harvard University Press, 1967).

Campbell, John C. *Tito's Separate Road.* New York: Harper and Row, 1967.

Crankshaw, Edward. *The New Cold War: Moscow vs. Peking.* Baltimore: Penguin Books, 1963.

Dallin, David J. *Soviet Foreign Policy After Stalin.* Philadelphia: J. B. Lippincott, 1961.

Dedijer, Vladimir. *Tito.* New York: Simon and Schuster, 1953.

Dimensions of Soviet Power. Hearings Before the Joint Economic Committee, Congress of the United States, December 10, 11, 12. Washington, D.C.: U.S. Government Printing Office, 1962.

Djilas, Milovan. *Conversations with Stalin.* New York: Harcourt Brace and World, Inc., 1962.

Eckstein, Alexander. *Communist China's Economic Growth and Foreign Trade.* New York: McGraw-Hill, 1966.

Economic Profile of Mainland China. Studies Prepared for the Joint Economic Committee, Congress of the United States, February, 1967. Washington, D.C.: U.S. Government Printing Office, 1967.

Farrell, R. Barry. *Yugoslavia and the Soviet Union 1948-1956.* Hamden, Conn.: Shoe String Press, 1956.

Fischer-Galati, Stephen (ed.). *Eastern Europe in the Sixties.* New York: Frederick A. Praeger, 1963.

_____. *The New Rumania.* Cambridge: MIT Press, 1967.

Fleron, Frederic J. (ed.). *Communist Studies and the Social Sciences: Essays on Methodology and Empirical Theory.* Chicago: Rand McNally, 1969.

Floyd, David. *Mao Against Khrushchev.* New York: Frederick A. Praeger, 1964.

_____. *Rumania.* New York: Frederick A. Praeger, 1965.

Frumkin, Abram. *Modern Theories of International Economics.* Moscow: Progress Publishers, 1969.

Garthoff, Raymond L. (ed.). *Sino-Soviet Military Relations.* New York: Frederick A. Praeger, 1966.

Goldman, Marshall I. *Soviet Foreign Aid.* New York: Frederick A. Praeger, 1967.

Griffith, William. *Albania and the Sino-Soviet Rift.* Cambridge: MIT Press, 1963.

_____. *Sino-Soviet Relations, 1964-65.* Cambridge: MIT Press, 1966.

_____. *The Sino-Soviet Rift.* Cambridge: MIT Press, 1964.

Grzybowski, Kazimierz. *The Socialist Commonwealth of Nations.* New Haven, Conn.: Yale University Press, 1964.

Hamm, Harry. *Albania: China's Beachhead in Europe.* New York: Frederick A. Praeger, 1963.

Hinton, Harold C. *Communist China in World Politics.* Boston: Houghton Mifflin, 1966.

Hoffman, George W., and Neal, Fred W. *Yugoslavia and the New Communism.* New York: Twentieth Century Fund, 1962.

Iklé, Fred Charles. *How Nations Negotiate.* New York: Harper and Row, 1964.

Ionescu, Ghita. *Communism in Rumania 1944-1962.* London: Oxford University Press, 1964.

Israelyan, V. (ed.). *Soviet Foreign Policy.* Moscow: Progress Publishers, 1967.

Kaser, Michael. *Comecon.* London: Oxford University Press, 1967.

Kertesz, Stephen D. (ed.). *East Central Europe and the World: Developments in the Post-Stalin Era.* Notre Dame, Ind.: University of Notre Dame Press, 1962.

Kindelberger, Charles P. *International Economics.* Homewood, Ill.: Richard D. Irwin, 1963.

Klochko, M. A. *Soviet Scientist in China.* New York: Frederick A. Praeger, 1964.

Kohler, Heinz. *Economic Integration in the Soviet Bloc.* New York: Frederick A. Praeger, 1965.

Kramer, Roland L., *et al.* (eds.). *International Trade.* Cincinnati: South-Western Publishing Co., 1959.

Labedz, Leopold (ed.). *International Communism after Khrushchev.* Cambridge: MIT Press, 1965.

————, and Laqueur, Walter (eds.). *Polycentrism.* New York: Frederick A. Praeger, 1962.

Lowenthal, Richard. *World Communism.* New York: Oxford University Press, 1964.

Mackintosh, James. *Strategy and Tactics of Soviet Foreign Policy.* New York: Oxford University Press, 1962.

Maclean, Fitzroy. *The Heretic.* New York: Harper and Brothers, 1957.

McNeal, Robert H. (ed.). *International Relations Among Communists.* Englewood Cliffs, N.J.: Prentice-Hall, 1967.

Mainland China in the World Economy. Hearings Before the Joint Economic Committee, Congress of the United States, April 5, 10, 11 and 12, 1967. Washington, D.C.: U.S. Government Printing Office, 1967.

Mehnert, Klaus. *Peking and Moscow.* New York: G. P. Putnam's Sons, 1963.

Muller, Kurt. *The Foreign Aid Programs of the Soviet Bloc and Communist China: An Analysis.* New York: Walker and Co., 1967.

Murphy, George G. S. *Soviet Mongolia.* Berkeley: University of California Press, 1966.

Nollau, Gunther. *International Communism and World Revolution.* New York: Frederick A. Praeger, 1961.

North, Robert C. *Moscow and the Chinese Communists.* Stanford, Calif.: Stanford University Press, 1963.

Nove, Alec, and Donnely, Desmond. *Trade with Communist Countries.* London: Hutchinson and Co., 1960.

Pano, Nicholas C. *The People's Republic of Albania.* Baltimore: Johns Hopkins Press, 1968.

Pertot, Vladimir. *Yugoslavia's Foreign Trade.* Belgrade: Yugoslav Ministry of Foreign Trade, 1958.

Pethybridge, Roger (ed.). *The Development of the Communist Bloc.* Boston: D. C. Heath and Co., 1965.

Pryor, Frederick. *The Communist Foreign Trade System.* Cambridge: MIT Press, 1963.

Remer, Charles Frederick. *Three Essays on the International Economics of Communist China.* Ann Arbor: University of Michigan Press, 1959.

Rusinow, Dennison I. *Yugoslavia and Stalin's Successors 1968-69.* Hanover: American Universities Field Staff Report, 1969.

Scalapino, Robert A. (ed.). *The Communist Revolution in Asia.* Englewood Cliffs, N.J.: Prentice-Hall, 1965.

Schelling, Thomas C. *International Economics.* Boston: Allyn & Bacon, 1958.

_____. *The Strategy of Conflict.* New York: Oxford University Press, 1963.

Schwartz, Harry. *Tsars, Mandarins and Commissars.* Philadelphia: J. P. Lippincott, 1964.

Segal, Ronald (ed.). *Sanctions Against South Africa.* Baltimore: Penguin Books, 1964.

Sergeev, S. D. *Ekonomicheskoe Sotrudnichestvo i Vzaimopomoshch' Sotsialisticheskikh Stran.* Moscow: Vneshtorgizdat, 1964.

Shulman, Marshall D. *Stalin's Foreign Policy Reappraised.* New York: Atheneum, 1965.

Skendi, Stavro. *Albania.* New York: Frederick A. Praeger, 1956.

Spulber, Nicholas. *The Economics of Communist Eastern Europe.* London: Chapman and Hall, 1957.

Stepanova, *et al.* (eds.). *Vneshniaia Torgovlia Stran Narodnoi Demokratii.* Moscow: Vneshtorgizdat, 1961.

Ulam, Adam B. *Titoism and the Cominform.* Cambridge: Harvard University Press, 1952.

Uren, Philip E. (ed.). *East-West Trade.* Toronto: Canadian Institute of International Affairs, 1966.

Vajda, Imre. *The Role of Foreign Trade in a Socialist Economy.* Budapest: Corvina Press, 1965.

Wei, Henry. *China and Soviet Russia*. Princeton: D. Van Nostrand, 1956.

Whiting, Alan S. *Sinkiang: Pawn or Pivot?* East Lansing: Michigan State University Press, 1958.

Wolff, Robert Lee. *The Balkans in Our Time*. Cambridge: Harvard University Press, 1956.

Wu, Yuan-li. *Economic Warfare*. New York: Prentice-Hall, 1952.

Zagoria, Donald. *The Sino-Soviet Conflict 1956-61*. Princeton: Princeton University Press, 1962.

Articles

Akimov, Y. "Problems of CMEA Countries' Economic Integration," *International Affairs* (Moscow), Vol. 15, No. 12 (December, 1969), pp. 7-11.

Aleksic, Milan. "Yugoslav Exports and Relations with Eastern Europe," *Review of International Affairs* (Belgrade), Vol. 6, No. 138 (January 1, 1956), pp. 16-18.

_____. "Yugoslav-Soviet Trade," *Review of International Affairs* (Belgrade), Vol. 6, No. 149 (June 15, 1956), pp. 6-7.

Alexeyev, A., and Ivanova, L. "15 Years of CMEA," *International Affairs* (Moscow), Vol. 10, No. 4 (April, 1964), pp. 55-59.

Andreev, I. "Druzhba i Sotrudnichestvo Sovetskogo i Kitaiskogo Narodov," *Vneshniaia Torgovlia*, Vol. 39, No. 2 (February, 1959), pp. 6-10.

Bakaric, Vladimir. "New Stage in the Development of Yugoslav-Soviet Relations," *Review of International Affairs* (Belgrade), Vol. 6 No. 149 (June 15, 1956), pp. 7-10.

Berghianu, Maxim. "Rumania's Economic Development at the Present Stage," *International Affairs* (Moscow), Vol. 14, No. 9 (September, 1968), pp. 12-20.

Bornstein, Morris. "Economic Sanctions and Rewards in Support of Arms Control Agreements," *American Economic Review*, Vol. 58, No. 2 (May, 1968), pp. 417-27.

Botsin, M. "Sovetsko-Koreiskoe Ekonomicheskoe Sotrudnichestvo," *Vneshniaia Torgovlia*, Vol. 46, No. 8 (August, 1966), pp. 22-23.

Braham, Randolph L. "Rumania: Onto the Separate Path," *Problems of Communism,* Vol. 13, No. 3 (May-June, 1964), pp. 14-20.

Brown, J. F. "Rumania Steps out of Line," *Survey,* No. 49 (October, 1963), pp. 19-34.

Cameron, Jules, "Albania: The Last Marxist Paradise," *Atlantic Monthly,* Vol. 211, No. 6 (June, 1963), pp. 41-50.

Charles, David A. "The Dismissal of Marshal P'eng Teh-huai," *China Quarterly,* No. 8 (October-December, 1961), pp. 63-76.

Chau, Kang, and Mah, Feng-Hwa. "A Study of the Ruble-Yuan Exchange Rate," *China Quarterly,* No. 17 (January-March, 1964), pp. 192-204.

Chen, Hai. "The Aggressive Nature of Soviet Revisionism's 'New Stage of Economic Integration,'" *Peking Review,* Vol. 12, No. 36 (September 3, 1969), pp. 16-19.

Chi-chang, Yeh. "China's Foreign Trade in the Past Ten Years," *Foreign Trade of the Peoples Republic of China,* No. 9 (September, 1959), pp. 2-7.

————. "Vneshniaia Torgovlia Nashei Strany za Desiat Let," *Vneshniaia Torgovlia,* Vol. 39, No. 10 (October, 1959), pp. 10-17.

Danilov, K. "Razvitie Ekonomiki Albanii," *Voprosy Ekonomiki,* Vol. 10, No. 11 (November, 1956), pp. 96-105.

Dmitrov, K. "Ekonomicheskie Uspekhi Narodno-Demokraticheskoi Albanii za Desiat Let," *Vneshniaia Torgovlia,* Vol. 34, No. 11 (November, 1954), pp. 73-82.

Dolina, Joseph. "[Yugoslavia's] Foreign Trade," in *Yugoslavia,* ed. Robert F. Byrnes (New York: Frederick A. Praeger, 1957), pp. 351-69.

Gamarnikow, Michael. "Comecon Today," *East Europe,* Vol. 13, No. 3 (March, 1964), pp. 3-9.

————. "The Future of Comecon," *East Europe,* Vol. 11, No. 6 (June, 1962), pp. 3-10.

Garthoff, Raymond L. "Sino-Soviet Military Relations 1945-66," *Sino-Soviet Military Relations,* ed. Raymond Garthoff (New York: Frederick A. Praeger, 1966), pp. 82-99.

————. "The Soviet Intervention in Manchuria," *Sino-Soviet Military Relations,* ed. Raymond Garthoff (New York: Frederick A. Praeger, 1966), pp. 57-81.

Glavinsky, Evgeny. "Soviet-Albanian Economic Relations," *Studies on the Soviet Union*, Vol. 2, No. 2 (Munich, 1962), pp. 66-77.

Golubkov, A. "Sovetsko-Kitaiskoe Nauchno-Tekhnicheskoe Sotrudnichestvo," *Vneshniaia Torgovlia*, Vol. 37, No. 7 (July, 1957), pp. 2-6.

Gormunov, F. "Uspeshnoe Razvitie Albanskoi Narodnoi Respubliki," *Veshniaia Torgovlia*, Vol. 32, No. 10 (October, 1952), pp. 25-32.

Haggard, M. T. "North Korea's International Position," *Asian Survey*, Vol. 5, No. 8 (August, 1965), pp. 375-88.

Hammond, Thomas T. "[Yugoslavia's] Foreign Relations since 1945," in *Yugoslavia*, ed. Robert F. Byrnes (New York: Frederick A. Praeger, 1957), pp. 18-41.

Heinman, Leo. "Peking's Adriatic Stronghold," *East Europe*, Vol. 13, No. 4 (April, 1964), pp. 15-17.

Hoeffding, Oleg. "Sino-Soviet Economic Relations in Recent Years," in *Unity and Contradiction*, ed. Kurt London (New York: Frederick A. Praeger, 1962), pp. 295-312.

_____. "Sino-Soviet Economic Relations, 1959-1962," *Annals of the American Academy of Political and Social Science*, Vol. 349 (September, 1963), pp. 94-105.

Iakovlev, M. "Razvitie Narodnogo Khoziaistva v Narodnoi Respublike Albanii," in *15 Let Narodnoi Albanii*, ed. Nesti Nase (Moscow: Institut Mezhdunarodnykh Otnoshenii, 1959), pp. 86-104.

Ivanov, E. "Shirokie Vozmozhnosti Razvitiia Sovetsko-Iaponskoi Torgovli," *Vneshniaia Torgovlia*, Vol. 41, No. 3 (March, 1961), pp. 3-6.

Jan, George P. "Japan's Trade With Communist China," *Asian Survey*, Vol. 9, No. 12 (December, 1969), pp. 900-918.

Kim, Joungwon A. "The 'Peak of Socialism' in North Korea: The Five and Seven Year Plans," *Asian Survey*, Vol. 5, No. 5 (May, 1965), pp. 255-69.

_____. "Soviet Policy in North Korea," *World Politics*, Vol. 22, No. 2 (January, 1970), pp. 237-55.

Kleimonov, F. "Plodotvornoe Sotrudnichestvo," *Vneshniaia Torgovlia*, Vol. 40, No. 2 (February, 1960), pp. 15-20.

Klein, Sydney. "Sino-Soviet Economic Relations 1949-1962," *Current Scene*, June 15, 1963, pp. 7-11.

Konstantinov, F. "Raskol'nicheskaia, Antimarksistskaia Deiatel'nost' Albanskikh Rukovoditelei," *Kommunist,* Vol. 38, No. 17 (November, 1961), pp. 38-53.

Korolenko, A. "Kompensatsionnoe Soglashenie Mezhdu Sovetskimi i Iugoslavskimi Vneshnetorgovlimi Organizatsiiami," *Vneshniaia Torgovlia,* Vol. 34, No. 11 (November, 1954), pp. 21-22.

"Krepnet Sovetsko-Kitaiskoe Sotrudnichestvo," *Vneshniaia Torgovlia,* Vol. 38, No. 3 (March, 1958), pp. 2-5.

Kronsten, Joseph A. "East-West Trade: Myth and Matter," *International Affairs* (London), Vol. 43, No. 2 (April, 1967), pp. 265-81.

Kuibyshev, A. "Upadok Ekonomiki Iugoslavii i Zakabalenie Strany Anglo-Amerikanskim Kapitalom," *Vneshniaia Torgovlia,* Vol. 29, No. 11 (November, 1949), pp. 27-43.

Kun, Joseph. "North Korea: Between Moscow and Peking," *China Quarterly,* No. 31 (July-September, 1967), pp. 48-58.

Kuplenski, V. "K Itogam Sovetsko-Kitaiskikh Torgovykh Peregovorov," *Vneshniaia Torgovlia,* Vol. 41, No. 5 (May, 1961), pp. 17-18.

Logoreci, Anton. "Albania and China: Incongruous Alliance," *Current History,* Vol. 52, No. 308 (April, 1967), pp. 227-31.

Lonamin, G. "Iugoslaviia na Puti k Ekonomicheskomu Krokhu," *Vneshniaia Torgovlia,* Vol. 32, No. 12 (December, 1952), pp. 11-20.

MacDougall, Colina. "China's Foreign Trade," *Far Eastern Economic Review,* September 26, 1963, pp. 801-3.

Mah, Feng-Hwa. "The Terms of Sino-Soviet Trade," *China Quarterly,* No. 13 (January-March, 1963), pp. 174-91.

Miroshnichenko, B. P. "Vneshniaia Politika i Ekonomicheskoe Sotrudnichestvo SSSR s Inostrannymi Gosudarstvami," in *Vneshneekonomicheskie Sviazi SSSR za 50 Let* (Moscow: Nauchno-Issledovatel'skii Kon"iunkturnyi Institut MVT, 1967), pp. 35-46.

Mishkov, V. "Razvitie Sovetsko-Iugoslavskikh Ekonomicheskikh Otnoshenii," *Vneshniaia Torgovlia,* Vol. 35, No. 10 (October, 1955), pp. 1-3.

Morozov, V. "Equality: Cornerstone of the Socialist Countries' Economic Co-operation," *International Affairs* (Moscow), Vol. 9, No. 12 (December, 1963), pp. 5-8.

Nase, Nesti. "The Albanian People's Fight for Socialism," *International Affairs* (Moscow), Vol. 5, No. 6 (June, 1959), pp. 24-28.

Nechaeva, R. "Ekonomika Albanii na Pod"eme," *Vneshniaia Torgovlia*, Vol. 30, No. 9 (September, 1950), pp. 1-6.

Partonic, Andrija. "The USSR Government's One-Sided Acts," *Review of International Affairs* (Belgrade), Vol. 9, No. 187 (June 16, 1958), pp. 3-5.

Pavlic, Stane. "Yugoslav Economic Relations with Foreign Countries in 1956," *Review of International Affairs* (Belgrade), Vol. 8, No. 162 (January 1, 1957), pp. 20-22.

_____. "Yugoslavia's Economic Relations with Foreign Countries," *Yugoslav Review*, Vol. 5, Nos. 3-4 (March-April, 1956), pp. 15-17.

Pekshev, Iu. "Ekonomicheskoe Sotrudnichestvo Sovetskogo Soiuza i Kitaiskoi Narodnoi Respubliki," *Vneshniaia Torgovlia*, Vol. 35, No. 2 (February, 1955), pp. 1-6.

Pericic, M. "Trade with the Countries of Eastern Europe," *Review of International Affairs* (Belgrade), Vol. 10, No. 216 (April 1, 1959), pp. 4-5.

Poliakova, A. "Rol' Vneshnei Torgovli v Ekonomike Albanii," *Vneshniaia Torgovlia*, Vol. 38, No. 10 (October, 1958), pp. 10-13.

Prybyla, Jan S. "Albania's Economic Vassalage," *East Europe*, Vol. 16, No. 1 (January, 1967), pp. 9-14.

_____. "The China Trade," *East Europe*, Vol. 16, No. 3 (March, 1967), pp. 15-20.

_____. "The Economic Causes of the Soviet-Albanian Quarrel," *Bulletin— Institute for the Study of the USSR* (Munich), Vol. 10, No. 3 (March, 1963), pp. 10-19.

_____. "Recent Trends in Sino-Soviet Economic Relations," *Bulletin— Institute for the Study of the USSR* (Munich), Vol. 14, No. 5 (May, 1967), pp. 11-21.

Ra'anan, Uri. "Peking's Foreign Policy 'Debate' 1965-66," in *China in Crisis*, Vol. II, ed. Tang Tsou (Chicago: University of Chicago Press, 1968), pp. 23-71.

Rupen, Robert A. "Mongolia in the Sino-Soviet Dispute," *China Quarterly*, No. 16 (October-December, 1963), pp. 75-85.

_____. "The Mongolian People's Republic and Sino-Soviet Competition," in *Communist Strategies in Asia,* ed. A. Doak Barnett (New York: Frederick A. Praeger, 1963), pp. 262-88.

Sajcic, Vladimir. "Yugoslav-Soviet Economic Relations," *Review of International Affairs* (Belgrade), Vol. 6, No. 131-2 (October 1, 1955), pp. 10-12.

Shiriaev, N. "K Itogam Sovetsko-Kitaiskikh Torgovykh Peregovorov," *Vneshniaia Torgovlia,* Vol. 38, No. 5 (May, 1958), pp. 2-6.

Shvartsshtein, I. "Rynok Sakhara—Problema Pereproizvodstva," *Vneshniaia Torgovlia,* Vol. 49. No. 2 (February, 1969), pp. 56-59.

Shvets, V. "Piatiletni Plan Razvitiia Narodnogo Khoziaistva Yugoslavii," *Vneshniaia Torgovlia,* Vol. 27, No. 6 (June, 1947), pp. 11-19.

_____. "Ukreplenie Ekonomiki Albanii," *Vneshniaia Torgovlia,* Vol. 28, No. 1 (January, 1948), pp. 24-28.

_____. "Uspekhi Albanskoi Narodnoi Respubliki," *Vneshniaia Torgovlia,* Vol. 31, No. 2 (February, 1951), pp. 7-13.

_____. "Zakabalenie Iugoslavii Anglo-Amerikanskim Kapitalom," *Vneshniaia Torgovlia,* Vol. 30, No. 9 (September, 1950), pp. 26-31.

Skrzypek, Stanislaw. "Notes on Soviet Bloc Trade," *East Europe,* Vol. 11, No. 2 (February, 1962), pp. 16-21.

Sladkovskii, M. "Nerushimaia Sovetsko-Kitaiskaia Druzhba," *Vneshniaia Torgovlia,* Vol. 37, No. 2 (February, 1957), pp. 2-4.

_____. "Razvitie Torgovli Sovetskogo Soiuza s Kitaiskoi Narodnoi Respublikoi," *Vneshniaia Torgovlia,* Vol. 39, No. 10 (October, 1959), pp. 2-10.

_____. "Uspekhi Sovetsko-Kitaiskoi Torgovli," *Vneshniaia Torgovlia,* Vol. 37, No. 10 (October, 1957), pp. 2-6.

Solomon, Anthony M. "The Revival of Trade between the 'Communist Bloc' and the West," *Annals of the American Academy of Political and Social Science,* Vol. 372 (July, 1967), pp. 105-12.

Spulber, Nicholas. "On Yugoslavia's Economic Ties with the Soviet Bloc," *Economia Internazionale,* Vol. 9, No. 2 (May, 1956), pp. 308-19.

Stolte, Stefan. "Three Problems Facing the Soviet Bloc," *Bulletin—Institute for the Study of the USSR* (Munich), Vol. 14, No. 7 (July, 1967), pp. 20-28.

Sylvester, Anthony. "Revisionists and Stalinists in the Balkans," *East Europe,* Vol. 16, No. 1 (January, 1967), pp. 2-8.

Teodosi, Kocho. "Stroitel'stvo Sotsialisticheskoi Ekonomiki v Narodnoi Respubliki Albanii," *Voprosy Ekonomiki,* Vol. 12, No. 11 (November, 1959), pp. 120-31.

Thompson, J. B. "Rumania's Struggle with Comecon," East Europe, Vol. 13, No. 6 (June, 1964), pp. 2-9.

Tretiak, Daniel. "The Founding of the Sino-Albanian Entente," *China Quarterly,* No. 10 (April-June, 1962), pp. 123-42.

"Velikie Uspekhi Kitaiskogo Naroda v Stroitel'stve Sotsialisma," *Vneshniaia Torgovlia,* Vol. 36, No. 2 (February, 1956), pp. 1-4.

Vicinich, Wayne. "The Albanian-Soviet Rift," *Current History,* Vol. 44, No. 261 (May, 1963), pp. 299-304.

Vladimirov, Yu. "The Question of Soviet-Chinese Economic Relations in 1950-1966," *Voprosy Istorii,* No. 6, 1969 (translated in *Current Digest of the Soviet Press,* Vol. 21, No. 33 [September 10, 1969], pp. 8-15).

Wa-doon, Chan. "Krepnet Sovetsko-Kitaiskaia Druzhba," *Vneshniaia Torgovlia,* Vol. 39, No. 6 (June, 1959), pp. 7-10.

Wan, Yeh Tsi. "Vneshniaia Torgovlia Kitaia," *Vneshniaia Torgovlia,* Vol. 35, No. 6 (June, 1955), p. 1-5.

Zagoria, Donald. "The Strategic Debate in Peking," in *China in Crisis,* Vol. II, ed. Tang Tsou (Chicago: University of Chicago Press, 1968), pp. 237-68.

Periodicals

Bulletin—Institute for the Study of the USSR, 1959-69.

East Europe, 1958-69.

Foreign Trade of the Peoples Republic of China, 1958-62.

International Affairs (Moscow), 1958-69.

The New York Times.

Peking Review, 1958-69.

Pravda.

Radio Free Europe Press Translations and Situation Reports
    (a) Yugoslavia   1955-69
    (b) Albania   1961-69
    (c) China   1958-69
    (d) North Korea   1962-69

Review of International Affairs (Belgrade), 1955-62.

Vneshniaia Torgovlia, 1947-69.

Voprosy Ekonomiki, 1949-69.

ABOUT THE AUTHOR

Dr. Robert Owen Freedman is Assistant Professor and the Russian Area Specialist in Marquette University's Department of Political Science. Until completion of his army service in July, 1970, he was Assistant Professor of Russian History and Government in the Department of Social Sciences at the United States Military Academy (West Point). Dr. Freedman has long been interested in Soviet control mechanisms within the Communist bloc.

Dr. Freedman received his B.A. from the University of Pennsylvania. He is a graduate of Columbia University's Russian Institute, and also received his M.A. and Ph.D. from Columbia University.